Prehistoric Settlement in the Lower Kennet Valley

Excavations at Green Park (Reading Business Park) Phase 3 and Moores Farm, Burghfield, Berkshire

by

Adam Brossler, Fraser Brown, Erika Guttmann,
Elaine L Morris and Leo Webley

with contributions by
*Leigh Allen, Hugo Anderson-Whymark, Kayt Brown, Sandy Budden,
Bethan Charles, Kate Cramp, Elizabeth Huckerby, Ruth Pelling, Mark Robinson,
Robert Scaife, Ruth Shaffrey, Maisie Taylor, Jane Timby and Annsofie Witkin*

illustrations by
Oxford Archaeology Graphics Office

Oxford Archaeology
Thames Valley Landscapes Monograph No 37
2013

The publication of this volume was generously funded by
Prudential Property Investment Managers Ltd and Caversham Bridge Group

Published for Oxford Archaeology by Oxford University School of Archaeology
as part of the Thames Valley Landscapes Monograph Series

Designed by Oxford Archaeology Graphics Office

Edited by Paul Booth

This book is part of a series of monographs which can be bought from all good bookshops
and internet bookshops. For more information visit www.oxfordarchaeology.com

Figures 1.1–4, 6.1 and 6.3 reproduced from the Ordnance Survey on behalf of the controller of
Her Majesty's Stationery Office, © Crown Copyright, AL100005569

Front cover: Extract from 'To pastures new' showing a late Bronze Age roundhouse; middle to late Bronze
Age ladle from Green Park; middle Bronze Age globular urn from Moores Farm; early Iron Age pit group
from Moores Farm; reconstruction of late Bronze Age weaving at Reading Business Park; middle Bronze
Age 'oven' at Moores Farm

Back cover: 'To pastures new' by Rosalyn Smith: reconstruction of late Bronze Age settlement at Green Park

ISBN 978-1-905905-29-4

Typeset by Production Line, Oxford
Printed in Great Britain by Berforts Information Press, Eynsham, Oxford

Contents

List of Figures vii
List of Tables ix
Summary xi
Acknowledgements xiii
Location of the archive xiii

Chapter 1: Introduction

Introduction 1
Site location, geology and circumstances of excavation 1
Archaeological background 2
    Survey work 2
    Previous Green Park investigations 2
    Other archaeological investigations 6
Fieldwork methods 6
    Green Park 3 6
    Moores Farm 6
    Excavation procedures 6
Layout of the volume 8

Chapter 2: Green Park 3 – Early Prehistoric and Bronze Age activity

Archaeological sequence 9
    Introduction 9
    Early prehistoric activity 9
    Middle to late Bronze Age 9
Artefacts 21
    Flint *by Kate Cramp* 21
    Bronze Age pottery *by Elaine L Morris* 24
    Quern *by Ruth Shaffrey* 34
    Shale bracelet *by Ruth Shaffrey* 35
    Wood *by Maisie Taylor* 35
Osteological and environmental evidence 38
    Human bone *by Annsofie Witkin* 38
    Animal bone *by Bethan Charles* 39
    Charred and waterlogged plant remains *by Ruth Pelling* 39
    Pollen *by Elizabeth Huckerby* 40
    Insects *by Mark Robinson* 43

Chapter 3: Green Park 3 – Iron Age, Roman and Post-Roman activity

Archaeological sequence 45
    Middle to late Iron Age 45
    Romano-British period 45
    Late medieval to post-medieval period 47

Artefacts and osteological evidence 47
    Iron Age pottery *by Elaine L Morris* 47
    Roman artefacts *by Leigh Allen, Ruth Shaffrey and Jane Timby* 49
    Late medieval to post-medieval artefacts *by Leigh Allen and Jane Timby* 50
    Animal bone *by Bethan Charles* 50

Chapter 4: Moores Farm

Archaeological sequence 53
    Introduction 53
    Mesolithic 53
    Middle Neolithic 53
    Late Neolithic to early Bronze Age 53
    Middle to late Bronze Age 53
    Early Iron Age 65
    Unphased prehistoric features 70
    Later activity and alluvial layers 70
Artefacts 70
    Flint *by Kate Cramp and Hugo Anderson-Whymark* 70
    Neolithic and early Bronze Age pottery *by Sandy Budden and Elaine L Morris* 74
    Middle and late Bronze Age pottery *by Elaine L Morris* 84
    Early Iron Age pottery *by Kayt Brown* 92
    Fired clay *by Sandy Budden* 97
    Querns *by Ruth Shaffrey* 97
Osteological and environmental evidence 98
    Animal bone *by Bethan Charles* 98
    Charred and waterlogged plant remains *by Ruth Pelling* 99
    Pollen *by Robert G Scaife* 99

Chapter 5: The Middle to Late Bronze Age ceramic transition in the Lower Kennet Valley and beyond *by Elaine L Morris*

Introduction 103
Pottery traditions 103
    Middle Bronze Age 103
    Late Bronze Age 105
    Post-Deverel-Rimbury (PDR) 106
The evidence: pots and dates 107
    The Lower Kennet Valley 107
    The Thames Valley: Berkshire, Oxfordshire, Surrey and Middlesex 109
    Wessex: the chalkland landscapes of Berkshire, Wiltshire, Hampshire, Dorset and Sussex 111
    Back to the Lower Kennet Valley: Green Park 1–3 and Moores Farm 114
Transitional later Bronze Age (TLBA) pottery 114
The future 114

Chapter 6: Prehistoric Settlement at Green Park and Moores Farm – an overview

Introduction 117
Land and water 117
Early prehistoric communities 117
    Mesolithic 117

Contents

Early Neolithic...118

Middle Neolithic to early Bronze Age...119

Later Bronze Age settlement and farming..121

Middle Bronze Age settlement at Green Park 3 and Moores Farm..................121

Waterholes: use and decommissioning...122

Interpreting the field systems of the Green Park/Moores Farm landscape.........123

The development of later Bronze Age settlement in the Green Park/Moores Farm landscape and beyond...126

Early Iron Age settlement shift...129

The end of prehistory..129

Bibliography...131

Index...137

List of Figures

Chapter 1
1.1 Location of sites 1
1.2 Cropmark evidence (after Gates 1975) and other archaeological investigations in the Green Park/Moores Farm area. Mapping of cropmarks does not extend eastwards of the SU 70 easting 2
1.3 Green Park: areas of archaeological fieldwork 4
1.4 Green Park: areas of watching brief 5
1.5 Moores Farm: areas of archaeological fieldwork 7

Chapter 2
2.1 Plan of all features, showing excavated interventions. 10
2.2 Middle to late Bronze Age features. 11
2.3 Distribution of finds from middle to late Bronze Age features 12
2.4 Waterhole 2690 14
2.5 Detail of timber structure within waterhole 2690, facing north, showing timbers 2770, 2774, 2790 and 2791 and ladle 2807. Scale: 0.2m. 15
2.6 Timber structure within waterhole 2690 after further excavation, facing north. Scale: 1m 15
2.7 Waterhole 3091 16
2.8 Wooden vessel 3255 within waterhole 3091, facing north. Scale: 0.2m. 17
2.9 Waterhole 3201; inset shows wooden bowl from Wessex Archaeology evaluation 18
2.10 Waterhole 2373 19
2.11 Waterhole 3263 19
2.12 Probability distributions of radiocarbon dates from Bronze Age waterholes 20
2.13 Probability distributions of radiocarbon dates: model providing an estimate for the duration of waterhole activity 21
2.14 Probability distribution providing an estimate for the length of time over which the waterholes were constructed 21
2.15 Burial 222. 21
2.16 Worked flint 23
2.17 Bronze Age pottery, nos 1–6. 31
2.18 Bronze Age pottery, nos 7–12. 32
2.19 Bronze Age pottery, nos 13–24. 33
2.20 Shale bracelet fragment. 35
2.21 Wooden objects. 37
2.22 Wooden ladle 2807. 38
2.23 Bronze Age waterhole 3091: percentage pollen diagram 41

Chapter 3
3.1 Middle to late Iron Age and Romano-British features. 46
3.2 Roman vessel containing cremated animal bone from ditch 3259, Wessex Archaeology evaluation 48
3.3 Post-medieval and modern features. 48
3.4 Iron Age pottery. 50

Chapter 4
4.1 Mesolithic and Neolithic features 54
4.2 Middle Bronze Age features. Waterholes are labelled in italics 55
4.3 Middle Bronze Age features in Areas 8 and 16. 56
4.4 Features in Area 9 57
4.5 Features in Area 13 58
4.6 Features in Area 14 59
4.7 Sections of middle Bronze Age pits 60

4.8   Plans and sections of middle Bronze Age 'ovens' 61
4.9   Middle Bronze Age 'oven' 2242, facing south. Scale: 0.5m 62
4.10   Middle Bronze Age 'oven' 2359, facing south. Scale: 0.5m 62
4.11   Sections of middle Bronze Age waterholes 63
4.12   Early Iron Age features 64
4.13   Early Iron Age features in Area 16 66
4.14   Pit group 2042 67
4.15   Early Iron Age pit group 2042, facing south. Scale: 1m 67
4.16   Sections of early Iron Age pits 68
4.17   Early Iron Age features in Area 12 68
4.18   Mesolithic flint assemblage: length/breadth ratio of broken and intact flints 72
4.19   Mesolithic flint assemblage: length/breadth ratio by context 72
4.20   Proportion of broken and intact flints 73
4.21   Mesolithic flint assemblage: proportion of broken and intact flints by context 73
4.22   Mesolithic flint assemblage: platform edge abrasion by context 73
4.23   Mesolithic flint assemblage: length/breadth ratio of flints with and without platform edge
       abrasion 73
4.24   Mesolithic flint assemblage: butt types by context 73
4.25   Mesolithic flint assemblage: length, breadth and butt type 74
4.26   Mesolithic flint assemblage: hammer mode by context 74
4.27   Mesolithic flint assemblage: termination type by context 74
4.28   Mesolithic flint assemblage: dorsal cortex extent by context 74
4.29   Mesolithic flint assemblage: flake type by context 74
4.30   Worked flint 77
4.31   Neolithic pottery, nos 1–2 82
4.32   Neolithic and early Bronze Age pottery, nos 3–9 83
4.33   Middle Bronze Age pottery, nos 1–11 89
4.34   Middle Bronze Age pottery, nos 12–19 90
4.35   Middle Bronze Age pottery, nos 20–24 91
4.36   Early Iron Age pottery, nos 1–7 94
4.37   Early Iron Age pottery, nos 8–14 95
4.38   Early Iron Age pottery, nos 15–18 96
4.39   Middle Bronze Age waterhole 824: percentage pollen diagram 101

Chapter 6
6.1   Excavated prehistoric and Romano-British sites in the Lower Kennet Valley mentioned
       in Chapter 6. 1: Aldermaston Wharf; 2: Amner's Farm, Burghfield; 3: Anslow's Cottages;
       4: Beenham; 5: Brimpton; 6: Cod's Hill; 7: Crane Wharf, Reading; 8: Cunning Man,
       Burghfield; 9: Diddenham Manor Farm, Grazeley; 10: Englefield; 11: Field Farm, Burghfield;
       12: Field Farm, Sulhamstead; 13: Hartley Court Farm, Shinfield; 14: Haywards Farm, Theale;
       15: Heron's House, Burghfield; 16: Knight's Farm, Burghfield; 17: Little Lea Park;
       18: Marshall's Hill, Reading; 19: Meales Farm, Sulhamstead; 20: Pingewood; 21: Reading
       Football Club; 22: Reading Sewage Treatment Works; 23: Shortheath Lane, Sulhamstead;
       24: Southcote; 25: Sulham; 26: Theale Ballast Hole; 27: Ufton Nervet (Allen and Allen 1997);
       28: Ufton Nervet (Manning 1974); 29: Wickhams Field, Burghfield 118
6.2   C-shaped ring ditch, Reading Sewage Treatment Works 120
6.3   The Green Park/Moores Farm landscape in the later Bronze Age 124-5
6.4   Pottery assemblages from later Bronze Age sites in the Lower Kennet Valley, quantification by
       numbers of sherds 127

List of Tables

Chapter 2
2.1   Summary of Bronze Age ditches 9
2.2   The dynamics of deposition in the Bronze Age waterholes 13
2.3   Radiocarbon dates from Bronze Age waterholes. Dates calibrated using OxCal v3.5
       (Bronk Ramsay 2000) and the data of Stuiver et al. (1998). 20
2.4   Results of chi-squared test on radiocarbon dates from Bronze Age waterholes. 20
2.5   Worked flint 22
2.6   Quantification of Bronze Age pottery by fabric 24
2.7   Correlation of fabric and form types for middle and late Bronze Age pottery by frequency
       of occurrences/vessels. * = perforated. 25
2.8   Occurrences of middle and late Bronze Age vessels by fabric within contemporary contexts
       (example in parentheses also represented in previous context). 28-9
2.9   Occurrences of middle and late Bronze Age vessels by form within contemporary contexts
       (number in parentheses also represented in previous context). 30
2.10   Wood from Bronze Age waterholes 36
2.11   Animal bone from middle to late Bronze Age contexts 39
2.12   Charred plant remains from Bronze Age waterholes 39
2.13   Waterlogged plant remains from Bronze Age waterholes 40
2.14   Insect remains from Bronze Age waterholes. + = present; ++ = several; A = aquatic 42

Chapter 3
3.1   Summary of Iron Age ditches 45
3.2   Summary of Roman ditches 45
3.3   Quantification of Iron Age pottery by fabric 49
3.4   Quantification of Roman pottery by fabric. 50
3.5   Animal bone from Iron Age and later contexts 51

Chapter 4
4.1   Summary of field system ditches 58
4.2   Summary of middle Bronze Age pits. 59
4.3   Radiocarbon dates from early Iron Age pit group 2042. Dates calibrated using
       OxCal v3.10 (Bronk Ramsey 2005) and atmospheric data from Reimer et al. (2004) 64
4.4   Summary of early Iron Age pits, excluding pit group 2042. 65
4.5   Worked flint 71
4.6   Worked flint from Mesolithic contexts 72
4.7   Quantification of Neolithic and early Bronze Age pottery by pottery date 78
4.8   Quantification of Neolithic and early Bronze Age pottery by fabric 79
4.9   Quantification of middle to late Bronze Age pottery by fabric 84
4.10   Middle to late Bronze Age pottery, quantification of sherds from each fabric type that
       have one or both surfaces missing 84
4.11   Middle to late Bronze Age pottery, quantification of vessel forms 85
4.12   Middle to late Bronze Age pottery, quantification of decoration types 86
4.13   Quantification of early Iron Age pottery by fabric 92
4.14   Early Iron Age pottery, correlation of fabric group and vessel class by rim count 93
4.15   Early Iron Age pottery, correlation of fabric group and decoration type by number of
       vessels 93
4.16   Saddle querns and rubbers 98
4.17   Animal bone. * = possibly intrusive. ** = 57 bones from a single skeleton 99
4.18   Charred and waterlogged plant remains. MBA: middle Bronze Age; EIA: early Iron Age 99

Chapter 5
5.1   Radiocarbon dating of middle and late Bronze Age pottery in south-central England 107

Summary

This volume presents the results of two excavations on the gravel terraces of the Lower Kennet Valley: the third phase of work at Green Park (Reading Business Park) and excavations nearby at Moores Farm, Burghfield, Berkshire. The Green Park excavations uncovered a field system and occupation features dating to the middle to late Bronze Age. Five waterholes or wells were distributed across the field system, the waterlogged fills of which preserved wooden revetment structures and valuable environmental evidence. The pottery assemblages from the waterholes are of significant interest for our understanding of the middle to late Bronze Age transition in the region. Later activity included middle to late Iron Age boundaries, a late Iron Age cremation burial, a Romano-British field system and post-medieval trackways. The Moores Farm excavations revealed occupation from the Mesolithic, Neolithic, middle Bronze Age and early Iron Age. The middle Bronze Age settlement included pits, ovens and possible post structures, and was again situated within a contemporary field system dotted with waterholes. As well as discussing these two individual sites, the volume provides an overview of all of the work to date in the Green Park Farm/Reading Business Park area (previously reported in Moore and Jennings 1992 and Brossler *et al*. 2004), exploring the development of this important prehistoric landscape. It is argued that significant changes in the inhabitation of this landscape between the middle and late Bronze Age can now be identified.

Acknowledgements

Oxford Archaeology would like to thank Prupim (originally Prudential Property Investment Managers Ltd) for funding the work at Green Park 3, and Caversham Restoration Ltd (originally the Caversham Bridge Group) for funding the work at Moores Farm. We would like to thank, in particular, Kevin Ashman at Prupim, and Lee Montague and Tony Butler at the Caversham Bridge Group.

The archaeology services of West Berkshire and Wokingham District Councils are thanked for their advice and curatorial role. Rob Bourne of Babtie also provided valuable advice. Richard Bradley and Duncan Coe are thanked for helpful comments on the draft report text.

This volume has had a long genesis and is the culmination of many people's work. The Green Park 3 excavations were managed by Greg Pugh and Richard Brown, and the Moores Farm excavations by Tim Allen. The contribution of all the OA site staff is acknowledged here. Those who have played a significant role in managing the post-excavation work and writing interim reports include Carol Allen, Angela Boyle, Philippa Bradley and Grace Jones among others. The draft excavation report was completed in 2008. Subsequent revision of the text has been on a limited scale; it has included some updating of references, but not substantive reworking of discussion to take account of very recent work. Peter Marshall of English Heritage is thanked for advice on the radiocarbon dating programme at Green Park 3. The Biology Department of Lancaster University is thanked for the use of laboratory facilities for the analysis of the Moores Farm charred plant remains. The final versions of the illustrations were produced by Julia Collins, Markus Dylewski and Magdalena Wachnik. The finds were illustrated by Adam Parsons

Location of the Archive

The finds and records from the Green Park 3 excavations have been deposited with Reading Museum under the accession code REDMG.2000.88, and those from Moores Farm with West Berkshire Museum (Newbury) under the accession code NEBYM.1998.63.

Chapter 1: Introduction

INTRODUCTION

This volume presents the results of two excavations on the gravel terraces of the Lower Kennet Valley, at Green Park (Phase 3) and Moores Farm, Burghfield, Berkshire. The excavations revealed a sequence of prehistoric activity that complements the results of the two previously published phases of work at Green Park (formerly known as Reading Business Park: Moore and Jennings 1992; Brossler *et al.* 2004). In particular, extensive evidence for later Bronze Age settlement and farming was revealed, which makes a significant contribution to our understanding of this period. The final chapter of the volume synthesises all of the work to date in the Green Park/Moores Farm area, in order to explore the development of this important prehistoric landscape.

SITE LOCATIONS, GEOLOGY AND CIRCUMSTANCES OF EXCAVATION

The Green Park Phase 3 excavation area is located in the south-western part of the Green Park development at SU 697696, and is bisected by the boundary between Burghfield and Shinfield parishes (Fig. 1.1). It lies on the first terrace gravels of the River Kennet, on level ground at 39m OD. The gravel is overlain by poorly drained, non-calcareous clay soils of the Loddon series (Jarvis 1968). Prior to the fieldwork the site was under arable cultivation. The site was excavated by Oxford Archaeology (OA) in advance of commercial development, on behalf of Caversham Project Management Ltd acting for Prudential Property Investment Managers Ltd (later as part of Prupim).

Moores Farm is located 1 km to the south-west of Green Park at SU 691687, within Burghfield parish (Fig. 1.1). It lies on ground sloping gently from north to south at *c* 40m OD. The underlying geology again consists of first terrace river gravels, capped by soils of the Loddon series and a series of red-brown alluvial deposits. Prior to the fieldwork the site was used partly for arable agriculture and partly as pasture. The site was excavated by OA in advance of gravel quarrying, on behalf of Caversham Project Management Ltd and the Caversham Bridge Group.

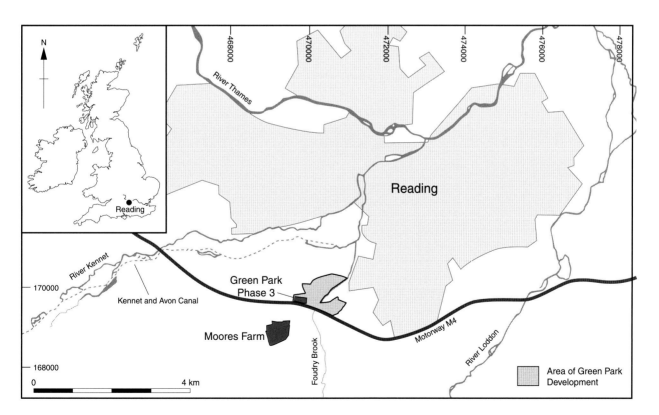

Fig. 1.1   Location of sites, © Crown Copyright 2013, Ordnance Survey 100005569

1

ARCHAEOLOGICAL BACKGROUND

The area of the Lower Kennet Valley around Green Park and Moores Farm has seen intensive archaeological investigation over the past two decades. The salient findings of this work are summarised below. For convenience, the first phase of excavation at Green Park – originally published as Reading Business Park (Moore and Jennings 1992) – will be referred to in this volume as Green Park 1, the second phase (Brossler *et al.* 2004) as Green Park 2, and the third phase (this volume) as Green Park 3.

Survey work

The archaeological richness of the area was first revealed in the mid 1970s by a survey of the aerial photographic evidence from the Middle Thames Valley, which showed that cropmark complexes extended across the gravel terraces of the Burghfield area. Green Park 3 lies within one of these cropmark complexes, which incorporates trackways, linear ditch systems and scattered pits (Fig. 1.2; Gates 1975, 32–3, pls 7–8).

Fieldwalking was subsequently carried out in the area by the Berkshire Archaeological Unit in 1983–84 as part of the Lower Kennet Valley Survey. The part of the survey area corresponding with Green Park 3

produced worked flint, prehistoric, Roman and medieval pottery and a Roman coin (Lobb and Rose 1996). Moores Farm was not surveyed.

Previous Green Park investigations

Wessex Archaeology evaluation 1986

In 1986 Wessex Archaeology carried out an evaluation of 1% of the Green Park development area (Fig. 1.3) (TWA 1986). The evaluation comprised a grid of 2m-square test pits, supplemented by longer trenches in areas where archaeological features and high artefact densities were found.

Within the south-western part of the evaluated area, corresponding to Green Park 3, 12 of the 31 excavated test pits contained archaeological features. The only stratified dating evidence was a group of medieval pottery sherds, although unstratified Bronze Age pottery was also recovered. Two of the five larger trenches in this area also produced archaeological remains. One trench revealed a crouched inhumation burial, a complex of intercutting ditches containing Bronze Age pottery, burnt flint and animal bone, and a large waterhole that produced a wooden bowl and two wooden stakes. A second trench revealed three Romano-British ditches.

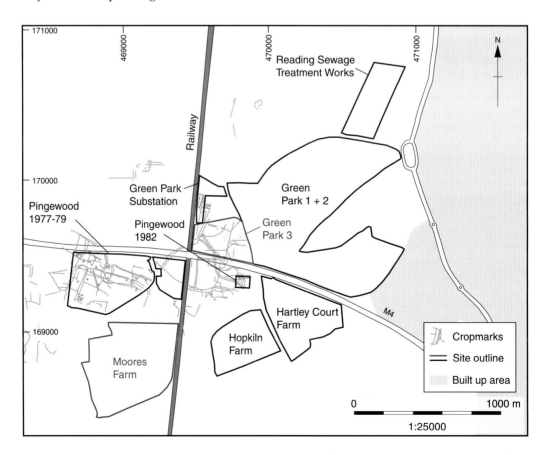

Fig. 1.2   Cropmark evidence (after Gates 1975) and other archaeological investigations in the Green Park/Moores Farm area. Mapping of cropmarks does not extend eastwards of the SU 70 easting. © Crown Copyright 2013, Ordnance Survey 100005569

Elsewhere within the evaluated area, to the west and north-west of Green Park 3, further evidence for later Bronze Age activity was discovered including an occupation layer adjacent to a palaeochannel. An area of Romano-British settlement close to Foundry Brook was also found.

Green Park 1 excavations 1987–88

As a consequence of the discoveries made during the evaluation, additional archaeological work was made a condition of the development. During 1987–88, further evaluation trenching and a series of open area excavations were carried out by OA (Fig. 1.3; Moore and Jennings 1992).

Excavation within Area 5 revealed a late Bronze Age settlement located on an island of gravel. Twenty roundhouses were excavated, together with two-, four-, and six-post structures and a large number of pits. Traces of an associated field system were found nearby in Areas 3 and 6.

In Area 2000 a number of intercutting ditches and pits proved to be mostly of Roman date. These were thought to represent the remains of field systems, enclosures, and other features associated with a nearby settlement.

Part of a late Bronze Age settlement was discovered in Area 3100, bounded to the north by a palaeochannel. Ten roundhouses were excavated, overlying an earlier field system. Other features associated with the settlement included two-, four-, and six-post structures, and a row of six possible flax-retting pits.

Area 4000 contained isolated pits and postholes associated with both late Bronze Age and Roman pottery. In Area 5000 four pit alignments were superseded by boundary ditches of Bronze Age date. Pits and postholes were also scattered across the excavated area. Area 6000 contained ditches and gullies thought to represent a Bronze Age field system.

Neolithic, late Bronze Age and Roman remains were located in Area 7000. A swathe of 118 pits of probable Neolithic date extended from north-west to south-east across the site. Other Neolithic features included postholes and a pit containing a complete cattle skeleton. Late Bronze Age activity in this area was represented by pits, a crouched inhumation burial, two cremation burials and several postholes, together with a U-shaped enclosure. Traces of four Roman enclosures were found in the northern and eastern parts of the site.

Green Park 2 excavations 1995

In 1995 OA carried out further excavation in advance of Phase 2 of the Green Park development (Brossler *et al.* 2004). Two sites with a total area of 2.2ha were investigated: Area 3017, located on a gravel island to the south-west of Area 7000, and Area 3000B, which represented an eastwards extension of Area 3100 (Fig. 1.3).

Area 3017 contained features predominantly dating to the Neolithic period. A segmented ring-ditch produced an assemblage of Neolithic flint-work, and animal bone from the upper ditch fills was radiocarbon dated to the early 3rd millennium cal BC. An unurned cremation burial from one of the upper fills may have been interred later, during the Bronze Age. Nineteen Neolithic pits similar to those excavated in Area 7000 to the north-east were recorded, together with postholes relating to a possible timber building. Other features included three late Bronze Age pits, and medieval ditches and pits associated with a field system.

Area 3000B showed a similar sequence to that recorded in Area 3100 immediately to the south-west, where a late Bronze Age settlement overlay part of an earlier field system. A cremation burial within a middle Bronze Age urn was found in a pit to the west of a large square field. To the south-east, another pit containing a fragmentary middle Bronze Age vessel was found, but there was no evidence of a cremation burial. A middle Bronze Age waterhole was also discovered. The late Bronze Age settlement was represented by a further five roundhouses, several two-, four-, and six-post structures, seven waterholes and a large number of pits. Immediately north-east of the roundhouses, a large burnt mound was uncovered, made up predominantly of burnt flint in a black sandy silt soil. This deposit produced significant amounts of late Bronze Age pottery, and had accumulated along the southern edge of the palaeochannel.

Watching brief work

Watching briefs were maintained on groundworks at various stages of the Green Park development (Fig. 1.4). Those carried out up to 1996 are reported on by Brossler *et al.* (2004). Between 1997 and 2002, watching briefs were carried out in intermittently the southern part of the development area, to the east of Kybe's Lane. In 1997 the watching brief covered two areas (P3 and P4) to the east and west of the palaeochannel covered by the 1996 watching brief. The southern part of the development (Zones 11 to 14) was covered by watching briefs carried out from 1998 to 2000. The watching briefs were carried out piecemeal as development progressed, sometimes covering only very small strips of land. The depth to which the areas were stripped varied, depending upon the impact of the development, but many areas were stripped only to shallow depths (rarely exceeding 0.50m, and sometimes to a depth of just 0.1m) which may have been insufficient to expose some archaeological features. After stripping, most of these areas were levelled with a grader and then covered with dense layers of gravel. Most areas had suffered from modern disturbance to some extent. Zones 11 and 12, which lay adjacent to the M4 had suffered particularly as the result of the removal of trees and shrubs. Not surprisingly, given these factors, the watching briefs

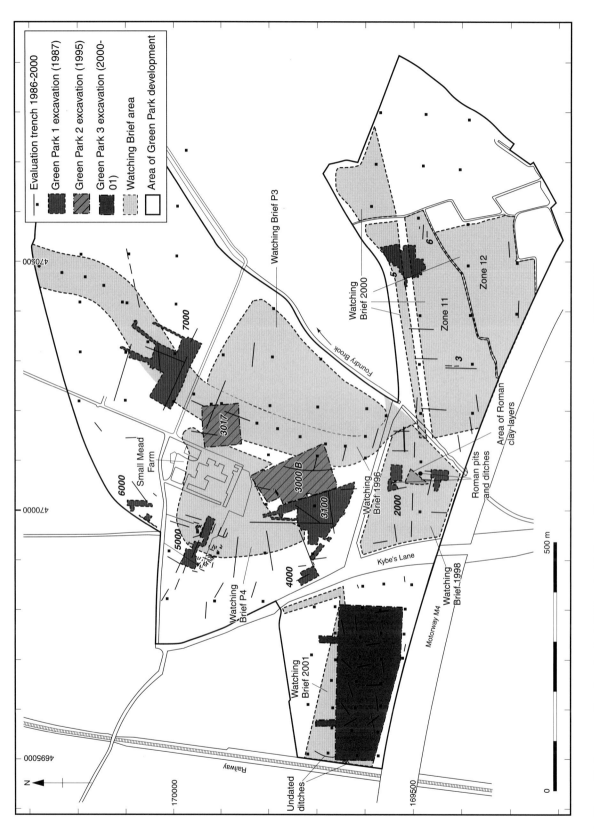

Fig. 1.3 Green Park: areas of archaeological fieldwork, © Crown Copyright 2013, Ordnance Survey 100005569

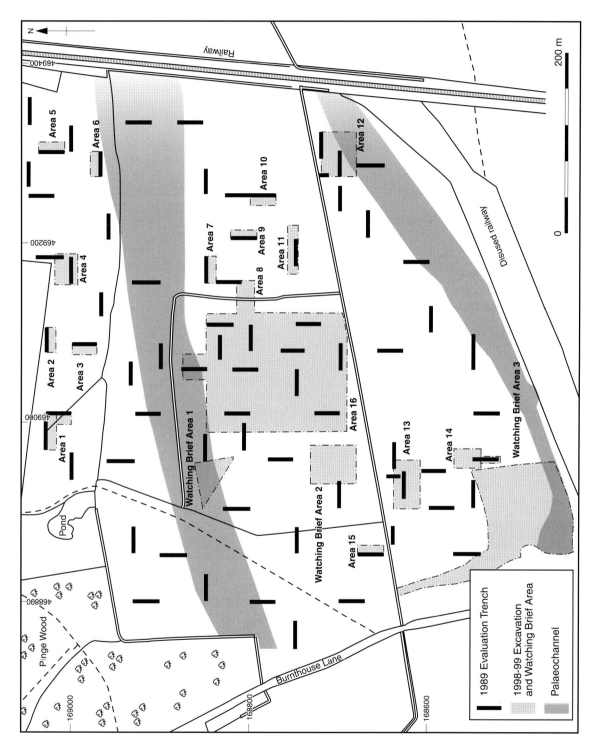

Fig. 1.4 Green Park: areas of watching brief, © Crown Copyright 2013, Ordnance Survey 100005569

revealed few features of archaeological interest, although modern drains and tree-throw holes were noted in most areas. Evidence for Romano-British activity was, however, found in 1998 in the immediate vicinity of the excavated Roman site at Area 2000 in a zone which was stripped between the two previous excavation areas (Fig. 1.4). Roman pottery and ceramic building material was recovered from two patchy silty clay layers that probably equate to the Roman plough soils identified in the earlier excavations (Moore and Jennings 1992, 62). The lower layer contained pottery dated to the 1st to 2nd centuries AD, while the upper layer was dated to after AD 240. A few sherds of 1st-century pottery were also found in an irregular pit or tree-throw hole that showed no stratigraphic relationship to the plough soils. Further watching brief work immediately to the east uncovered a curvilinear gully and three clusters of intercutting pits, which produced small amounts of pottery dated to the 2nd century or later. The remaining features revealed in the watching briefs consisted of a very small number of undated ditches and pits which contained no finds.

Other archaeological investigations

A number of other archaeological investigations have been carried out in the immediate vicinity of Green Park and Moores Farm (Fig. 1.2). These include work carried out by the Berkshire Archaeological Unit at Pingewood in 1977–82 in advance of gravel quarrying. The first stage of excavation, located 200m to the north-west of Moores Farm, uncovered later Bronze Age occupation, late Iron Age cremation burials and a Roman settlement consisting of a series of enclosures backing onto a trackway (Johnston 1985). A subsequent watching brief immediately to the east revealed further Bronze Age activity and a concentration of medieval occupation close to Pingewood House (Lobb and Mills 1993). A further small-scale excavation carried out 150m to the south of Green Park 3 uncovered a ring ditch presumed to be of prehistoric date and a number of Romano-British ditches (ibid.).

More recently, fieldwork has been carried out by OA at several locations in the area (Fig. 1.2). An evaluation at Hartley Court Farm, 200m to the south-east of Green Park 3, has revealed later Bronze Age occupation, a Romano-British settlement producing late 3rd- to 4th-century pottery, and a small medieval settlement dating to the 12th to 14th centuries (OA 1991a; Keevill 1992). Fieldwalking to the west of this site at Hopkiln Farm produced prehistoric worked flint, Roman finds including pottery and a shale vessel fragment, and a sparse scatter of medieval pottery (OA 1991b). Evaluation trenching at the Green Park Substation site, immediately to the north of Green Park 3, uncovered two ditches of probable Bronze Age date, along with two ditches containing late 11th-century pottery that are likely to be associated with a cropmark complex to the east (OA 2001). Finally, at Reading Sewage Treatment Works, 1km to the north-east of Green Park 3, a watching brief revealed a C-shaped ring ditch which produced no finds but is likely to be of prehistoric date (OA 2002).

FIELDWORK METHODS

Green Park 3

The third phase of OA fieldwork at Green Park comprised evaluation trenching followed by open area excavation in the south-western part of the development area (Fig. 1.3). Thirteen evaluation trenches were excavated in August 2000 (OA 2000), to add to the information gained from the earlier Wessex Archaeology evaluation of the site (see above). A total area of 3ha, divided into two discrete zones either side of a drainage ditch, was then excavated between October 2000 and April 2001. A watching brief was subsequently carried out immediately to the north of the excavation area (Fig. 1.3). This revealed few significant archaeological features; the majority of the relevant area was scheduled to be used for dumping, and topsoil removal was not complete across the whole area. Features were revealed in the north-west corner of this area (Fig. 1.3) but were not dated.

Moores Farm

Evaluation trenching was undertaken at Moores Farm in 1989 (OA 1989). A total of 83 trenches were excavated, representing a 1% sample of the site; where archaeological deposits were encountered the number of trenches was increased to a 2% sample (Fig. 1.5). The results from the evaluation trenches formed the basis for the placement of 16 excavation areas, investigated between October 1998 and July 1999. The largest of these, Area 16, measured 165 x 135m, and corresponded with an area of later Bronze Age activity identified by the evaluation. The other 15 excavation areas were much smaller, ranging from 50 x 40m to 30 x 10m in size. In total, an area of 3ha was uncovered. In addition, a limited watching brief was maintained on groundworks carried in various other parts of the site between July and September 1999. Subsequently, in 2000, three discrete areas in the western part of the site were stripped and subjected to a more rigorous watching brief. Archaeological features within these areas were planned and limited sample excavation carried out.

Excavation procedures

The excavations at both Green Park 3 and Moores Farm followed standard procedures set out by the OA field manual (Wilkinson 1992) and IFA guidelines (IFA 1999). The topsoil was removed mechanically down to the first significant archaeological horizon or to the surface of the underlying natural silts and gravel, under the supervision of an archae-ologist. Subsequently, archaeological features and deposits were excavated by hand. Linear ditches were sample excavated in segments, and discrete features were usually half-sectioned. Some signifi-cant discrete features were subjected to 100%

excavation. All archaeological deposits were allocated a unique context number. Finds were recorded by context, with objects of special interest additionally being given a unique small find number (eg SF 10). Environmental sampling targeted features with a high potential for the

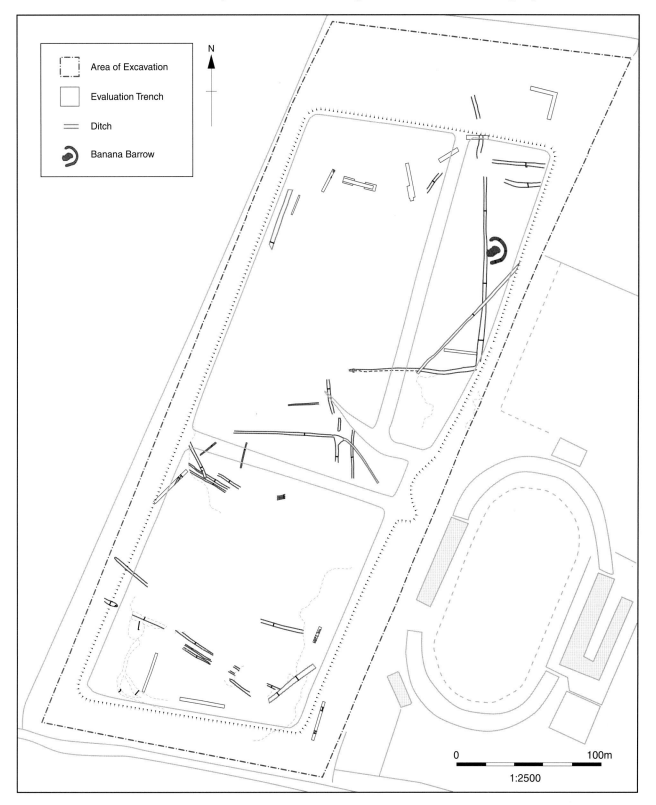

Fig. 1.5   Moores Farm: areas of archaeological fieldwork

recovery of charred remains or waterlogged macroscopic plant remains. Pollen columns were also taken from waterlogged features at both sites.

LAYOUT OF THE VOLUME

The next two chapters of this volume present the stratigraphic sequence, finds and environmental evidence from Green Park 3, with Chapter 2 covering the early prehistoric and Bronze Age evidence and Chapter 3 the later Iron Age to post-medieval activity. The evidence from Moores Farm is presented in Chapter 4. In Chapter 5, Elaine Morris considers the significance of the assemblages from Green Park and Moores Farm for our understanding of the middle to late Bronze Age ceramic transition in southern Britain. The final chapter discusses the development of prehistoric settlement in the Green Park/Moores Farm area, synthesising the results of all of the fieldwork to date.

Chapter 2: Green Park 3 –
early Prehistoric and Bronze Age activity

ARCHAEOLOGICAL SEQUENCE

Introduction

The Green Park 3 excavations revealed multi-period activity including middle to late Bronze Age occupation, later Iron Age ditches, a Romano-British field system and post-medieval trackways. This chapter deals with the pre-Iron Age archaeology. Most of the features occurred at the eastern and western ends of the site, with a 'blank' area in the centre (Fig. 2.1). It is possible that this central area was genuinely avoided in the past, although as it contained many modern service trenches archaeological features may have been lost to truncation.

Early prehistoric activity

Low-level early prehistoric activity is evinced by small quantities of residual Mesolithic and Neolithic flintwork found scattered across the site (see Cramp below). A single sherd of Beaker pottery (late Neolithic/early Bronze Age) was also recovered from middle Bronze Age waterhole 2690 (see Morris below).

Middle to late Bronze Age

A fragmentary Bronze Age field system extended across much of the excavated area, incorporating five large waterholes or pit-wells (Fig. 2.2). The chronology of these features requires comment, as they produced both middle Bronze Age pottery in the Deverel-Rimbury (DR) tradition of *c* 1700–1150 cal BC, and non-Deverel-Rimbury pottery that would traditionally be ascribed to the late Bronze Age (*c* 1150–750 cal BC). The two pottery types occurred together in a number of contexts in both the waterholes and field boundary ditches, making it difficult to dismiss the DR material as residual or the non-DR material as intrusive. A programme of radiocarbon dating of waterhole deposits was thus carried out in order to clarify ceramic chronology at the site. The radiocarbon dates clearly show that the waterholes belong to the middle Bronze Age, implying an earlier origin for the non-DR elements of the pottery assemblage than previously accepted. This important finding is discussed at length by Morris (see below and Chapter 5), who argues that the non-DR material from the waterholes represents a class of 'transitional' pottery belonging to the second half of the second millennium BC, overlapping with the DR tradition and predating the classic late Bronze Age

'plain ware' assemblages of the 10th–9th centuries BC. No material suitable for radiocarbon dating was available from the field system ditches. While it seems likely that the field system was directly contemporary with the waterholes, the possibility that it continued in use later, into the late Bronze Age 'proper', cannot be discounted.

Field system

The field system was divided into two discrete blocks, in the eastern and western parts of the site, and generally followed a NNE-SSW/ESE-WNW or N-S/E-W alignment (Fig. 2.2). The status of linear features in the extreme north-west corner of the watching brief area is uncertain, and it is possible that some of these undated features, although on slightly different alignments, were related to the western block of field boundaries. The ditches positively identified as components of the field system were up to 0.62m deep, with a U-shaped profile. They typically had a fill of silty clay, sometimes overlying a basal gravel-rich erosion deposit. None of the ditches had been recut, and there were no stratigraphic indications of any alterations to the field system over time. The sparse finds from the ditches included small amounts of

Table 2.1 Summary of Bronze Age ditches

Feature	Finds and dating evidence
2436	Burnt flint. Dated by alignment
2495	15 sherds DR and non-DR pottery
2505	Dated by alignment
2511	25 sherds DR (from 1 vessel?)
	10 sherds of DR and non-DR pottery
2538	Saddle quern
2539	Dated by alignment
2540	Dated by alignment
2571	1 sherd later Bronze Age pottery
2638	23 sherds DR and 3 sherds non-DR pottery
2736	Flint
2797	Cut by Iron Age ditch 2798
2806	Aligned with 2797
3033	4 sherds ?non-DR pottery
3051	2 sherds later Bronze Age pottery
3082	Aligned with 3033
3149	8 sherds non-DR pottery
3260	Flint and burnt stone
3383	1 sherd non-DR pottery

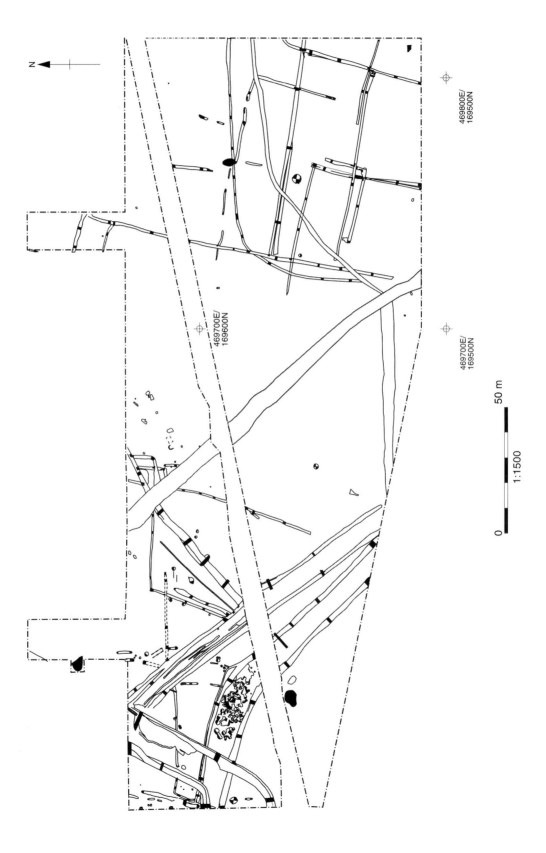

Fig. 2.1   Plan of all features, showing excavated interventions

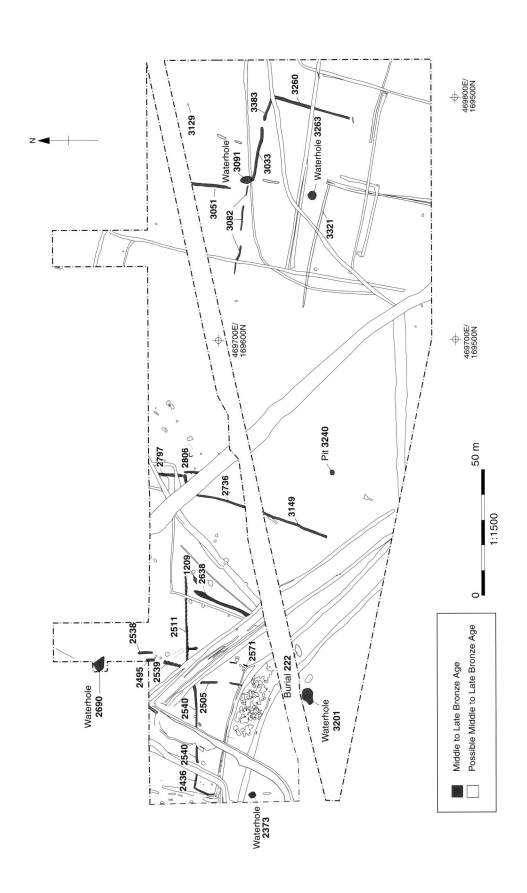

Fig. 2.2 Middle to late Bronze Age features

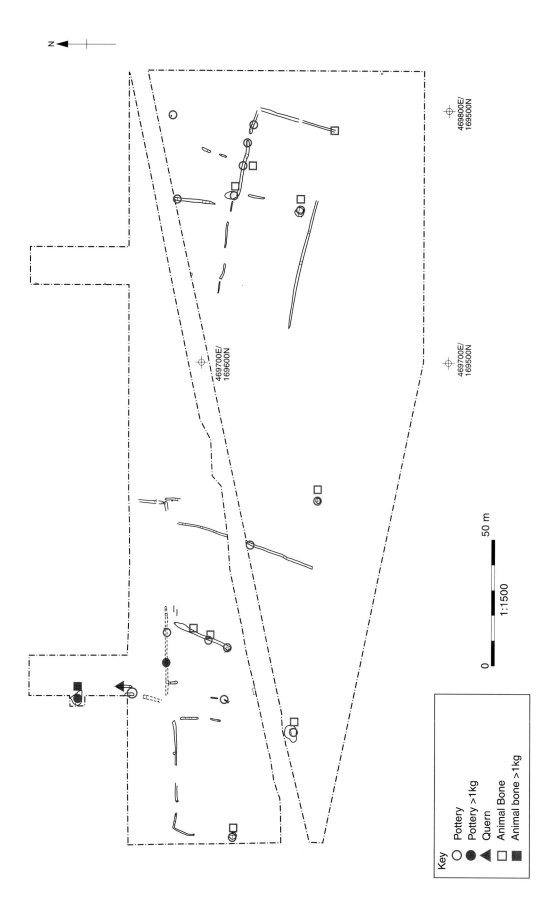

Fig. 2.3 Distribution of finds from middle to late Bronze Age features

pottery, worked flint and animal bone (Table 2.1). One much larger group of pottery weighing 2.4 kg and including a perforated vessel base was recovered from one intervention in ditch 2511 (Fig. 2.3); this may represent a deliberate deposit. A complete saddle quern found nearby at the base of the northern terminus of ditch 2538 was probably also deliberately placed. As noted above, the pottery from the ditches includes both DR and non-DR material, with the two clearly occurring together within ditch 2511 (see Morris below). Ditch 3321 produced no finds and could equally well be associated with the later Romano-British field system, which followed a similar alignment (see Chapter 3).

Waterholes

Three waterholes or pit-wells were associated with the western block of the field system (2373, 2690 and 3201) and two with the eastern block (3091 and 3263) (Fig. 2.2). These were up to 5.5m in diameter and 0.85–1.08m deep, and appear to have largely filled through natural processes of silting and erosion. The lower fills of the waterholes were waterlogged, and aquatic plant and insect species in environmental samples from these deposits confirms the presence of standing water during their period of use (see below).

Work elsewhere in the Thames Valley has suggested that later Bronze Age waterholes can generally be divided into two broad categories: steep-sided features, and large, teardrop-shaped features accessed by a gently-sloping ramp (Framework Archaeology 2006; Yates 2007, 16; Lambrick 2009, 267). Both types were represented at this site, with the large waterholes 2690, 3091 and 3201 falling into the ramped category and the smaller waterholes 3263 and especially 2373 being steep-sided. The two categories of waterhole had a number of distinct characteristics. The ramped features all contained remains of wooden structures, which probably represent revetted platforms used to draw water when the level within the waterhole was low. Each of them also produced some unusual finds from their fills (Table 2.2). Artefacts deposited while the waterholes were still in use included wooden vessels and, in the case of waterhole 2690, human bone. After the waterholes had gone out of use, material

deposited in their upper fills included a large group of pottery sherds (waterhole 2690) and a shale bracelet fragment (waterhole 3091). Small amounts of cremated human bone were also recovered from the upper fills of two of the ramped waterholes. The steep-sided waterholes, in contrast, showed no traces of any wooden structures. They contained no finds other than a few small fragments of pottery and animal bone from the middle and upper fills, which may have been incidental inclusions. The role of these waterholes and the nature of the deposits within them is discussed in more depth in Chapter 6.

Ramped waterholes

Waterhole 2690 was 3.00–4.40m in diameter and 1.08m deep (Fig. 2.4). It was teardrop-shaped, with a gently sloping ramp to the south-east. It appeared to cut a shallow, undated ditch (2810) that continued beyond the limit of excavation to the west.

The waterhole had a primary, waterlogged, gravel-rich clay fill (2689), overlain by three further layers of clay (2686–8). The primary fill contained the *in situ* remains of a structure made up of wooden planks and stakes, forming a right-angled arrangement along the southern and eastern sides of the waterhole, just above the base of the feature (Figs 2.4–6). This structure probably served both to revet the waterhole and provide a platform for the extraction of water. The main element of the southern side of the structure was a large horizontal oak plank (2766) with a mortice hole at its western end. This was held in position by a vertical stake (2768), set into the base of the waterhole and running through the broken mortice hole. Two further vertical stakes (2789 and 2790) supported the northern edge of the plank. Similar horizontal planks pegged into position using mortice holes have been found in later Bronze Age waterholes at Stanwell, Middlesex (O'Connell 1990) and Swalecliffe, Kent (Masefield 2003), and have been interpreted as 'steps' used as a standing place while drawing water. The eastern side of the structure was quite different, incorporating a revetment formed by a plank set on edge lengthways (2787) and held in position on its western side by a vertical post set into the base of the waterhole (2772). Five further planks on the eastern side of the structure might also have originally formed part of this revetment, although they had

Table 2.2 The dynamics of deposition in the Bronze Age waterholes

Water-hole type	Feature	Use					Decommissioning/disuse			
		Pottery	Wooden vessel	Animal bone	Buzzard bone	Human tibia	Pottery	Shale bracelet	Cremated human bone	Animal bone
1	2690	●	●	●	-	●	●	-	-	●
1	3091	●	●	●	-	-	●	●	●	●
1	3201	-	●	●	●	-	-	-	●	●
2	2373	-	-	-	-	-	●	-	-	●
2	3263	-	-	-	-	-	●	-	-	●

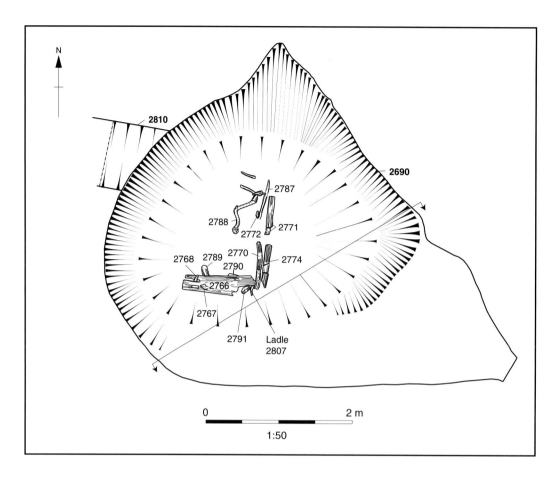

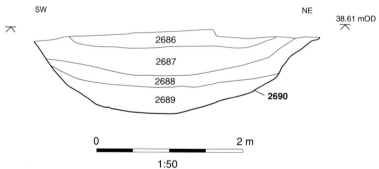

Fig. 2.4 Waterhole 2690

since slumped to a near-horizontal position. Four of the planks lay one above the other (from top to bottom: 2769, 2714, 2770 and 2774; only 2770 and 2774 are shown on Fig. 2.4).

Other wooden objects from the primary fill included a wooden ladle or dipper (2807) found adjacent to plank 2766 (Fig. 2.5), a fragmentary wooden vessel (2767) resting on top of the same plank, and a piece of roundwood possibly deriving from a hedge (2788; see Taylor below). Sherds of DR and non-DR pottery, 500g of animal bone and a human tibia fragment were also recovered. Two radiocarbon dates of 1412–1218 cal BC (KIA19182: 3068 ± 34 BP) and 1518–1318 cal BC (KIA19183: 3152 ± 39 BP) were obtained from waterlogged seeds from this deposit.

The remaining three fills of the waterhole

contained no waterlogged material. In each case, animal bone, burnt flint and pottery in both the DR and non-DR traditions was recovered. The bulk of the pottery (1.6 kg) and burnt flint (322g) occurred in penultimate fill 2687. It is possible that the pottery deposited within the waterhole was carefully selected, with a preponderance of decorated body sherds from DR vessels and rim sherds from non-DR vessels (see Morris below).

Waterhole 3091 was up to 4.60m in diameter and 0.90m deep (Fig. 2.7). It cut an earlier irregular pit or tree throw hole (3249) with a burnt fill, and was in turn later cut along its southern edge by ditch 3015 (a component of ditch 3033 on Fig. 2.2). The primary fill of the waterhole (3250) was a gravel-rich erosion deposit producing no finds. This was overlain by

Fig. 2.5 Detail of timber structure within waterhole 2690, facing north, showing timbers 2770, 2774, 2790 and 2791 and ladle 2807. Scale: 0.2m

Fig. 2.6 Timber structure within waterhole 2690 after further excavation, facing north. Scale: 1m

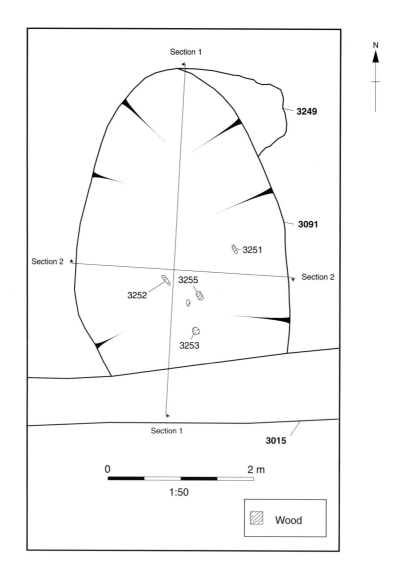

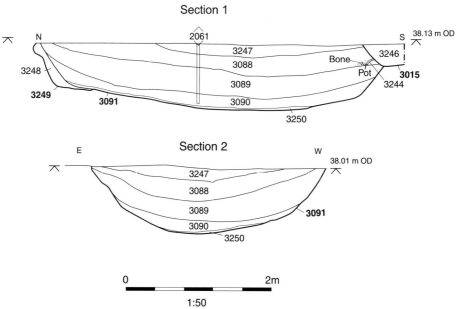

Fig. 2.7 Waterhole 3091

Fig. 2.8 Wooden vessel 3255 within waterhole 3091, facing north. Scale: 0.2m

four layers of clay (3088–90 and 3247), each of which produced pottery and animal bone. The first of these (3090) was a peaty, waterlogged deposit, which contained DR pottery, animal bone, fragments of a wooden vessel (3255; Fig. 2.8), and pieces of worked timber possibly deriving from a revetment structure (3252–3). Two radiocarbon dates of 1388–1130 cal BC (KIA19180: 3018 ± 35 BP) and 1395–1047 cal BC (KIA19181: 2997 ± 59 BP) respectively were obtained from seeds from this fill. The penultimate fill (3088) of the waterhole contained a shale bracelet fragment and, at the southern edge of the feature, a discrete scatter of cremated human bone, charcoal and DR pottery sherds (3244), possibly representing an urned cremation burial truncated by the digging of ditch 3015. The only certain non-DR pottery from the feature came from the uppermost fill (3247).

Waterhole 3201 was 5.50m in diameter and 1.00m deep (Fig. 2.9). It was teardrop-shaped, with a gently sloping access ramp to the south-west. The northern half of the waterhole had previously been partially investigated during the Wessex Archaeology evaluation, when a wooden bowl (Fig. 2.9) and two worked wooden stakes (oak and willow) were recovered from what was described as the primary fill (TWA 1986, 7). Excavation of the remainder of the feature revealed a sequence of four silty clay fills (3209–12). The initial fill (3212) was an organic-rich, waterlogged deposit which contained

two oak stakes driven into the base of the feature (3233 and 3235), along with several other wooden stake and plank fragments not *in situ* (3231–2, 3234 and 3237–8). These are likely to represent the remains of a revetment structure similar to that seen in waterhole 2690. Other finds were limited to fragments of animal bone, including a buzzard bone. Two radiocarbon dates of 1411–1214 cal BC (KIA19178: 3060 ± 36 BP) and 1393–1114 cal BC (KIA19179: 3006 ± 43 BP) were obtained from water-logged seeds from this fill. Finds from the middle and upper fills of the waterhole were limited. Fragments of animal bone and some tiny sherds of later Bronze Age pottery were recovered from fill 3210, and a small amount of cremated human bone was retrieved from an environmental sample from the uppermost fill (3209).

Steep-sided waterholes

Waterhole 2373 was 3.10m in diameter and 0.85m deep (Fig. 2.10). It was unique among the water-holes for showing evidence for at least two recuts. The original cut and first recut (2822) contained a series of silty clay fills. Two radiocarbon determinations of 1501–1307 cal BC (KIA19184: 3130 ± 35 BP) and 1383–1051 cal BC (KIA19185: 2991 ± 46 BP) were obtained from waterlogged seeds from the basal fill (2394) of the recut. No finds were recovered other than a few sherds of non-DR pottery from fill 2364. The second recut (2823) contained an initial layer of

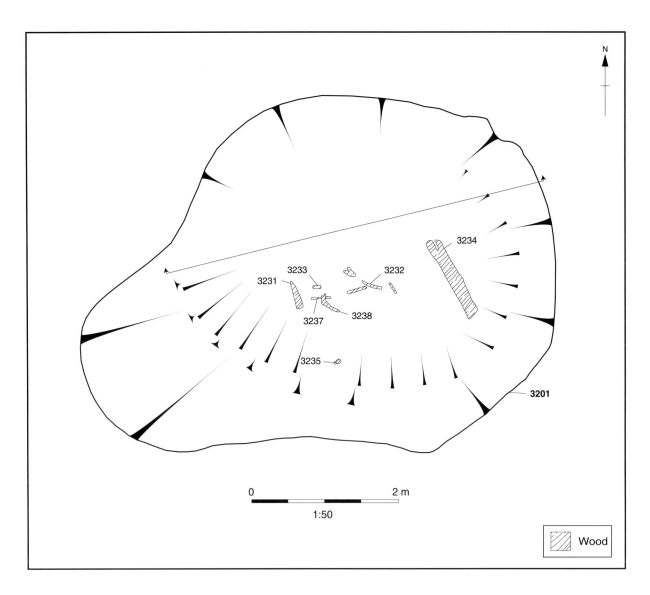

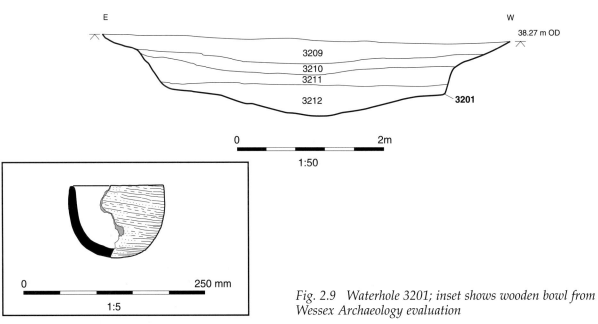

Fig. 2.9   Waterhole 3201; inset shows wooden bowl from Wessex Archaeology evaluation

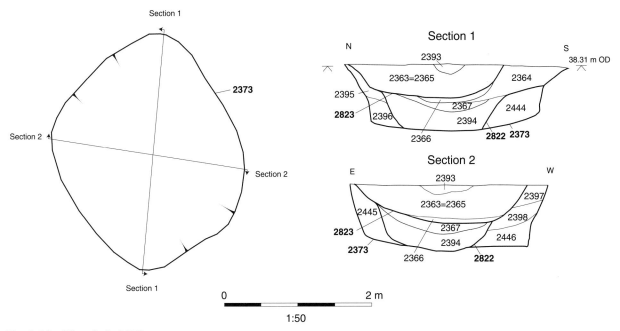

Fig. 2.10   Waterhole 2373

greenish silty clay (2366), possibly cess-like in character, overlain by a dumped deposit (2363/2365) containing large amounts of burnt flint (c 40%) and a few fragments of non-DR pottery and animal bone.

Waterhole 3263 was 3.60m in diameter and 0.85m deep (Fig. 2.11). It contained an initial erosion deposit of gravel (3272), overlain by two layers of clay. The lower clay fill (3271) was an organic-rich, waterlogged deposit. Seeds from this layer produced two radiocarbon dates of 1434–1214 cal BC (KIA19186: 3081 ± 43 BP) and 1388–1129 cal BC (KIA19187: 3014 ± 38 BP). The uppermost fill (3264) contained sherds of probable DR pottery and fragments of animal bone.

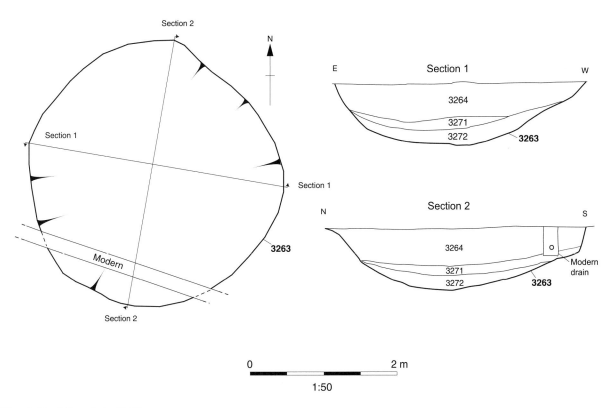

Fig. 2.11   Waterhole 3263

Table 2.3 Radiocarbon dates from Bronze Age waterholes

Feature	Context	Laboratory number	Material	$\delta^{13}C$ (‰)	Uncalibrated date (BP)	Calibrated date (1σ)	Calibrated date (2 σ)
2373	2394	KIA19184	Woody seeds	-25.2	3130 ± 35	1435–1320 BC	1501–1307 BC
2373	2394	KIA19185	*Crataegus* (hawthorn) fruits	-30.3	2991 ± 46	1366–1129 BC	1383–1051 BC
2690	2689	KIA19182	Seeds	-24.1	3068 ± 34	1393–1265 BC	1412–1218 BC
2690	2689	KIA19183	Weed seeds	-27.1	3152 ± 39	1492–1324 BC	1518–1318 BC
3091	3090	KIA19180	Woody seeds	-26.8	3018 ± 35	1371–1134 BC	1388–1130 BC
3091	3090	KIA19181	Seeds	-26.3	2997 ± 59	1370–1129 BC	1395–1047 BC
3201	3212	KIA19178	Woody seeds	-26.6	3060 ± 36	1388–1264 BC	1411–1214 BC
3201	3212	KIA19179	Weed seeds	-28.7	3006 ± 43	1369–1132 BC	1393–1114 BC
3201*	204	HAR-8561	Wooden stake	-25.0	2830 ± 80	1120–900 BC	1260–820 BC
3263	3271	KIA19186	Woody and weed seeds	-26.9	3081 ± 43	1408–1265 BC	1434–1214 BC
3263	3271	KIA19187	*Ranunculus repens* type seeds	-23.9	3014 ± 38	1370–1133 BC	1388–1129 BC

* = Determination from Wessex Archaeology evaluation 1986.
Dates calibrated using OxCal v3.5 (Bronk Ramsay 1995; 2001) and the data of Stuiver *et al.* (1998)

Table 2.4 Results of chi-squared test on radiocarbon dates from Bronze Age waterholes

Feature	Samples (laboratory number)	Results of chi-squared test (Ward and Wilson 1978)
2373	KIA19184/KIA19185	v =1 T'=5.8 (5% 3.8)
2690	KIA19182/KIA19183	v =1 T'=2.6 (5% 3.8)
3091	KIA19180/KIA19181	v =1 T'=0.1 (5% 3.8)
3201	KIA19178/KIA19179	v =1 T'=0.9 (5% 3.8)
3263	KIA19186/KIA19187	v =1 T'=1.4 (5% 3.8)

Radiocarbon dating of waterholes

The ten AMS radiocarbon dates obtained from the waterholes (two from each feature) all derive from waterlogged organic material found within the primary silting fills. They should therefore relate to the active use of these features. The date ranges all fell between 1492 cal BC and 1129 cal BC at the 68% confidence level (1 σ), and between 1518 cal BC and 1047 cal BC at the 95% confidence level (2 σ), indicating a middle Bronze Age attribution for the features (Table 2.3; Fig. 2.12). Four of the five sample pairs gave ages that showed no statistically significant difference, confirming the reliability of the results obtained, the exception being the pair from waterhole 2373 (Table 2.4). The samples from 2373 (unlike those from the other waterholes) derived from the fill of a recut, and as such it is possible that material of different ages had become incorporated into this fill.

Modelling of the dates (Fig. 2.13) provides support for the assumption that the waterholes represents a single phase of activity (A=88.4%). It provides an estimate for the start of waterhole activity on the site of 1500–1310 cal BC (95% probability), and an estimate for the end of activity of 1370–1130 cal BC (95% probability). Further mathematical analysis (Fig. 2.14) provides an estimate for the length of time over which the waterholes were

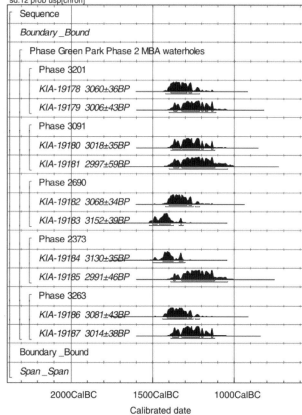

Fig. 2.12 Probability distributions of radiocarbon dates from Bronze Age waterholes

constructed of 20–200 years (68% probability) or 1–320 years (95% probability).

In addition to the ten dates discussed above, a further radiocarbon date had previously been obtained during the Wessex Archaeology evaluation, from a wooden stake recovered from waterhole 3201 (Table 2.3). This gave a date range of 1260–820 cal BC at 2σ(HAR8561: 2830 ± 80 BP),

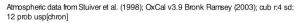

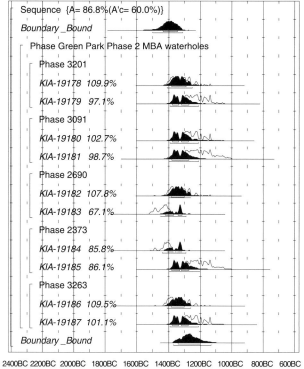

Fig. 2.13 *Probability distributions of radiocarbon dates: model providing an estimate for the duration of waterhole activity*

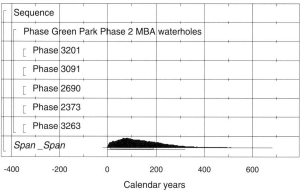

Fig. 2.14 *Probability distribution providing an estimate for the length of time over which the waterholes were constructed*

which is later in emphasis than the date ranges from the two samples from basal fill 3212 of the same waterhole. This difference is difficult to interpret given the uncertain stratigraphic relationship of the wooden stake to fill 3212.

Pits

Two pits of differing character were recorded (Fig. 2.2). Pit 3129 was 0.30m in diameter and 0.08m

deep, and contained the upstanding base of a DR vessel, placed flush within the cut. No bone was present within the vessel to suggest that it was a cremation urn. Pit 3240 was a bowl-shaped feature measuring 2.00m in diameter and 0.50m deep. It contained a gravel-rich lower fill overlain by two deposits of silty clay. The middle fill contained a single sherd of non-DR pottery and small fragments of animal bone.

Inhumation burial

A single crouched inhumation burial within an oval grave (222) was found in the south-western part of the site during the Wessex Archaeology evaluation (Figs 2.2 and 2.15). The body lay on its left side on an east-west alignment, with the head to the east. The individual was aged 35–45 years and was probably male. There were no associated finds, but a date no later than the middle to late Bronze Age is suggested by the fact that the grave was cut by a gully ascribed to that period (TWA 1986). Two similar crouched inhumation burials were found at Green Park 1, one of which contained late Bronze Age pottery (Moore and Jennings 1992, 11).

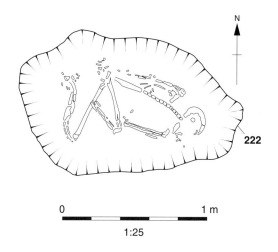

Fig. 2.15 *Burial 222*

ARTEFACTS

Flint *by Kate Cramp*

Introduction

A total of 70 struck flints and 523 pieces (6.01kg) of burnt unworked flint were recovered from the evaluation and the excavation (Table 2.5). Technologically, the majority of the material probably dates broadly to the Neolithic and Bronze Age. A very small amount of possible Mesolithic flintwork was also identified. The absence of large *in situ* assemblages and the paucity of diagnostic implement types have precluded more precise dating.

Table 2.5 Worked flint

Category	No. of pieces
Flake	14
Blade	1
Blade-like	3
Irregular waste	3
Chip	36
Multi-platform flake core	1
Tested nodule	3
Retouched flake	4
End scraper	2
End and side scraper	1
Scraper/piercer	1
Piercer	1
Total	70

Context and condition

The struck flint came from 27 contexts; with the exclusion of the chips recovered from sieving, the largest assemblage comprised four pieces. The burnt unworked flint was also thinly distributed across the site. A sizeable assemblage was retrieved from Bronze Age waterhole 2690 (612g), and a large proportion of the upper fill of waterhole 2373 (40%) was recorded as comprising burnt flint, although this was not collected.

The condition of the flint is varied. A small number of flints are in a fresh condition and, as such, are unlikely to have been subjected to a significant degree of post-depositional movement. Many pieces, however, exhibit some post-depositional damage or surface abrasion. Numerous pieces are in a poor, rolled condition with extensive edge-damage consistent with repeated redeposition.

Raw material

As at Green Park 2 (Bradley 2004) and Moores Farm (Cramp and Lamdin-Whymark, Chapter 6), gravel flint appears to have been the main source of raw material for the production of the debitage and tools in the assemblage. These nodules are characterised by an abraded cortex and the occasional presence of thermal fractures and were probably available locally, perhaps from the river gravels. An incomplete flake recovered from Iron Age context 2172 (pit 2173, pit group 2117) may be of bullhead flint or a related flint type.

Technology and dating

The general technological and morphological appearance of the assemblage suggests a later Neolithic or Bronze Age date. A small number of possible earlier Neolithic or Mesolithic pieces were also identified, although few diagnostic retouched forms were recovered from any period.

Flakes and blades are the most numerous class (Table 2.5). The majority of flakes are undiagnostic (eg Fig. 2.16.1), and can tentatively be ascribed to the Neolithic or Bronze Age. One flake, recovered from context 2656 (ditch 2638), may be earlier. Blades and blade-like flakes are less numerous, which probably reflects the under-representation of Mesolithic and earlier Neolithic material (Pitts and Jacobi 1979; Ford 1987, 79). A total of three blade-like flakes and one blade were recovered, combining to provide around 10% of the assemblage. The blade (pit 2078, pit group 117) is probably a Mesolithic or early Neolithic product, and exhibits extensive platform edge abrasion.

A single multi-platform core, probably dating to the later Bronze Age, was recovered from context 2612 (ditch 2640). It has been worked using a hard-hammer percussor, and no evidence for platform edge abrasion was identified. Three burnt tested nodules were also recovered, two from context 1207 (ditch 1209) and a third from the subsoil. None of the cores or tested nodules exceeded 55g in weight.

Context 2172 (pit 2173, group 2117) contained 36 chips, several of which are in a reasonably fresh, uncorticated condition. The recovery of chips from this context may be indicative of a limited amount of knapping activity in the vicinity, although the full range of knapping debitage is not represented. It is possible that the absence of chips from other features constitutes a product of the sieving strategy rather than a true reflection of the spatial distribution of knapping microdebitage. However, it seems likely that the assemblage does not contain a significant *in situ* knapping element.

The retouched component consists of nine pieces and includes edge-retouched flakes/blades, scrapers (Fig. 2.16.2–3) and piercers (Fig. 2.16.4). The majority of these pieces probably range in date from the Neolithic to the Bronze Age. The broad retouched blade (Fig. 2.16.5), recovered from context 2365 (waterhole 2373), may date to the Mesolithic or Neolithic. The end scraper (Fig. 2.16.6) from context 2687 (waterhole 2690) is unusually robust, consisting of a broad, square-shaped secondary flake of heavily corticated gravel flint in reasonable condition. Areas of discontinuous retouch have been applied to the distal flake margin to provide an abrupt scraping edge.

A number of flints, including several flakes and retouched tools, exhibit macroscopically detectable use-wear. Both hard and soft material use-wear appears to be represented. A total of nine flints have been burnt (26%) and 15 broken (43%). The presence of utilised, retouched, burnt and broken flints within the assemblage suggests a certain amount of domestic activity.

Discussion

The majority of the flint assemblage is probably of Neolithic or Bronze Age date. A date in the latter half of this range would be consistent with the low numbers of blades in the collection (Pitts and Jacobi 1979; Ford 1987, 79). In fact, given the under-representation of chalk flint artefacts it is possible that a significant component of the assemblage dates to the later Bronze Age. This would be consistent with the apparent decline in the use of good quality raw material over time seen in the lithic assemblages from Green Park 1 and 2 (Bradley and Brown 1992; Bradley 2004) and Moores Farm (Cramp and Anderson-Whymark, Chapter 6). Given the paucity of datable artefacts from Green Park, however, this cannot easily be borne out by a quantification of flints by raw material type and date.

Although the recovery of Neolithic and Bronze Age flintwork implies a human presence in these periods, it does not appear to represent intensive or prolonged levels of occupation. With the exception of a few minor concentrations of burnt flint and chips, the distribution of the flintwork does not reveal distinct foci of activity, but instead constitutes a relatively uniform and diffuse spread of material.

Catalogue of illustrated flint (Fig. 2.16)

1 Flake. Iron Age(?) pit group 2117, pit 2173, context 2172
2 End and side scraper. Post-medieval trackway 3123, context 3093
3 End scraper. Middle Bronze Age waterhole 2690, context 2687
4 Scraper/piercer. Iron Age(?) pit group 2117, pit 2295, context 2294
5 Retouched blade. Middle Bronze Age waterhole 2373, context 2365
6 End scraper. Middle to late Bronze Age ditch 3383, context 3371

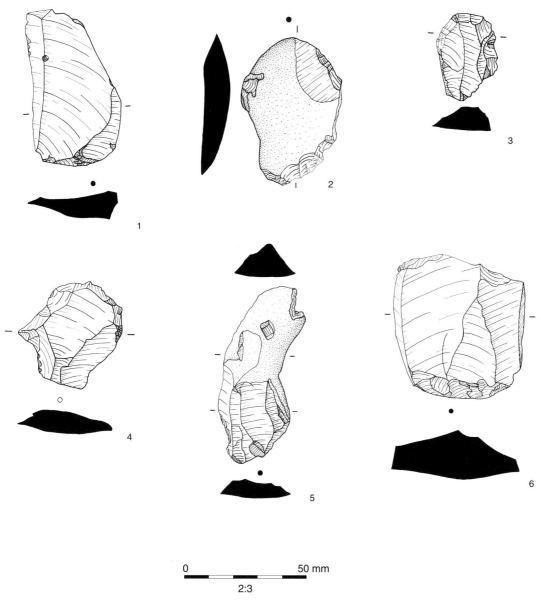

0   50 mm

2:3

Fig. 2.16   Worked flint

Bronze Age pottery *by Elaine L Morris*

Introduction

A total of 585 sherds (6.8 kg) of Bronze Age pottery was recovered (Table 2.6). The assemblage is significant because it represents the transition from the middle Bronze Age Deverel-Rimbury to late Bronze Age post-Deverel-Rimbury ceramic traditions, a phenomenon which has only recently been recognised amongst a limited number of prehistoric pottery assemblages from sites within the wider Upper-Middle Thames Valley region. The pottery has been analysed and recorded using the methodology recommended by the Prehistoric Ceramics Research Group for study of later prehistoric pottery (PCRG 1997). Where possible the Green Park 3 pottery fabric and vessel form types have been assigned the same code numbers as those used for the Green Park 2 assemblage (Morris 2004).

Late Neolithic/Early Bronze Age

A single sherd of Beaker pottery was identified (context 2687, waterhole 2690). This is an undecorated body sherd 7–9mm thick, which derived from a vessel that had been softly fired in an oxidising atmosphere for a short period of time. This produced an orange-coloured exterior surface, an unoxidised core within the vessel wall and an irregularly-coloured interior surface. No sherds of

Beaker type were specifically identified at Green Park 1, but a grog-tempered fabric with 20–30% temper was recorded, which was presumably associated with plain body sherds only (Hall 1992; Fabric Group 9, fabric AA). A single sherd of grog-tempered pottery was found in the Green Park 2 assemblage, but the vessel had been hard-fired and was consequently interpreted as of late Bronze Age date (Morris 2004).

Grog-tempered group

G2: a fine to intermediate-grade, softly-fired fabric consisting of a common amount (20–25% concentration) of grog measuring ≤ 2mm across in an only very slightly sandy clay matrix bearing rare to sparse amounts (2-3%) of subrounded to subangular quartz/quartzite grains measuring ≤ 0.2mm across and possibly finer mica flecks

Middle to late Bronze Age

Fabrics

The middle-late Bronze Age pottery assemblage is dominated by fabrics tempered with crushed, calcined flint fragments (Tables 2.6–8). Amongst the fabrics used to make middle Bronze Age vessels only, several (F15–17) were identified previously in the Green Park 2 assemblage. There were four new middle Bronze Age fabrics defined from amongst the Green Park 3 assemblage (F18–22). The new fabrics

Table 2.6 Quantification of Bronze Age pottery by fabric

Date	Fabric group	Fabric type	Number of records	Number of sherds	Weight of sherds (g)	Mean sherd weight (g)
Late Neolithic/early Bronze Age	Grog-tempered	G2	1	1	3	3.0
Middle-late Bronze Age	Flint-tempered/gritted	F1	13	27	92	3.4
		F3	21	89	999	11.2
		F5	34	184	1396	7.6
		F6	3	4	29	7.3
		F8	5	8	31	3.9
		F9	2	9	7	0.8
		F10	6	15	99	6.6
		F11	1	3	11	3.7
		F15	1	3	15	5.0
		F16	8	30	2027	67.6
		F17	12	154	1881	12.2
		F18	3	13	28	2.2
		F19	1	1	12	12.0
		F20	4	4	36	9.0
		F21	2	5	23	4.6
		F22	3	13	76	5.8
		F99	1	11	1	0.1
Middle-late Bronze Age	Flint and grog-tempered	FG1	1	5	7	1.4
Middle-late Bronze Age	Iron oxide and flint-tempered	IF2	2	3	12	4.0
		IF3	1	1	4	4.0
Middle-late Bronze Age	Sandy	Q1	2	2	6	3.0
		Total	127	585	6795	11.6

included a coarse ware (F18) which was used to make a barrel urn found in pit 1209. This had a high density of moderately-sorted inclusions and was not dissimilar to the bucket urn fabric F15 from Green Park 2. An unusual intermediate ware (F19) had very well-sorted temper with a narrow measurement range from 1–3mm across, and was classified as middle Bronze Age due to this distinctive characteristic of the temper. The temper was similar to that used to make globular urns. F21 was a fine to intermediate fabric with well-sorted temper, and was used to make a globular urn. The fourth new middle Bronze Age fabric (F22) was extraordinarily densely tempered (40–50% concentration) with a narrow size range of well-sorted, selected inclusions.

In the Green Park 2 assemblage one fabric, F5, was recognised as having been used to make both middle and late Bronze Age vessels. At Green Park 3 both F5 and an additional fabric, F3, were used to make pottery of both ceramic traditions. Fabric F3 was regarded as a late Bronze Age fabric in the Green Park 2 assemblage, but was used during both ceramic periods at Green Park 3. It may actually represent the use of both groups of vessels at the same time. These two fabrics are coarsewares within the fabric range of later Bronze Age production techniques. In addition, one new, very fine flint-tempered fabric, F20, was used to make both middle Bronze Age globular urns and late Bronze Age bowls. Only four sherds were assigned to fabric type F20, but these derive from four different thin-walled vessels.

The likelihood of coterminous occupation in the areas excavated at Green Park 1–3 is supported by the use of three middle Bronze Age (F15–17), two

middle-late Bronze Age (F3 and F5) and nine late Bronze Age (F1, F6, F8, F10, F11, FG1, IF2, IF3 and Q1) pottery fabrics defined amongst the Green Park 1 and 2 assemblages (Hall 1992; Morris 2004) which were also found within the Green Park 3 assemblage.

Flint-tempered/gritted group

F1: identical to fabric type F1 at Green Park 2 (late Bronze Age)

F3: identical to fabric type F3 at Green Park 2 (middle and late Bronze Age)

F5: identical to fabric type F5 at Green Park 2 (middle and late Bronze Age)

F6: identical to fabric type F6 at Green Park 2 (late Bronze Age)

F8: identical to fabric type F8 at Green Park 2 (late Bronze Age)

F10: identical to fabric type F10 at Green Park 2 (late Bronze Age)

F11: identical to fabric type F11 at Green Park 2 (late Bronze Age)

F15: identical to fabric type F15 at Green Park 2 (middle Bronze Age)

F16: identical to fabric type F16 at Green Park 2 (middle Bronze Age)

F17: identical to fabric type F17 at Green Park 2 (middle Bronze Age)

F18: a coarse fabric characterised by a micaceous clay matrix containing a common to very common (25–30% concentration) amount of moderately-

Table 2.7 Correlation of fabric and form types for middle and late Bronze Age pottery by frequency of occurrences/vessels.

Form					Fabric					
	F1	F3	F5	F10	F16	F17	F18	F20	F21	TOTAL
R3	-	-	-	-	-	-	-	1	-	1
R11	1	-	1	1	-	-	-	-	-	3
R14	-	-	1	-	-	-	-	-	-	1
R16	-	-	1	-	-	-	-	-	-	1
R18	-	-	1	-	-	-	-	-	-	1
R19	-	-	1	1	-	-	-	-	-	2
R31	-	-	-	-	-	-	1	-	-	1
R32	-	-	-	-	-	-	-	-	1	1
R33	-	-	-	-	-	-	-	1	-	1
L4	-	-	-	-	-	-	-	-	1	1
L99	-	-	1	-	1	-	-	-	-	2
B1	-	-	1	-	-	1	-	-	-	2
B2	-	-	1	-	1*	-	-	-	-	2
B99	-	1	-	-	-	2	-	-	-	3
D1	-	3	2	1	-	-	1	-	-	7
Total	1	4	10	3	2	3	2	2	2	29

* = perforated

sorted, angular, crushed, burnt flint fragments with the majority measuring from 2–4mm across with finer fragments also present; this fabric is similar to F15 at Green Park 2 but is coarser grained in texture (middle Bronze Age)

F19: an intermediate fabric distinctively characterised by a common to very common amount (20–30%) of very well-sorted, angular, crushed burnt flint fragments measuring between 1–3mm across (there are no larger or smaller fragments visible using a binocular microscope at x10 power in the single sherd identified in this assemblage) (middle Bronze Age)

F20: a very fine fabric containing a common amount (20%) of very well-sorted, angular, crushed burnt flint fragments measuring ≤1mm across (middle and late Bronze Age)

F21: a fine to intermediate fabric containing a common amount (25%) of well-sorted, angular, crushed, burnt flint fragments measuring ≤2mm across, with only very rare fragments measuring up to 3mm across (middle Bronze Age)

F22: an intermediate fabric which contains an abundant amount (40–50%) of very well-sorted, angular, crushed burnt flint fragments measuring ≤2mm across with the majority of fragments measuring between 1–2mm across which emphasises the very well-sorted texture of this very harsh feeling fabric (?middle Bronze Age)

F99: fragments of pottery, each bearing more than one angular burnt flint inclusion, which are too small to provide representative detailed fabric type descriptions

Flint and grog-tempered group

FG1: identical to fabric type FG1 at Green Park 2 (late Bronze Age)

Iron oxide and flint-gritted group

IF2: identical to fabric type IF2 at Green Park 2 (late Bronze Age)

IF3: identical to fabric type IF3 at Green Park 2 (late Bronze Age)

Sandy group

Q1: identical to fabric type Q1 at Green Park 2 (late Bronze Age)

Vessels

Traditionally, sherds from later Bronze Age assemblages can be classified either as middle Bronze Age Deverel-Rimbury bucket, barrel and globular urns or as late Bronze Age post-Deverel-Rimbury plain ware comprising shouldered and ovoid jars and shouldered, slack-profiled, and hemispherical bowls with occasional cups (Barrett 1980). However, the assemblages from excavations at Green Park 2 (Morris 2004), Pingewood (Johnston 1985) and Eynsham Abbey, Oxfordshire (Barclay 2001) now

demonstrate that in the Upper Thames and Kennet Valley regions it is possible to see a transitional form. This is characterised by a straight-sided, neutral vessel shape reminiscent of the bucket urn tradition but which is thinner-walled and often has an incurving effect near the rim, suggestive of the convex ovoid jar tradition of the late Bronze Age. For the Green Park 2 assemblage, this vessel type was coded R16 (Morris 2004) and the fabrics associated with that form (F1, IF2 and IF5) were interpreted as belonging to the late Bronze Age tradition. In the Green Park 1 assemblage, the form is known as types 14 and 15 and decorated examples are both slashed and fingertipped on the rim (Hall 1992, figs 44.14, 44.19, 44.46 and 45.53). At Green Park 3 this vessel shape has been encountered again, but with a fabric type (F5) which was both middle and late Bronze Age in date, and with decoration on the rim which is commonly seen on middle Bronze Age urns. The Green Park 3 ceramics therefore show a greater mixture of middle and late Bronze Age characteristics than was observed in the Green Park 2 examples. This combination of form and fingertip decoration has also been found in the Lower Kennet Valley at Aldermaston Wharf (Bradley 1980, fig. 18.160B) and Pingewood, where numerous examples were recovered (Johnston 1985, figs 7–8). Examination of the Green Park 3 assemblage has revealed a more complex pattern within what is being interpreted as an exciting period of ceramic transition, which can now hopefully be identified elsewhere in future. This phenomenon is discussed in detail below, after the more common types for each major period are described. The vessels are illustrated by key groups from specific features (Figs 2.17–19).

A small number of diagnostic middle Bronze Age vessels were identified in the Green Park 3 assemblage from rim, lug/handle sherds and decorated sherds specifically. These include one barrel urn (Fig. 2.17.1) and two globular urns (Fig. 2.18.9 and 2.19.23). These vessels are typical of middle Bronze Age examples often found in the Middle Thames and Kennet Valley region as at sites in Middlesex (Barrett 1973) and at Field Farm, Burghfield and Shortheath Lane, Sulhamstead in Berkshire (Butterworth and Lobb 1992). One sherd has a vertically applied and horizontally perforated small lug with incised horizontal decoration at the lug, which is a typical combination of characteristics for globular urns. The barrel urn sherd has a flat-topped rim and a raised horizontal cordon bearing fingertip impressions along the vertical wall, a regular combination of characteristics for these large vessels. It was recovered from the upper fill of field boundary ditch 1207.

There are several other vessels in the Green Park 3 assemblage which probably represent middle Bronze Age urns. The applied cordon with fingertip impressions on a decorated sherd (Fig. 2.19.19) could have derived from a bucket or barrel urn, but what is most significant is that the vessel was made from fabric F3, originally interpreted as a late Bronze Age fabric in the Green Park 2 assemblage (Morris 2004). The base from an urn made from a middle Bronze Age fabric reflects the size diameter, 240mm, expected of a middle Bronze Age bucket or barrel urn (Fig. 2.17.5). It may represent a truncated cremation burial (3129), although no cremated bone survived. This large urn base contrasts with a much smaller one, also made from a middle Bronze Age fabric, measuring only 140mm in diameter (Fig. 2.17.2) which had been roughly perforated in the base centre after firing; the hole measures *c* 14–16mm across. One vessel, found in association with the perforated base urn, is from a very large thick-walled vessel bearing the stub of a handle joining the vessel wall (Fig. 2.17.3). The girth diameter of this pot is *c* 240mm, and it is likely to represent another urn based on size, wall thickness and fabric type (F16). These vessels were recovered from ditch 2511. The central flat part of another probable large urn (not illustrated) made from a middle Bronze Age fabric (F17) was found in ditch 2638. This sherd was 22–3mm thick.

A very specific range of late Bronze Age vessel types, one bowl and four jar forms, was found in the Green Park 3 assemblage, but none of these are the usually very common shouldered jars and bowls. The bowl form is the wide open, slack-profile type R3, and only one example was found (Fig. 2.18.11). It had been made from a very fine fabric, F20, which was also used to make a globular urn (Fig. 2.19.23). This R3 form is very similar to examples from Green Park 1 (Hall 1992, fig. 45.50) and Aldermaston Wharf (Bradley 1980, fig. 14.48G).

Jar type R11 is an ovoid or convex-profile shape, and three examples were identified at Green Park 3 (Figs 2.17.4, 2.17.6 and 2.19.24). Jar type R14 is a necked form, with a single example identified (Fig. 2.18.8); this form was also found at Eynsham Abbey (Barclay 2001). A sherd was recovered from what was probably a large shouldered form, R18 (Fig. 2.18.12), and the fourth jar type is very reminiscent of barrel urns, with its flat-top rim and bulging or expanded profile (Fig. 2.19.15–16). This type was first identified at Green Park 1 (Hall 1992, fig. 47.114 and 47.118), but none were found in the Green Park 2 assemblage. The R14, R18, one of the R19 and one of the R11 jars from Green Park 3 were made from the middle to late Bronze Age transition fabric type F5, while the second R19 jar and two of the R11 jars were made from late Bronze Age fabrics (F1 and F10).

The most significant vessel form which displays characteristics of both the middle Bronze Age and the late Bronze Age ceramic traditions is the straight-sided, nearly convex-profile vessel type R16. The example from Green Park 3 (Fig. 2.18.7), found in waterhole 2690, is amongst the larger vessels in the assemblage. The rim diameter is 200mm and is therefore of smaller bucket urn dimensions, but at 8–10mm the vessel walls are thinner than those of the typical bucket urn, which normally measure more than 12mm thick. The vessel is decorated with

fingertip impressions on the top of the rim, which is typical of middle Bronze Age bucket urns, while the fabric, F5, is part of the middle-late Bronze Age tradition at the Green Park complex. At Green Park 2, however, the five examples of R16 vessels were all made from late Bronze Age fabrics (F1, IF2 and IF5). An identical example to the Green Park 3 vessel was found at Pingewood in association with a middle Bronze Age urn with a boss (Bradley 1985, fig. 7.4–5). An extremely similar example was found at Green Park 1 in the same context as a decorated body sherd from a middle Bronze Age urn (Hall 1992, fig. 45.53–54). A similar vessel with slashed decoration on the rim was found in association with a bucket urn at Knights Farm subsite 3, Berkshire (Lobb *et al.* 1980, fig. 32.39–42). Several examples of slashed or fingernail decorated vessels of this type were found at Eynsham Abbey (Barclay 2001, fig. 16, 34, 36, 38–9).

Another fabric F5 special correlation (Table 2.7) is a decorated sherd with one vertical and one horizontal row of oval-shaped, toothed comb impressions (Fig. 2.19.21). This technique of decoration is not found on middle Bronze Age urns in the Middle Thames valley region (cf. Barrett 1973). The vessel is very thick-walled, which suggests that the sherd comes from an urn. The presence of combed decoration is also just faintly visible on another decorated, thick-walled urn sherd with an applied horizontal cordon decorated with fingertip impressions (Fig. 2.19.22). These combed impressions, however, were made with a square-toothed implement and the vessel had been made from the other middle-late Bronze Age coarse fabric, F3. There could well be some merit to a very detailed, magnified examination of the different types of fingertip decoration, cordon application, and toothed-comb impressions correlated to fabric variations in assemblages of this period, with the aim of identifying different potters' hand/fingerprints or signatures (cf. Tomalin 1995) on vessels recovered from the same site.

There are two decorated body sherds which may belong to the transition from middle to late Bronze Age traditions. One, decorated with an incised geometric grid pattern (Fig. 2.18.10), was from a large, thin-walled vessel with a possible 240mm girth diameter. This is an unusual combination of fineware-style decoration but extremely coarseware fabric (F3). In addition, the vessel was abraded on the interior surface, which suggests that something acidic had been stored in this vessel or that whatever had been stored in it was scraped out. The second sherd (Fig. 2.19.20) was made from the other middle-late Bronze Age fabric, F5, and appears to have a cordon onto which short, slashed marks have been incised, and might represent a shouldered vessel. It may be that this sherd is from the junction between two manufacturing coils, one representing the upper half of the vessel (missing) and the other the lower half. A very similar sherd was found at Field Farm, Burghfield (Mepham

1992a, fig. 19.19). A third sherd from Green Park 3 (Fig. 2.17.6) bears a single horizontal, incised line from the lower part of a vessel with medium girth size, but it was made from a fine-intermediate late Bronze Age fabric (F10). All of these decorated sherds were recovered from waterhole 2690.

There are three examples of perforated vessels in the Green Park 3 assemblage, two of which were perforated before the vessels had been fired (one illustrated; Fig. 2.19.17) and one of which was perforated after firing (Fig. 2.17.2), probably as a secondary use for the vessel. Some of the latter vessel's body sherds were found in the same context. In addition, there is a single sherd with an attempted perforation which was made prior to firing (Fig. 2.19.18). All of the pre-firing perforated sherds were found in waterhole 2690 and were from vessels made from middle to late Bronze Age fabrics F3 and F5. A similar range of perforations or attempted perforations was recorded in the Eynsham Abbey late Bronze Age assemblage (Barclay 2001, figs 14.9, 15.18 and 15.27). One was also recovered from Green Park 1 (Hall 1992, fig. 44.10), and one from Aldermaston Wharf (Bradley 1980, fig. 12.4D). There are no examples of sooted

sherds or sherds with carbonised residues in this assemblage, but two vessels display evidence which could be interpreted as interior vessel wall scraping from use (Fig. 2.18.10 and 2.19.14; see above).

In summary, this modest assemblage of later Bronze Age pottery is dominated by classic examples of middle Bronze Age Deverel-Rimbury pottery with a small component of fragments from late Bronze Age vessels including jars and a bowl. The most exciting contribution, however, is the identification of the transitional middle to late Bronze Age pottery style, deposited within one principal feature on the site. If the Eynsham Abbey site was occupied between *c* 1270–1040 cal BC (Barclay *et al.* 2001), the end of Bronze Age occupation at the Green Park site is likely to have been contemporary with the beginning of that at Eynsham Abbey, due to the similarity of straight-sided vessels and the presence of at least a few truly late Bronze Age vessel forms. It is also likely to have been contemporary with the occupation at Pingewood, due to the presence of so many straight-sided vessels or 'tubs' at that site, several directly associated with decorated sherds from middle Bronze Age urns (Bradley 1985).

Table 2.8 Occurrences of middle and late Bronze Age vessels by fabric within contemporary contexts (example in parentheses also represented in previous context)

Feature	Context	F1	F3	F5	F6	Fabric Type F8	F9	F10	F11	F15	F16
Ditch 1209	1207	-	-	-	-	-	-	-	-	-	-
Ditch 2495	2494	-	-	1	-	-	-	-	-	-	-
Ditch 2511	2486	-	1	-	-	-	-	-	-	-	1
Ditch 2511	2487	1	-	-	-	-	-	-	-	-	2
Ditch 2511	2604	-	-	-	-	-	-	-	-	-	-
Ditch 2571	2570	-	-	1	-	-	-	-	-	-	-
Ditch 2638	2656	-	-	-	-	-	-	-	-	-	-
Ditch 2638	2698	1	-	-	-	-	-	-	-	-	-
Ditch 3033	3029	-	1	-	-	-	-	-	-	-	-
Ditch 3033	3377	-	-	-	-	-	-	-	-	-	-
Ditch 3051	3061	1	-	1	-	-	-	-	-	-	-
Ditch 3149	3053	-	-	2	-	-	-	-	-	-	-
Ditch 3383	3371	-	-	1	-	-	-	-	-	-	-
Pit 3129	3130	-	-	-	-	-	-	-	-	-	-
Pit 3240	3242	-	1	-	-	-	-	-	-	-	-
Waterhole 2373	2363	1	-	-	-	-	-	-	-	-	-
"	2364	1	-	-	-	-	-	-	-	-	-
"	2365	1	1	-	1	-	-	-	-	-	-
Waterhole 2690	2686	-	1	3	-	-	-	1	-	-	-
"	2687	-	6	11	1	3	1	1 (1)	-	-	-
"	2688	-	2	1	-	-	-	-	1	-	-
"	2689	-	-	1	1	-	-	-	-	-	-
Waterhole 3091	3088	-	1	-	-	-	-	-	-	-	-
"	3089	-	1	1	-	-	-	-	-	-	-
"	3090	-	-	-	-	-	-	-	-	-	-
"	3247	-	-	-	-	-	-	-	-	-	-
Waterhole 3201	3210	-	-	-	-	-	-	-	-	-	-
Waterhole 3263	3264	-	-	-	-	-	-	-	-	-	-

Middle Bronze Age urn forms

R31: flat-topped, square-shaped rim on inward sloping neck; from barrel urn with mid-wall decoration of fingertip impressions along horizontal raised cordon (Fig. 2.17.1)

R32: rounded rim from neckless vessel; ?globular urn; this rim profile is similar to the late Bronze Age biconical bowl type 4 from Green Park 1 (Hall 1992, 64, fig. 41.4) which ranges from 110–150mm in diameter (Fig. 2.18. 9)

R33: incurved, upright, thin-walled rim from globular urn (Fig. 2.19.23)

L4: horizontally perforated, vertically applied small, lug with narrow cross-section; middle Bronze Age ceramic tradition (Fig. 2.18.9)

L99: junction zone of uncertain handle type with vessel body wall (Fig. 2.17.3 and 2.19.13)

Late Bronze Age bowl forms

R3: identical to bowl rim type R3 at Green Park 2 (Fig. 2.18.11)

Late Bronze Age jar forms

R11: identical to jar rim type R11 at Green Park 2 (Fig. 2.17.4, 2.17.6 and 2.19.24)

R14: identical to jar rim type R14 at Green Park 2 (Fig. 2.18.8)

R16: identical to jar rim type R16 at Green Park 2 (Fig. 2.18.7)

R18: very similar if not identical to jar types 10 and 11 from Green Park 1 (Hall 1992, 64–8, figs. 42.10 and 43.11) based on rim shape and upper body profile as well as apparently large vessel size (Fig. 2.18.12)

R19: similar to vessel type 16 at Green Park 1 (Hall 1992, 68, figs 43.16, 47.114 and 47.118) (Fig. 2.19.15–16)

Middle-late Bronze Age base forms

B1: identical to base type B1 at Green Park 2 (Fig. 2.17.5)

B2: identical to base type B2 at Green Park 2 (Figs 2.17.2 and 2.19.14)

B99: central flat zone of base (not illustrated)

Discussion

The analysis of this modest assemblage of middle and late Bronze Age pottery was a challenge, due to the infrequency of featured sherds and the similarities with variations amongst the fabrics. This

					Fabric Type						
F17	F18	F19	F20	F21	F22	F99	FG1	IF2	IF3	Q1	Date
-	1	-	-	-	-	-	-	-	-	-	MBA
-	-	-	-	-	-	-	-	-	-	-	?M/LBA
-	-	-	-	-	-	-	-	-	-	-	MBA
-	-	-	-	-	-	-	-	-	-	-	MBA & LBA
-	-	1	-	-	-	-	-	-	-	-	?LBA
-	-	-	-	-	-	-	-	-	-	-	M/LBA
2	-	-	1	-	-	-	-	-	-	-	MBA
-	-	-	-	-	-	-	-	-	-	-	LBA
-	-	-	-	-	-	-	-	-	-	-	?LBA
1	-	-	-	-	-	-	-	-	-	-	MBA
-	-	-	-	-	-	-	-	-	-	-	?M/LBA
-	-	-	-	-	-	-	-	-	-	2	LBA
-	-	-	-	-	-	-	-	-	-	-	LBA
1	-	-	-	-	-	-	-	-	-	-	MBA
-	-	-	-	-	-	-	-	-	-	-	LBA
-	-	-	-	-	-	-	-	-	-	-	?LBA
-	-	-	-	-	-	-	-	-	-	-	LBA
-	-	-	-	-	-	-	-	-	-	-	LBA
1	-	-	-	-	-	-	-	-	-	-	MBA & LBA
-	-	-	1	1	1	-	-	-	-	-	MBA & LBA
-	-	-	1	-	1	-	-	-	-	-	MBA & LBA
-	-	-	1	-	-	-	-	-	-	-	MBA & LBA
3	-	-	-	-	-	-	-	-	-	-	MBA
-	-	-	-	-	-	-	-	-	-	-	MBA (?LBA)
-	-	-	1	-	-	-	-	-	-	-	MBA
-	-	-	-	-	-	-	1	-	-	-	LBA
-	-	-	-	-	-	1	-	-	-	-	Uncertain
-	-	-	-	-	1	-	-	-	-	-	?MBA

'struggle with the fabrics' suggests that the Green Park 3 assemblage in particular may reflect a similar effort for the Bronze Age potters who could have been responding to changes in their society at that time; they were wrestling with finding a way to express the life which they were experiencing. Eventually we can clearly see the ceramic change from globular, barrel and bucket urns to biconical bowls and shouldered or ovoid jars, but undoubtedly this did not take place overnight. Why these shape changes were being experimented with is at present unknown.

The assemblage from Green Park 2 first suggested that this change could be recognised as a transition from straight-sided, thick-walled bucket and barrel urns to straight-sided, thinner-walled vessels of neutral form, which evolved into plain assemblage post-Deverel-Rimbury ovoid jars including hooked rim varieties and shouldered jars. Similar straight-sided, neutral-profile vessel forms have recently been published from the late Bronze Age site of Eynsham Abbey, and directly radiocarbon dated to *c* 1270–1040 cal BC by assay of burnt residue on the pottery (Barclay *et al.* 2001). This indicates that the late Bronze Age pottery style originated earlier than was previously supposed, first appearing towards the end of the second millennium BC in this region. Two other sites where both middle Bronze Age urns and these transitional forms have been found are nearby at Field Farm, Burghfield (Butterworth and Lobb 1992, fig. 19) and Knights Farm subsite 3, where the sherds were found in a deposit which has been radiocarbon dated to 1750–1200 cal BC (Lobb *et al.* 1980, 268, fig. 32.39–42). There were no globular urns at Green Park 2, so the assemblage there cannot contribute to the argument that this form developed into the late Bronze Age bowl form, but at Green Park 3 the same fabric, F20, was used to make both a globular urn and a late Bronze Age bowl. This suggests continuity within change; a transformation within acceptable parameters.

The Green Park 3 assemblage suggests a dramatic or complicated action, simply by the use of the same fabrics for making pots for both 'diagnostic' ceramic traditions and for the deposition of similar sized sherds, ie specific fragments (J. Chapman, pers. comm.), from both middle Bronze Age urns and late Bronze Age vessels into the same large feature. Waterhole 2690 contained fragments of several middle Bronze Age vessels (Figs 2.18.9, 2.19.13, 2.19.19 and 2.19.21–3) and fragments of even more late Bronze Age vessels (Figs 2.17.6, 2.18.7–8, 2.18.11–12 and 2.19.14–16). Other features generally contained either middle or late Bronze Age sherds, but at least one ditch context contained sherds from both ceramic traditions (context 2487, ditch 2511) (Tables 2.8–9). This pattern did not occur at Green Park 2, where a small amount of middle Bronze Age pottery was found only in a few field boundary ditches and cremation burials but large quantities of late Bronze Age pottery occurred in dozens of settlement features, including several waterholes. At Green Park 2, middle Bronze Age pottery was the minority pottery in frequency and was not found in any waterholes.

What is most important to emphasise about the sherds recovered from waterhole 2690 is that they represent at least 18 vessels (Table 2.8), that each vessel is represented by only one or just a few sherds and that many of the vessels are decorated sherds from the bodies of the pots. In particular, it is the middle Bronze Age vessels which are primarily represented by decorated body sherds (with one exception), while the late Bronze Age vessels are represented by rims (with one exception) including the straight-sided transition form which is decorated. This range of forms, presence and absence of decoration by ceramic tradition, selection of vessel parts and fragmentation all found within a waterhole deposition context must be significant. The manufacture of these vessels and their destruction and deposition could represent creation/procreation and death or change/alteration respectively. The Green Park 3 assemblage may be one of the best archaeological examples we have of the use of pottery as a

Table 2.9 Occurrences of middle and late Bronze Age vessels by form within contemporary contexts (number in parentheses also represented in previous context)

Feature	Context	R3	R11	R14	R16	R18	R19	R31	R32	R33	L4	L99	B1	B2	B99	D1	Date
Ditch 1209	1207	-	-	-	-	-	-	1	-	-	-	-	-	-	-	1	MBA
Ditch 2511	2486	-	-	-	-	-	-	-	-	-	-	-	-	1	-	-	MBA
Ditch 2511	2487	-	1	-	-	-	-	-	-	-	1	-	-	-	-	-	MBA & LBA
Ditch 2495	2494	-	-	-	-	-	-	-	-	-	-	-	1	-	-	-	?M/LBA
Ditch 2638	2656	-	-	-	-	-	-	-	-	-	-	-	-	-	1	-	MBA
Pit 3129	3244	-	-	-	-	-	-	-	-	-	-	-	1	-	-	-	MBA
Waterhole 2690	2686	-	1	-	1	-	-	-	-	-	-	-	-	-	1	-	MBA & LBA
Waterhole 2690	2687	1	-	1	(1)	1	2	-	1	-	1	1	-	1	1	5	MBA & LBA
Waterhole 2690	2688	-	-	-	-	-	-	-	-	-	-	-	-	-	-	1	MBA & LBA
Waterhole 3091	3090	-	-	-	-	-	-	-	-	1	-	-	-	-	-	-	MBA

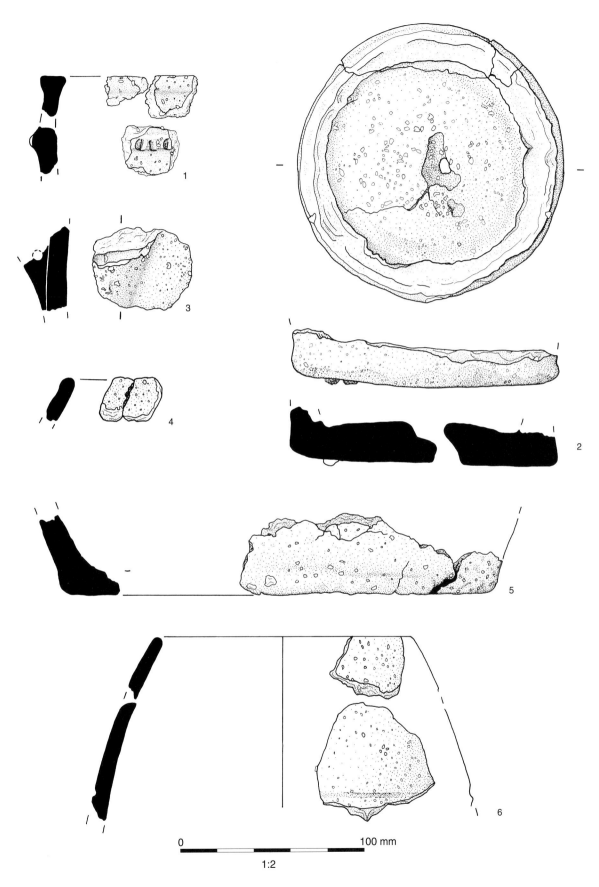

Fig. 2.17   Bronze Age pottery, nos 1–6

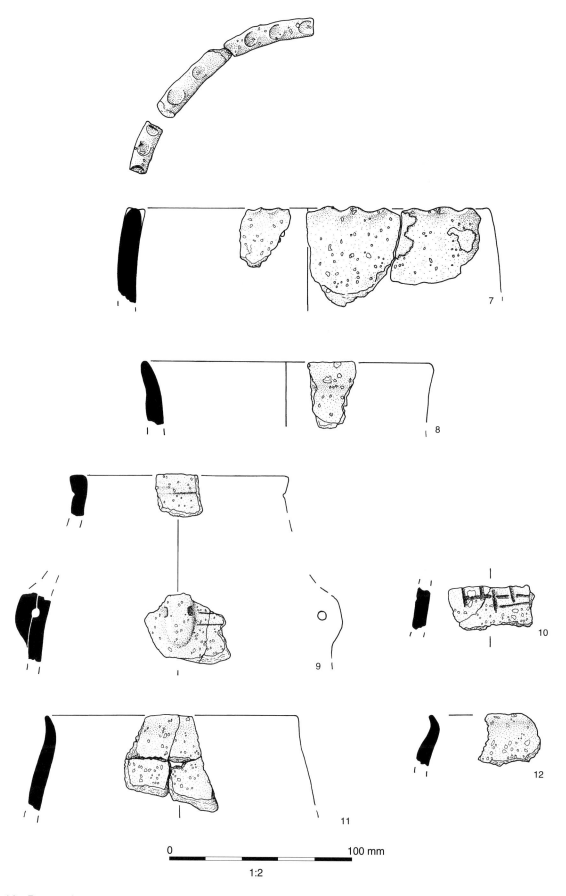

Fig. 2.18   Bronze Age pottery, nos 7–12

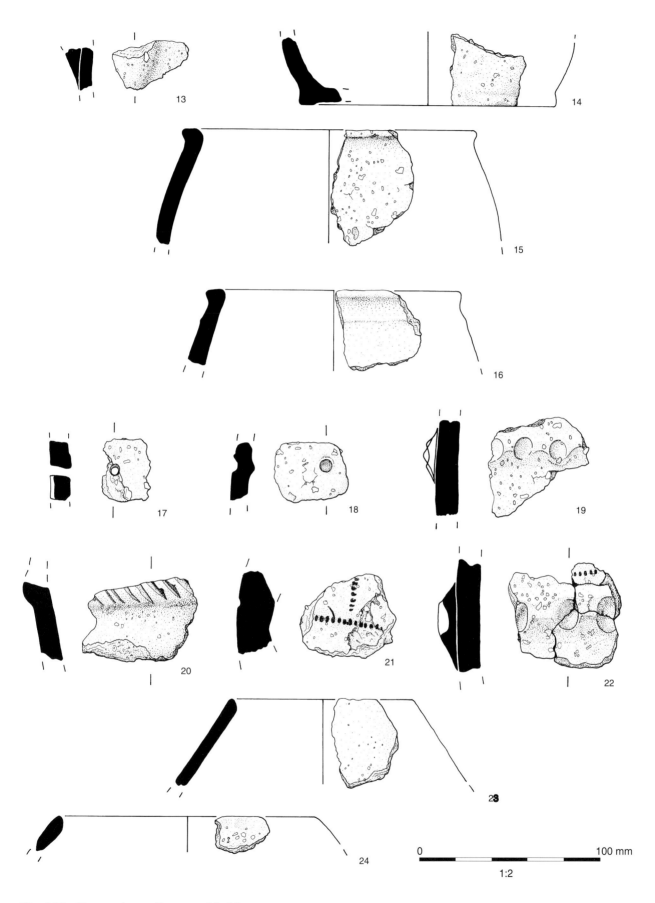

Fig. 2.19   Bronze Age pottery, nos 13–24

metaphor for life, people and ancestors (cf. Sterner 1989; Morris 1994; Brown 1995). Future research in this area might consider the transformation of earthly matter, such as flint, a vital element in this system of change since it is such an important element of both landscapes and ceramic production in the region. The study of fabric variation as a demonstration of social identity or ethnicity is in its infancy (cf. Raymond 1994).

Catalogue of illustrated middle to late Bronze Age pottery (Figs 2.17–19)

1 Rims/decorated sherd, barrel urn; R31, less than 5% present; fabric F18; fingertip impressions on raised, horizontal cordon; unoxidised exterior and core, oxidised interior. Ditch 1209, context 1207.

2 Base, urn; B2, 100% of 140mm diameter present; fabric F16; irregularly-fired exterior, unoxidised interior and core; post-firing perforation c 145–165mm in diameter. Ditch 2511, context 2486.

3 Lug/handle stub, urn; L99; fabric F16; irregularly-fired exterior, unoxidised interior and core. Ditch 2511, context 2487.

4 Rim, ovoid jar; R11, 5% of 140mm diameter; fabric F1; unoxidised. Ditch 2511, context 2487.

5 Base, urn; B1, 35% of 240mm diameter; fabric F17; oxidised exterior, unoxidised interior and core. Pit 3129, context 3130.

6 Rim/decorated body, ovoid jar; R11/D11, 6% of 140mm diameter; fabric F10; incised line on lower vessel zone; oxidised. Waterhole 2690, context 2686 and 2687.

7 Rim, straight-sided jar; R16; 15% of 200mm diameter; fabric F5; decorated with fingertip impressions on rim top; oxidised. Waterhole 2690, context 2686 and 2687.

8 Rim, necked jar; R14, 5% of 160mm diameter; fabric F5; oxidised. Waterhole 2690, context 2687.

9 Rim/lug, globular urn; R32/L4, 6% of 120mm diameter; fabric F21; incised at rim/neck join and at lug girth. Waterhole 2690, context 2687.

10 Decorated sherd; D1; fabric F3; oxidised on exterior and interior, unoxidised core; possible use wear abrasion on interior. Waterhole 2690, context 2687.

11 Rim, bowl; R3; 6% of 140mm diameter; fabric F20; irregularly-fired exterior, unoxidised interior and core. Waterhole 2690, context 2687.

12 Rim, necked jar; R18, less than 5% present; fabric F5; irregularly-fired exterior, unoxidised core, oxidised interior. Waterhole 2690, context 2687.

13 Lug/handle stub; L99; fabric F5; oxidised on exterior and interior, unoxidised core. Waterhole 2690, context 2687.

14 Base, jar; B2, 7% of 140mm diameter; fabric F5; oxidised on exterior and interior, unoxidised core; possible use wear abrasion on interior. Waterhole 2690, context 2687.

15 Rim, barrel jar; R19, 5% of 160mm diameter; fabric F5; oxidised. Waterhole 2690, context 2687.

16 Rim, barrel jar; R19, 6% of 140mm diameter; fabric F10; cordon effect at neck; unoxidised. Waterhole 2690, context 2687.

17 Sherd with pre-firing perforation; P1; fabric F3; oxidised. Waterhole 2690, context 2687.

18 Sherd with partial pre-firing perforation; P1; fabric F3; oxidised. Waterhole 2690, context 2687.

19 Decorated sherd, urn; D1; fabric F3; applied cordon with fingertip impressions; oxidised. Waterhole 2690, context 2687.

20 Decorated sherd, possible urn or shouldered jar; D1; fabric F5; slashed decoration; oxidised. Waterhole 2690, context 2687.

Decorated sherd, possible biconical urn; D1; fabric F5; perpendicular impressions made from an oval-toothed comb; oxidised. Waterhole 2690, context 2687.

22 Decorated sherd, urn; D1; fabric F3; applied cordon with fingertip impressions and possible square-toothed comb impressions above; oxidised. Waterhole 2690, context 2688.

23 Rim, globular urn; R33, 7% of 100mm diameter; fabric F20; smoothed surfaces; irregularly-fired exterior, unoxidised exterior and core. Waterhole 3091, context 3090.

24 Rim, ovoid jar; R1, 5% of 140mm; fabric F5; oxidised exterior and interior, unoxidised core. Ditch 3258, context 3336 (residual in Romano-British context).

Quern *by Ruth Shaffrey*

A complete saddle quern of Sarsen was recovered from ditch 2538 (context 2537). The stone had been worked into a roughly rectangular shape (280 x 170 x 87mm), though the underneath of the quern had been left in its natural state, revealing that it was made from a small boulder or large cobble. The quern would have been fixed in position as its base is uneven. The concave grinding surface was pecked but extremely well worn, and showed signs of polish caused by extensive use. The item was possibly discarded because the grinding surface had become so smooth that it had ceased to be effective, and the very concave nature of the surface may have made the quern difficult to use and therefore not worth repecking. However, the disposal of the quern is suggestive of ritual deposition, as it had been placed in the base of a ditch terminal before the ditch was backfilled, and was not associated with other 'refuse'.

Sarsen occurs locally as blocks and boulders (Blake 1903, 68–9) and would have been easily obtainable. It was the most common material for querns from later Bronze Age contexts at Green Park 1 and 2 (Jennings 1992, 94; Roe 2004), and has been found elsewhere in the local area at Moores Farm (Shaffrey, Chapter 4) and Pingewood (Lobb and Mills 1993, 87). It was also used at sites where it was not immediately available, for example at Bray in east Berkshire, where the nearest source was at least 5 km away (Montague 1995, 25).

Shale bracelet *by Ruth Shaffrey*

About one quarter of a well-preserved, undecorated shale bracelet (Fig. 2.20) was recovered from middle Bronze Age waterhole 3091 (context 3088). This has an off-round cross section (*c* 8 x 7mm) and an external diameter of approximately 92mm. A fragment of a similar shale bracelet was recovered from the late Bronze Age burnt mound at Green Park 2 (Boyle 2004a). Elsewhere in the Thames Valley, there are a few examples of shale bracelets from middle Bronze Age contexts, for example at Petters Sports Field, Egham, Surrey (Johnson 1975), but they are more commonly found during the late Bronze Age, as at Runnymede Bridge, Surrey (Longley 1980, 31) and Eynsham, Oxfordshire (Boyle 2001). The shale is likely to come from the outcrop at Kimmeridge, Dorset (Lawson 1976, 242).

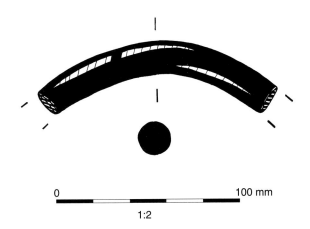

Fig. 2.20   Shale bracelet fragment

Wood *by Maisie Taylor*

An important assemblage of waterlogged wood was recovered from the lower fills of Bronze Age waterholes 2690, 3091 and 3201 (Table 2.10). The wood was examined visually and measured where possible. Field measurements have been used in those cases where pieces were too damaged or fragile to measure. Over 30 pieces of wood were received for analysis together with 11 bags of sampled material.

The assemblage includes a few pieces of worked roundwood, but most of it is unworked. One piece of unworked roundwood is almost certainly derived from a hedge. Most of the timber is radially split from fairly small trees, with a few pieces of tangentially split timber, possibly from larger trees. There are also a few pieces of woodworking debris, mostly woodchips, though there is one piece of timber debris. There are five artefacts, all of which were recovered from waterholes 2690 and 3091. These include two vessels and a ladle or dipper.

Condition

Using the scoring scale developed by the Humber Wetlands Project (Van de Noort *et al.* 1995, table 15.1) most of the material scores 1 or 2, indicating a poor condition. The artefacts were better preserved, possibly scoring 4 or 5. Waterhole 3201 had been partly excavated during the 1986 evaluation, and this may go some way to explaining the condition of the wood recovered from this feature, which was very brittle and crumbly. Disturbance of a waterlogged context in this way will often lead to oxygen activating bacterial activity. The distorted diameters of some of the roundwood can be taken as an indicator of desiccation (Taylor 1998, 142).

The wood

Sixty pieces of roundwood were examined. One, 2788 from waterhole 2690, clearly shows a right-angled bend, which is diagnostic of laid hedges (Taylor 1998, 147, fig. 156). Other pieces of roundwood seem to be derived from branch wood; some of these are trimmed, presumably to be used as stakes. A tree trunk (3253) recovered from waterhole 3091 had been felled and trimmed with two axes. An axe with a blade 45mm wide was used to fell the tree whilst another (34mm wide) was used for trimming off side branches. The dimensions of the axe blades fall within the range most frequently associated with middle and late Bronze Age axes (Taylor 2001, 197).

Thirteen planks were examined. Most had been radially split from small, fast-grown trees. There were occasional tool facets surviving. These facets show that surfaces had been worked but give little indication of the size and shape of axes.

The site did not produce a large enough assemblage of woodworking debris to make statistical analysis practical, but there are woodchips of all kinds: one tangentially aligned, two radially aligned and four which could not be categorised. There was one 'slab' which is a type of woodchip diagnostic of debarking a tree.

There was some evidence that the surviving planks and stakes were the remains of timber structures constructed in the base of the three waterholes. In features 3091 and 3201 fragments of broken planking, probably not *in situ*, and a few stakes driven into the natural at the base of the waterholes had survived. The structure in feature 2690 was better preserved, however. Here, two sides of a rectangular wooden structure (2765) survived, with planks held in position by stakes driven into the natural. Frames and revetments are relatively common in the bases of Bronze Age waterholes and seem to be related to the instability of the gravel into which the holes are dug. Sometimes they incorporate a step or platform for standing on. In many cases these timbers are reused.

The ladle or dipper (2807; Fig. 2.21.1; Fig. 2.22) is small and appears to have been carved from a piece of wood with a naturally bulbous shape, possibly

Table 2.10 Wood from Bronze Age waterholes

Feature	Cxt	Description	Dimensions and condition
2690	2691	Horizontal oak planking/fragment, 1/8 split, trimmed squarish	
2690	2692	10+ small fragments of radially split oak plank.	? x 90 x 20 mm. Both ends missing.
2690	2714	Horizontal plank, radially split, both ends trimmed square. Tool marks recorded in field not now measurable	670 x 160 x 30 mm. Broken
2690	2766	Horizontal oak plank, half-split and hewn flat, with broken mortice at one end. Tool marks recorded in field no longer discernible.	975 x 325 x 40 mm. Broken and heavily decayed.
2690	2767	Base of sewn or two-piece vessel, probably unused, cut edge slightly curved and unworn.	Broken into 48 pieces with much missing, therefore not reconstructable
2690	2768	Roundwood stake, two ends trimmed/all directions, possibly retaining plank 2766.	382 x 52 x 50mm
2690	2769	Radially split oak fragment, trimmed one end/all directions.	436 x 84 x 25mm. One end missing.
2690	2770	Oak plank, radially split and trimmed square, trimmed one end/two directions.	734 x 85 x 40mm. Broken into four fragments, one end and other parts missing.
2690	2771	Oak plank, radially split and trimmed square.	
2690	2772	Oak post, radially split and trimmed square, trimmed one end/two directions.	Field measurements: 565 x 70 x 30 mm. One end missing.
2690	2773	Radial oak chip. Tool mark recorded in field no longer discernible.	187 x 46 x 16 mm. One end missing.
2690	2774	Timber, radially split and trimmed square.	600+ x 105 x 35 mm
2690	2787	Radially split, trimmed square and 1 end/blunt	620 x 100 x 25 mm
2690	2788	Roundwood with 90 degree bends, possibly from a laid hedge.	630 x 50 mm
2690	2791	Roundwood oak stake retaining plank 2776.	186 x 78/60mm diameter. Heavily charred
2690	2807	Ladle. Probable Pomoideae (apple/pear/hawthorn; identified by Jennifer Jones).	140 x 60mm. End of handle missing
2690	2808	Vertical oak fragment, roughly squared, tangentially split.	473 x 80 x 59 mm
2690	2809	Timber, radially split and trimmed square.	Much broken. Field measurements: 210 x 225 x 50–55mm x 20–28mm.
2690	2812	(1) Timber fragment, 1/8 split, trimmed to near circular dowel. (2) 11 fragments of thin, radially split oak.	(1) 120 x 65 x 50 mm. Broken and both ends missing. (2) all broken.
2690	2813	(1) 50 small pieces of roundwood, some oak, some alder, some unidentified. (2) oak woodchip, (3) woodchip, (4) slab (including bark with sapwood).	(1) 20–100 x 5–20 mm diameter, (2) 70 x 30 x 20 mm, very poor condition, (3) 30 x 20 x 10 mm, (4) 100 x 50 x 25 mm).
3091	3251	Tangential oak woodchip.	156 x 47 x 17 mm
3091	3252	Timber fragment, possibly vertical, tangentially split.	280 x 49 x 18 mm. Broken.
3091	3253	Felled tree, end trimmed off. Two axes used: tree felling (45:3) and trimming (34:4).	155 x 130 mm diameter.
3091	3255	Carved vessel, possibly oval, steep-sided, very finely made.	Broken into large number of small pieces and much missing. Impossible to reconstruct profile.
3091	3262	32 fragments from a very good quality object or objects now too shattered for further analysis. Evidence for hewing and splitting. Alder (*Alnus glutinosa*) or willow (*Salix* sp.)	
3201	3231	Vertical roundwood fragment (stake?), trimmed one end/three directions.	
3201	3232	Horizontal roundwood fragment, trimmed one end/all directions.	307 x 28/41 mm diameter. Broken.
3201	3233	Vertical oak roundwood fragment (stake), trimmed one end/all directions.	360 x 40/45 mm diameter. Very soft.
3201	3234	Plank fragment, tangentially split with ends trimmed square.	1210 x 200 x 30 mm. Very soft.
3201	3235	Vertical oak roundwood fragment (stake?), trimmed one end/one direction.	420 x 60/70 mm diameter.
3201	3237	Vertical roundwood fragment (stake?), trimmed one end/three directions.	303 x 25/29 mm diameter.
3201	3238	Vertical roundwood fragment (stake?) with trimmed side branch, trimmed one end/all directions.	340 x 45/50 mm diameter. Broken.

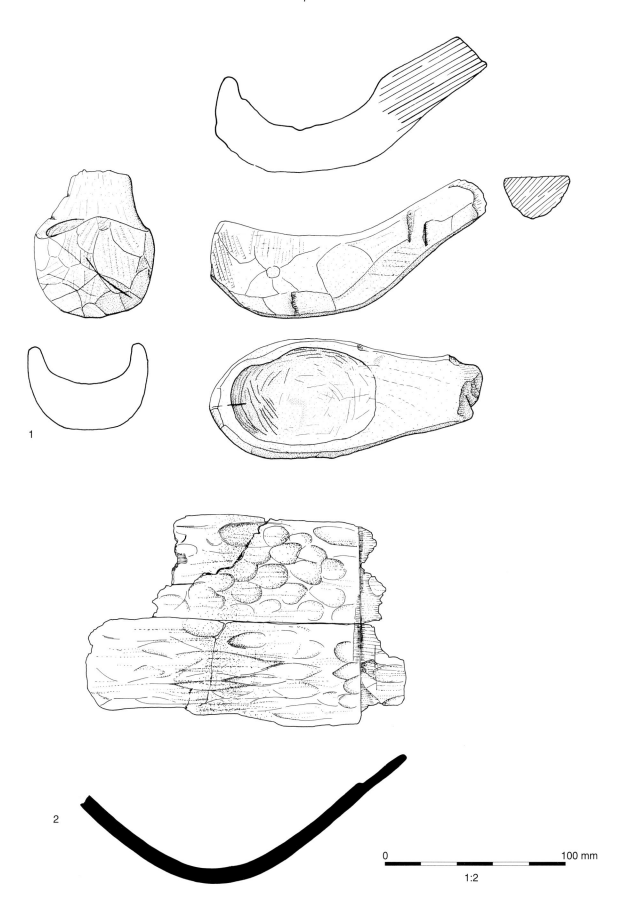

Fig. 2.21 Wooden objects

Fig. 2.22   Wooden ladle 2807

the join between a side branch and the trunk of a small tree. The wood is probably Pomoideae (apple/pear/hawthorn). An object interpreted as the bowl of a small ladle was found at Runnymede Bridge, Surrey (Heal 1991, 141, pl. 54, fig. 63), but other Bronze Age ladles tend to be larger (Taylor 2001, 226, fig. 7.65). Fragments of another artefact from the primary fill of the same feature are from a two-part vessel (2767). The fragments are from the vessel base, which shows evidence for having been sewn. Sewn two-piece vessels were found near the base of the Wilsford Shaft, Wiltshire (Earwood 1993, 54–6, fig. 30). The bases were made of single pieces of split wood, fastened to the body with fibres. A slightly different method of making sewn two-piece vessels has been seen in Ireland, but the fragmentary state of the present piece makes it impossible to be sure how it was fabricated. In addition to these items a short length of a dowel was retrieved from the same feature and layer. Both of its ends were missing, making it impossible to estimate the original length. It appears to have been made in the conventional way with a radially split piece of wood carved down to a virtually round section. The diameter of the dowel is 50mm, which is much larger than required for artefacts such as spear shafts or handles, and although closer in size to that required for a socketed axe foreshaft, it is still too large (Taylor 2001, fig. 7.62). Its use must, therefore, remain speculative.

The fragmentary remains of another vessel, possibly a box (3254–5), came from feature 3091 (Fig. 2.21.2; Fig. 2.8). This carved vessel is very unusual, and may have been oval with straight sides. The rebated top implies a lid and anticipates the lidded, carved or turned boxes of later periods. It is not possible to reconstruct the profile of the vessel because it is so badly damaged and large

pieces are missing. It was almost certainly of two-piece construction originally, although one-piece vessels do occur in the Bronze Age (Taylor 2001, fig. 7.66). An oval box would be a unique middle to late Bronze Age artefact. Waterhole 3091 also produced the damaged fragments of another good quality artefact.

Although the preservation of wood in Bronze Age waterholes is reasonably common in Britain, it is less common to find fine artefacts. A well-made trough was retrieved from a waterhole at Yarnton, Oxfordshire (Hey forthcoming) and a well made two piece vessel and an artefact have come from waterholes and ponds at Pode Hole, Cambridgeshire (Daniel 2009) but sites such as these are the exception.

OSTEOLOGICAL AND ENVIRONMENTAL EVIDENCE

Human bone *by Annsofie Witkin*

A right tibia fragment (84g) consisting of the mid shaft only was recovered from the primary fill (2689) of middle Bronze Age waterhole 2690. Using size as a guide, the bone appears to be from an adult. The only pathological lesion present is slight periostitis present on the distal medial side. The lesion appears not to have been active at the time of death of the individual.

Cremated human bone was recovered from two further middle Bronze Age waterholes. The penultimate fill of waterhole 3091 contained a discrete scatter of cremated bone, charcoal and middle Bronze Age pottery sherds (context 3244), possibly representing an urned cremation burial truncated by the digging of a later ditch. The deposit was subject to 100% recovery as a whole-earth sample and subsequently wet-sieved; only 10g of bone was recovered. The uppermost fill of waterhole 3201 (context 3209) produced a very small amount (<10g) of cremated bone from an environmental sample. In both cases, the bone fragments were heavily abraded. None of the fragments could be identified, and no age or sex estimate could be obtained. An average adult cremation weighs between 1000–2400g (McKinley 1997, 68), and it is therefore clear that neither of these deposits represents anything like the entire remains of any one individual. This may be explained by truncation of the deposits, although it is possible that they only ever contained a sample of the cremated remains. A number of very small deposits of cremated bone occurred in later Bronze Age features at Green Park 1 and 2 (Boyle 1992; 2004b).

Animal bone *by Bethan Charles*

A small and poorly preserved assemblage of animal bone comprising 71 refitted fragments (2171g) was recovered from middle to late Bronze Age contexts (Table 2.11). Only 26 fragments (37%) could be identified to species. The most abundant species was cattle, although this may not be representative of the animals eaten and kept at the site due to the poor condition of the assemblage. Smaller and more fragile fragments such as those from sheep and pigs will not have survived as well. Where possible, age data have been obtained using epiphyseal closure (Silver 1969) and tooth eruption and wear stages (Grant 1982; Halstead 1985).

A cattle mandible from a senile individual was recovered from waterhole 3091 (context 3088). Two further cattle mandibles from Bronze Age contexts were from an adult from waterhole 3201 (context 3210) and another aged 18–30 months from pit 3240 (context 3242). An unfused distal humerus from waterhole 2690 (context 2689) suggests that at least one animal died before reaching 1–1.5 years of age. A tibia from the same feature (context 2688) had been chopped, probably for marrow extraction. Carnivore gnawing on a cattle femur from waterhole 3091 (context 3090) suggests that the bone was exposed for a time before its final deposition.

Table 2.11 Animal bone from middle to late Bronze Age contexts

Species	No. fragments
Cattle	16
Sheep/goat	7
Horse	1
Red deer	1
Buzzard	1
Unidentified	45
Total	71

A sheep/goat mandible from waterhole 2690 (context 2688) was from an animal aged 3–5 years, and one from waterhole 2373 (context 2365) was aged 5–8 years. An unfused distal tibia from waterhole 3201 (context 3212) suggests that at least one sheep/goat died before reaching 1.5–2 years.

Horse is represented by a single femur fragment from waterhole 3091 (context 3089). Wild species comprise red deer, represented by a mandible from ditch 2638, and buzzard, represented by a single tibio-tarsus from waterhole 3201 (context 3212). This suggests that some hunting of wild animals occurred.

Charred and waterlogged plant remains
by Ruth Pelling

Twelve samples were taken for the recovery of charred plant remains and eight samples for the recovery of waterlogged remains from middle Bronze Age waterholes. The samples were processed using a modified Siraf type flotation machine. The volume of material processed for charred remains ranged from 9–40 litres. Sub-samples of 1kg were processed for waterlogged plant remains. Flots were collected onto 250μm meshes and residues retained on 1mm mesh.

Charred plant remains were generally sparse, and roots and modern weed seeds were present in several samples (Table 2.12). Charcoal was present in low or moderate quantities in 11 of the 12 samples, with oak (*Quercus* sp.) and Pomoideae (apple/pear/hawthorn) noted. Single grains of barley (*Hordeum vulgare*) were present in three samples.

The waterlogged plant remains are summarised in Table 2.13. Aquatic species were limited, being represented by crowfoot (*Ranunculus* subgen

Table 2.12 Charred plant remains from Bronze Age waterholes.

Sample	Context	Feature	Sample volume (litres)	Barley (Hordeum vulgare) grain	Charcoal	Notes
2016	2365	2373	40	0	++	*Quercus*, other
2017	2366	2373	36	0	++	cf. Pomoideae, modern weeds
2028	2686	2690	32	+	0	
2029	2687	2690	32	+	+	Pomoideae
2030	2688	2690	32	0	+	*Quercus*
2056	3209	3201	40	0	+	
2057	3210	3201	35	0	+	
2058	3211	3201	32	0	+	
2060	3244	3091	4	0	+	
2067	3247	3091	29	0	+	Modern weeds
2068	3088	3091	35	+	+	
2069	3089	3091	32	0	+	cf. Pomoideae

+ = 0–10, ++ = 11–50

Table 2.13 Waterlogged plant remains from Bronze Age waterholes

| | | | Sample 2012 | 2018 | 2019 | 2031 | 2055 | 2059 | 2070 | 2072 |
| | | | Context 2396 | 2367 | 2394 | 2689 | 3212 | 3212 | 3090 | 3271 |
			Feature 2373	2373	2373	2690	3201	3201	3091	3263
Ranunculus acris/reprens/bulbosus	Buttercup	Gd	-	-	-	+	+	+	+	+
Ranunculus subgen *batrachium*	Crowfoot	Aq	-	-	-	+	-	-	+	-
Stellaria media	Chickweed	R	-	-	+	+	+	+	-	+
Stellaria graminea	Lesser Stitchwort	GW	-	-	-	++	-	-	-	-
Chenopodium album	Fat hen	R	+	-	+	+	+	-	-	-
Atriplex sp.	Orache	R	-	-	-	-	-	-	+	-
Rubus sp.	Blackberry/Raspberry	RSc	+	+	+	+	-	-	+	-
Prunus spinosa	Sloe	Sc	-	-	+	-	-	-	-	-
Crataegus monogyna	Hawthorn	Sc	+	-	++	+	+	+	+	+
Oenanthe aquatica	Fine-leaved Water Dropwort	Aq	-	-	-	+	+	+	+	+
Aethusa cynapium	Fools Parsley	C	+	-	-	+	-	-	-	-
Polygonum persicaria/lapathifolium	Red Shank/Pale Persicaria	R	-	-	-	-	+	+	-	+
Polygonum aviculare	Knotgrass	R	-	-	-	-	+	-	-	-
Rumex sp.	Docks	R	-	-	+	+++	+	+	+	+
Rumex sp.	Docks, charred seed		-	-	-	-	+	-	-	-
Urtica dioica	Common Nettle	R	+	-	+	++	+	-	+	-
Alnus glutinosa	Alder	W d	-	-	-	-	-	-	-	+
Solanum sp.	Nightshade	R	-	-	+	-	-	-	+	-
Lycopus europeaus	Gipsywort	AqM	-	-	-	+	-	-	-	-
Lamium sp.	Dead Nettle	C	+	-	-	-	-	-	-	-
Galeopsis sp,	Hemp Nettle	CR	-	-	-	+	-	-	+	-
Sambucus nigra	Elder	RSc	+	+	++	+	+	+	+	+
Carduus/Cirsium sp.	Thistle	R	+	-	-	+	-	-	-	-
Juncus sp.	Rushes	GMd	-	-	-	-	-	+	-	+
Eleocharis palustris	Common Spikerush	GMd	-	-	-	-	+	-	-	-
Cerealia indet.	Charred cereal grain		-	+	-	-	-	-	-	-
Carex spp.	Sedges	GMd	+	-	+	+	-	-	+	-
Tree bud			+	-	+	-	-	-	-	-
Leaf fragments			-	-	-	-	+	-	-	-
Wood fragments			-	-	-	++	+++	+	+	+
Charcoal fragments			++	+	-	-	-	-	-	-

+ = 1-10, or present, ++ = moderate, +++ = frequent, ++++ = abundant

Habitat key: Aq - aquatic C - cultivated soils G - grassland M - marsh R - ruderal

Batrachium), fine-leaved water dropwort (*Oenanthe aquatica*) and gipsy wort (*Lycopus europeus*). These species are suggestive of a local environment of muddy and/or still water, as might be expected in features of this kind. Rushes (*Juncus* sp.), sedges (*Carex* sp.) and common spikerush (*Eleocharis palustris*) are likely to have been growing in wet conditions on the edges of the waterholes. Plants of cultivated or disturbed habitats include chickweed (*Stellaria media*), fat hen (*Chenopodium album*), fool's parsley (*Aethusa cynapium*), docks (*Rumex* sp.), nettle (*Urtica dioica*), dead nettle (*Lamium* sp.), hemp-nettle (*Galeopsis* sp.) and thistle (*Carduus/Cirsium* sp.). These plants may all have been growing in nitrogen-rich disturbed soils around the edge of the waterholes. Ruderal species such as red shank/pale persicaria (*Polygonum persicaria/lapathifolium*) and some dock species also occur on the banks of ponds or rivers. Scrubby vegetation, also associated with nitrogen-rich disturbed soils, is

suggested by seeds of bramble (*Rubus* sp.) and elder (*Sambucus nigra*), while alder (*Alnus glutinosa*), a species of damp ground, is represented by a single seed in waterhole 3263 (context 3271). Occasional fragments of charcoal, a charred cereal grain of indeterminate species and a charred dock seed were also recovered. These remains must derive from human activity within the vicinity but are not sufficient to suggest cereal processing on any scale.

Pollen *by Elizabeth Huckerby*

Introduction

Palynological analysis was undertaken on a monolith sample (sample 2061) taken through the fills of Bronze Age waterhole 3091 (Fig. 2.7). Ten subsamples were taken at depths of between 0.10m and 0.705m from the top of the monolith, and were

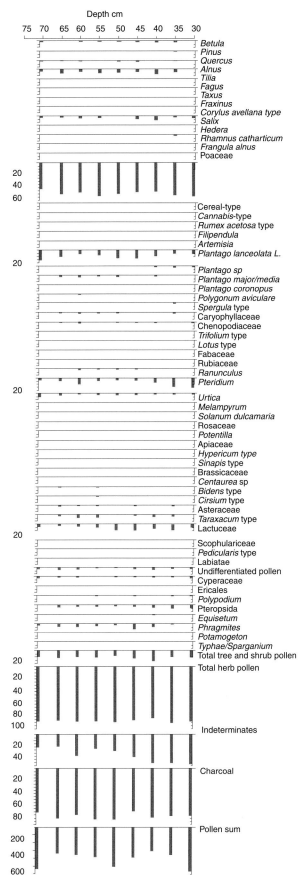

Fig. 2.23 Bronze Age waterhole 3091: percentage pollen diagram

prepared and analysed using standard techniques (Faegri and Iversen 1989; Brooks and Thomas 1967; Andersen 1979; Birks 1973). Plant nomenclature follows Stace (1991).

The results are presented as a percentage pollen diagram of selected taxa (Fig. 2.23). The pollen sum, on which the percentages are calculated, includes all land pollen and bracken spores. The diagram has not been divided into local pollen zones because there are no obvious differences in the pollen assemblages from the individual spectra.

The major pollen and spore types are grass (Poaceae), ribwort plantain (*Plantago lanceolata*), dandelion-type (Lactuaceae) and bracken (*Pteridium*). Low values of cereal-type (less than 2%) and arable weeds, for example corn spurrey-type (*Spergula*-type) and charlock/mustard-type (*Sinapis*), were recorded at some depths but in general the herb pollen types identified suggest grassland or ruderal communities and not intensive arable cultivation. Tree and shrub pollen was recorded at low values in all the pollen spectra, suggesting that the environs of the site had been cleared of woodland when the fills of the waterhole were accumulating. Alder (*Alnus*) and hazel (*Corylus*) pollen were recorded at higher values than other tree taxa.

As would be expected some marsh and aquatic taxa were recorded, including common reed (*Phragmites*), sedges (Cyperaceae) and sporadic occurrences of pondweed (*Potamogeton*). The absence of high values of marsh or true aquatic plants suggests that the waterhole was not becoming overgrown whilst the fills were accumulating.

High levels of charcoal were recorded in all samples. The numbers of indeterminate pollen grains, predominately of crumpled or corroded ones, were very high above 0.50m and lower from the deeper samples, although the values were still between 20% and 35% in these samples.

Discussion

The source of pollen recorded in fills from archaeological features is complicated by a number of factors. Unlike natural deposits, such as mires or lakes, fills of features such as waterholes may contain material that has been imported into the site from outside the immediate geographical area. Other factors include disposal of material from the site itself, and the deposition of the regional and local pollen rain through natural atmospheric dispersion. These factors combine to give a complex taphonomy of the deposits and therefore make the interpretation of the pollen data more difficult. However, the smaller the diameter of a naturally formed basin, the more local the pollen record with fewer grains from the regional pollen rain recorded (Jacobson and Bradshaw 1981). Therefore waterholes, because of their relatively small size, can theoretically provide an excellent record of the local vegetation.

At this site the interpretation of the data is further complicated by the high values of indeterminate grains recorded. Several factors may cause these high percentages. As mentioned above pollen may have been imported onto the site, and oxygen levels in the water may be relatively high, thus causing more corrosion than would occur if conditions were more anaerobic. Also the pollen grains of several taxa recorded (eg grass, alder, plantain and dandelion-type) have stronger and more resistant exines (outer covering) or are very distinctive and more readily identified if preservation is poor. Both these factors, the easily identifiable grains and the resistant ones, give rise to a skewed data set.

However, the results from waterhole 3091 can be compared with those from late Bronze Age waterhole 1015 at Green Park 2 (Scaife 2004) and middle Bronze Age waterhole 824 at Moores Farm (Scaife, Chapter 7). There are broad similarities in the results from each site, although also some differences. Woodland had probably been cleared from the local area when the fills of these waterholes were accumulating. The low values of tree and shrub pollen identified from all three sites provide evidence for this. However, the character of the remaining trees and shrubs at Green Park 3 differs from that at Moores Farm and Green Park 2. At this site more alder pollen with some hazel was recorded, whereas at the two other sites oak and hazel pollen were more important.

Both at this site and at Moores Farm the major components of the pollen sum are grasses (Poaceae), ribwort plantain (*Plantago lanceolata*), dandelion-type (Lactuceae) and bracken (*Pteridium*). At both sites arable weeds, including corn spurrey (Spergula-type) and cereal-type pollen are recorded but the values are low. This pollen assemblage suggests extensive grassland or ruderal plant communities with little arable cultivation. In contrast, higher percentages of cereal-type pollen and arable weeds were identified from waterhole 1015 at Green Park 2 (Scaife 2004). This suggests that cultivation was more important in that locality at this later date, although Scaife discusses the possibility that pollen from arable weeds and cereals may have been introduced into the deposits indirectly as a result of crop processing, when

Table 2.14 Insect remains from Bronze Age waterholes

Sample		2012	2019	2031	2059	2070	2072
Context		2396	2394	2689	3212	3090	3271
Feature		2373	2373	2690	3201	3091	3263
Coleoptera							
Agonum sp.	A	-	-	+	-	-	-
Haliplus sp.	A	-	+	-	-	-	-
Hydroporus sp.	A	-	+	-	-	-	-
Agabus bipustulatus	A	-	+	-	-	-	-
Helophorus sp. (*brevipalpis* size)	A	+	++	+	+	+	+
Hydrobius fuscipes	A	-	+	+	-	-	-
Ochthebius cf. *bicolon*	A	+	-	-	-	-	-
O. minimus	A	-	+	-	-	-	-
O. cf. *minimus*	A	-	++	+	-	-	-
Hydraena testacea	A	-	+	+	-	-	-
Limnebius sp.	A	-	+	-	-	-	-
Stenus sp.		-	+	-	-	-	-
Tachyporus sp.		-	-	-	-	+	-
Geotrupes sp.		-	-	+	-	-	-
Colobopterus erraticus		-	-	+	-	-	-
Phyllopertha horticola		-	+	+	-	-	-
Cetonia aurata		-	+	-	-	-	-
Agriotes sp.		+	+	-	-	-	-
Chrysolina sp.		-	-	-	-	+	-
Longitarsus sp.		-	+	-	-	-	-
Alophus triguttatus		+	-	-	-	-	-
Tychius sp.		-	+	-	-	-	-
Other insects							
Forficula auricularia		-	+	-	-	-	-
Aphrodes bicinctus		-	+	-	-	-	-
Diptera puparium		-	-	+	-	-	-

+ = present; ++ = several; A = aquatic

42

pollen trapped in the cereal inflorescences could have been released into the atmosphere as the result of threshing activities (Scaife, Chapter 7; Robinson and Hubbard 1977).

Insects *by Mark Robinson*

Insect remains were noted in the flots of six of the eight samples assessed for waterlogged plant remains from the middle Bronze Age waterholes (see above). These flots were then separately assessed for insects. The flots were scanned in water under a binocular microscope and those insects observed were identified. Their relative abundance is listed in Table 2.14. Nomenclature for Coleoptera follows Kloet and Hincks (1977).

The concentrations of insect remains are low and preservation is poor in all but context 2394 (waterhole 2373), which contains a much higher concentration of well-preserved fragments. Unsurprisingly, the majority of the insects in this, and indeed all, the samples are aquatic beetles characteristic of standing water. *Helophorus* sp. (*Brevipalpis* size) and *Ochthebius*

minimus are particularly numerous, and probably reflect conditions in the open waterholes. The relatively few terrestrial insects are mostly beetles of open habitats, such as *Phyllopertha horticola* and *Agriotes* sp., which occur in grassland. Scarabaeoid dung beetles which tend to be associated with the dung of domestic animals, such as *Colobopterus erraticus*, are present but not as abundant as from some prehistoric waterholes.

The evidence that the waterholes held standing water is hardly unexpected. One useful result, however, is the evidence from context 2394, which indicates open conditions around waterhole 2373. This contrasts somewhat with the macroscopic plant remains from the same sample, which provides evidence for scrub, although the terrestrial insects are likely to have been derived from a larger catchment than the macroscopic plant remains. It therefore seems probable that there was some scrub immediately around the waterhole but that the general landscape was relatively open. The preponderance of aquatic insects in context 2394 meant that it was unsuitable for further analysis.

Chapter 3: Green Park 3 –
Iron Age, Roman and Post-Roman activity

ARCHAEOLOGICAL SEQUENCE

Middle to late Iron Age

Features dated to the middle to late Iron Age included ditches, pits and a cremation burial. The sparse distribution of features and the paucity of finds suggests that the main focus of occupation may lie outside the excavated area.

Ditches

A group of shallow ditches in the western half of the site (2639, 2640, 2719 and 2798) contained small amounts of handmade middle to late Iron Age pottery (Fig. 3.1 and Table 3.1). While ditches 2640 and 2719 ran parallel to each other on a NE-SW axis, 2639 and 2798 followed a different alignment that seems to mirror that of the Bronze Age field system. It is therefore possible that the alignment of 2639 and 2798 was influenced by surviving earthworks, or that the Iron Age pottery from these features is in fact intrusive. In the eastern half of the site, curvilinear ditch 3015 produced no datable finds, but could date to the Iron Age as it cut across a middle Bronze Age waterhole and was subsequently cut by a Roman ditch.

Pits

Iron Age pottery was recovered from three pits in the western part of the site (2173, 2178 and 2613). Pit 2613 was a small, bowl-shaped feature, 0.23m deep, cut by ditch 2639. Pits 2173 and 2178 lay within group 2117, a dense cluster of 66 bowl-shaped or irregular pits up to 0.42m deep, many of them inter-cutting. Most of the other pits within group 2117 lacked datable finds, except for a single sherd of Roman pottery from the upper fill of pit 2078, and it is thus plausible that the primary use of the group

as a whole lay in the later Iron Age. The function of the pits is unclear.

Cremation burial

A heavily truncated late Iron Age cremation burial (3121) was found in the north-eastern corner of the site. The remains had been interred within a wheel-thrown vessel, and were associated with a few tiny fragments of copper alloy sheet (1g) which could represent the remains of a pyre good or grave good. The bones were heavily fragmented and abraded and could not be aged or sexed. Three environmental samples taken from the burial contained abundant oak charcoal. The presence of a wheel-made, grog-tempered pot could suggest that this burial is slightly later in date than the other Iron Age features at the site, although it is also possible that finer, wheel-made vessels would have been specifically selected for deposition in funerary contexts.

Romano-British period

During the Romano-British period, a rectilinear field system was laid out across the the site, on a NNE-SSW/ENE-WSW alignment (Fig. 3.1). The sparse dating evidence for the field system centres

Table 3.2 Summary of Roman ditches

Feature	Width (m)	Depth (m)	Finds and dating
2388	0.40-0.70	0.10-0.18	Parallel to 2390
2389	1.00-1.50	0.30-0.31	2 sherds Roman pottery
2390	1.32-1.54	0.30-0.44	2 sherds Roman pottery
2657	1.80-1.86	0.50-0.68	3 sherds Iron Age and Roman pottery
3060	1.00-1.10	0.30-0.31	15 sherds 2nd-3rd century pottery
3183	0.85-1.35	0.30-0.40	10 sherds 2nd century pottery
3184	0.60	0.20	Cut by 3183
3256	0.90-1.20	0.25-0.50	Rotary quern fragment
3257	0.62-1.15	0.20-0.32	Cuts 3256, cut by 3320
3258	1.10	0.30-0.43	5 sherds Roman pottery
3259	1.26-2.00	0.48-0.62	Cut by 3060, cuts 3184
3281	0.85-1.10	0.28-0.37	Recut of 3283
3282	0.50-0.60	0.12-0.15	Cut by 3183
3283	0.60-0.80	0.30	Same as 3257
3320	1.06-1.66	0.32-0.66	1 sherd Roman pottery
3400	1.20	0.46	Cut by 3259

Table 3.1 Summary of Iron Age ditches

Feature	Width (m)	Depth (m)	Finds and dating
2639	0.60-0.88	0.10-0.20	7 sherds MIA-LIA pottery
2640	0.25-0.65	0.04-0.20	3 sherds MIA-LIA pottery
2719	>1.50	0.38	6 sherds MIA-LIA pottery
2798	0.78	0.10	1 sherd MIA-LIA pottery
3015	0.70-0.85	0.11-0.30	Cuts MBA waterhole 3091 Cut by Roman ditch 3060

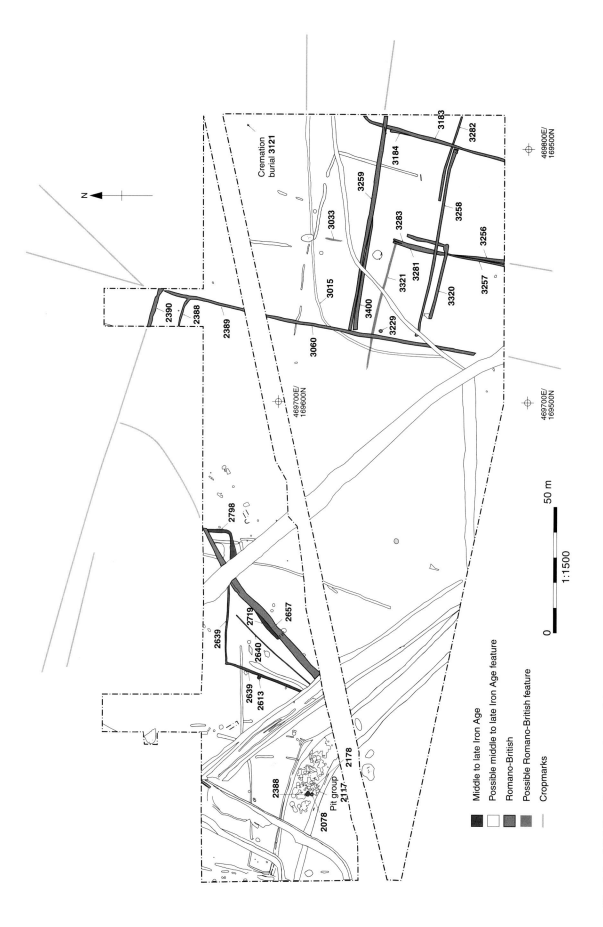

Fig. 3.1 Middle to late Iron Age and Romano-British features

around the 2nd century AD, although some later activity at the site is indicated by two unstratified sherds of late 3rd to 4th century pottery.

The ditches demarcating the field system were up to 0.66m deep, with a U-shaped profile (Table 3.2). The ditch fills often showed a sequence of an initial erosion deposit, rich in gravel, followed by a longer period of silting. Maintenance of the field system over a significant period of time is suggested by the fact that some of the ditches had been recut. For example, ditch 3400 had been recut as ditch 3259, and ditch 3256/3283 had been recut as ditch 3257/3281. Finds from the ditches were generally sparse, comprising pottery and animal bone, along with a rotary quern fragment from ditch 3256 and part of a copper alloy earring or bracelet from ditch 2390. However, one deliberate deposit was identified during the 1986 evaluation within ditch 3259, comprising three semi-complete ceramic jars. One of these – a burnished, necked jar in a reduced sandy fabric (Fig. 3.2) – contained cremated animal remains, probably belonging to an immature sheep or goat (TWA 1986). The necked jar can be dated to the 1st to 2nd centuries AD, while the other datable pottery from the field system has been attributed to the 2nd or 2nd–3rd centuries.

Ditch 2657 followed a differing alignment to the rest of the field system, and appears to have been a recut of Iron Age ditch 2719. Cropmark evidence suggests that the ditch curved northwards to meet ditch 2390 (Fig. 3.1), but this could not be observed on the ground as topsoil removal in this part of the watching brief area was incomplete, a factor which precluded examination of the northward continuation of other ditches (such as Iron Age feature 2798) in this area. The only datable finds comprised three sherds of Roman pottery from the upper fill. It is therefore possible that the ditch was

dug during the Iron Age but remained partly open into the Roman period. Three environmental samples taken from the ditch produced no plant remains other than sparse oak charcoal from the basal fill.

Two pits were the only potentially contemporary features within the field system. Pit 3229 was a bowl-shaped feature, 1.36m in diameter and 0.44m deep, which contained a single small sherd of Roman pottery. A single sherd of Roman pottery was also recovered from the upper fill of pit 2078 within pit group 2117.

Late medieval to post-medieval period

Three trackways defined by parallel ditches were present in the western part of the site (2541, 3123 and 3408) (Fig. 3.3). These are clearly visible on the cropmark plot of the area (Fig. 1.2), and the southward continuation of trackway 2541 had previously been investigated in the 1982 Pingewood excavations (where it was mistakenly regarded as Romano-British: Lobb and Mills 1993, 90, fig. 2). All three trackways produced late medieval to post-medieval finds, including pottery, tile, clay tobacco pipe and horseshoe fragments. Trackways 2541 and 3408 correspond with lanes depicted on the earliest detailed cartographic source for the area, John Rocque's 1761 map of Berkshire; they were erased by the inclosure of Burghfield parish in 1853 (Berkshire Record Office: Q/RDC/99A-B). Trackway 3123 does not appear on any maps, but excavation showed that it was cut by 3408, and it probably represents an earlier alignment of 2541. Wheel ruts were evident within 2541, but otherwise no traces of any road surfaces were present.

ARTEFACTS AND OSTEOLOGICAL EVIDENCE

Iron Age pottery *by Elaine L Morris*

A total of 39 sherds (225 g) of later Iron Age pottery was recovered (Table 3.3). The assemblage includes only a limited range of forms and is typical of the local area.

Fabrics

Six fabrics were defined amongst this small assemblage, representing four different fabric groups. The flint-tempered fabric is virtually identical to one of the types first recognised as late Bronze Age in date. This similarity in definition demonstrates the difficulties encountered when attempting to date plain body sherds of later prehistoric pottery recovered from fieldwalking in the Berkshire region. The single example with a naturally-gritted iron oxide and sandy clay matrix is quite similar to one from the sandy group (Q2), but the lack of form types for these groups precludes any discussion of the significance other than to suggest that these two fabrics

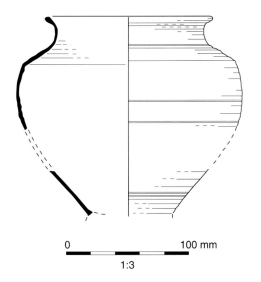

0   100 mm

1:3

Fig. 3.2 Roman vessel containing cremated animal bone from ditch 3259, Wessex Archaeology evaluation

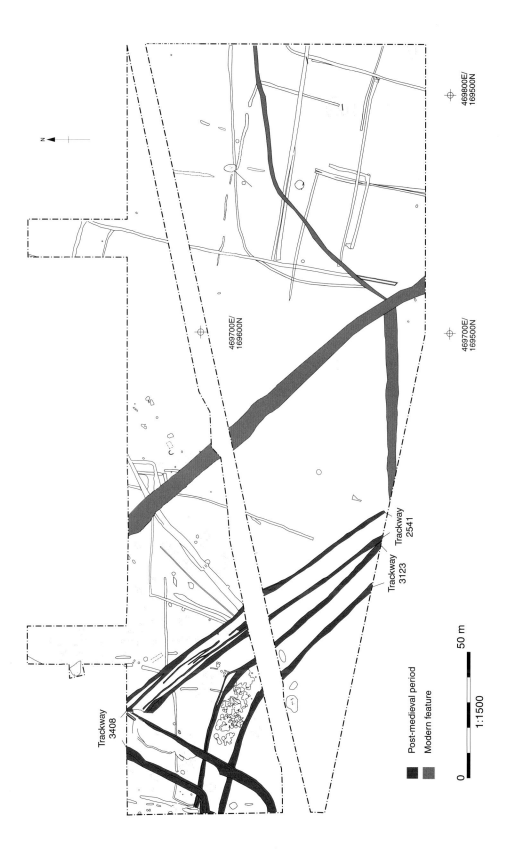

Fig. 3.3 Post-medieval and modern features

(and possibly all the sandy fabrics) are probably of local origin. The grog-tempered fabric is a very common type of the late Iron Age wheel-thrown tradition of the first century AD (if not earlier) in southern Britain.

These four different fabric groups can be paralleled at later Iron Age sites elsewhere in the local area. Grog-tempered ware and the Silchester ware have been found specifically in late Iron Age deposits at Ufton Nervet (Manning 1974), Riseley Farm, Swallowfield (Lobb and Morris 1993) and Silchester (Timby 1989; 2000), for example.

Grog-tempered group

G3: a moderate amount (10%) of fine to medium grog temper measuring ≤2mm across in a softly-fired clay matrix containing a sparse amount (5%) of fine quartz/quartzite grains, rare (2%) iron oxides and rare (< 1%) flint fragments measuring ≤ 1mm across (late Iron Age)

Flint-tempered group

F10: identical to fabric type F10 at Green Park 2. The description of this fabric type is identical to that for the late Bronze Age examples and therefore has not been assigned a new code, despite the dating differences (late Iron Age)

Iron oxide and sandy group

IQ1: an intermediate fabric characterised by a sandy clay matrix containing a moderate to common amount (15–20%) of naturally-occurring, subrounded iron oxides or the voids where these once existed measuring ≤ 2mm across and a sparse amount (10%) of fine-medium grains of quartz/quartzite sand, ≤ 0.5mm across, and a rare to sparse amount (1–3%) of flint detritus which is ill-sorted, rounded to angular in shape and ≤ 6mm across (middle-late Iron Age)

Sandy group

Q2: the same basic description as for Q1 at Green Park 2 but also bearing a sparse amount (5–10%) of rounded, iron oxide fragments measuring ≤ 2mm across. This fabric is distinctively sandy in texture. The low density of iron oxide fragments distin-

guishes this fabric from IQ1 above (middle-late Iron Age)

Q3: a sandy clay matrix containing a sparse (5%) concentration of poorly-sorted burnt flint fragments including rounded large pieces with cortex adhering (6mm across) and others which are subangular to angular in shape and ≤ 4mm across; the quartz/quartzite sand grains are moderately-sorted, subrounded to subangular in shape, measure ≤ 1mm across and are found in common density (25%), along with a rare amount (1%) of subrounded iron oxide fragments, ≤ 1mm across (middle-late Iron Age)

Q4: a very common to abundant amount of medium-fine, well-sorted, subrounded quartz/quartzite grains, < 0.5mm across, and a rare amount (1%) of subangular flint detritus measuring ≤ 2mm across (middle-late Iron Age)

Vessel forms

Amongst the 39 Iron Age sherds there are only three different identifiable vessel forms. The two represented by rims are dated to the late Iron Age and represent contemporary handmade (R90) and wheelthrown (R91) vessels.

R90: an upright or pulled, beaded rim jar with sloping shoulder; this is a common handmade form which dates to the late Iron Age (Fig. 3.4.1).

R91: a long-necked, wheelthrown cordoned bowl or jar; this is a common form which dates to the late Iron Age (Fig. 3.4.2).

A2: identical to rounded shoulder type A2 at Green Park 2; this is a simple handmade form which can be found from the late Bronze Age through the Iron Age.

Catalogue of illustrated pottery (Fig. 3.4)

1 Rim, beaded-rim jar; R90, less than 5% present; fabric F10; unoxidised throughout and appears to be extremely hard fired. Handmade. Pit group 2117, pit 2173, context 2172.

2 Rim, cordoned bowl/jar; R91, 5% of 140mm diameter; fabric G3; cordon at lower neck; oxidised exterior and interior, unoxidised core. Wheelthrown. Late Iron Age cremation burial 3121, context 3127.

Roman artefacts *by Leigh Allen, Ruth Shaffrey and Jane Timby*

The Roman pottery assemblage comprises 119 sherds (1054 g), and includes material spanning the 2nd to 4th centuries AD (Table 3.4). The bulk of the assemblage comprises grey sandy wares, largely from the Alice Holt industry, grog-tempered storage jars and one sherd of Dorset black burnished ware, the products of long-lived industries spanning the

Table 3.3 Quantification of Iron Age pottery by fabric

Fabric group	Fabric type	No. of records	No. of sherds	Weight of sherds (g)	Mean sherd weight (g)
Grog-tempered	G3	4	10	22	2.2
Flint-tempered	F10	2	2	21	10.5
Iron oxide and sandy	IQ1	9	20	119	6.0
Sandy	Q2	3	5	54	10.8
	Q3	1	1	6	6.0
	Q4	1	1	3	3.0
	Total	20	39	225	5.8

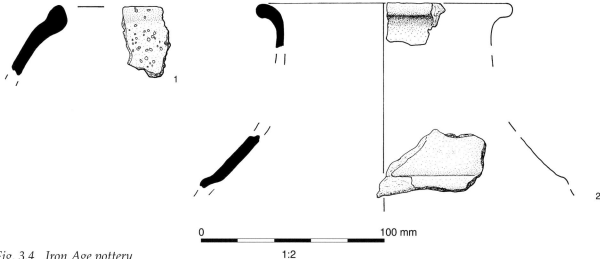

Fig. 3.4   Iron Age pottery

1st to 4th centuries AD. Recognisable 2nd-century wares include 14 sherds of Central Gaulish samian ware, ten of which belong to a single cup (Dragendorff form 33) from ditch 3183. A burnt Oxfordshire white ware mortarium (Young 1977, form M17) from a post-medieval ditch indicates later 3rd-century activity, whilst two sherds of Oxfordshire colour-coated ware from the subsoil are of later 3rd or 4th century date.

Two small rotary quern fragments of disc type were retrieved; both were made from the Quartz Conglomerate type of Old Red Sandstone from the Forest of Dean. The first item was from Roman ditch 3256 and was fairly fresh, while the second specimen was recovered from the subsoil. Both are fragments of upper stones. Old Red Sandstone was widely used for rotary querns in this area during the Roman period (Shaffrey 2006). Examples were found in Romano-British contexts

at Green Park 1 (Moore and Jennings 1992, 97) and it is one of the most common materials at the town of Silchester, 10 km to the south-west (Shaffrey 2003).

Ditch 2390 produced a curved fragment of twisted, square-sectioned copper alloy wire. The fragment measures 18mm long and is up to 2.5mm in thickness. It is likely to represent part of an earring or bracelet.

Late medieval to post-medieval artefacts
by Leigh Allen and Jane Timby

Twenty sherds (152 g) of later medieval and post-medieval pottery were recovered. At least five pieces from trackway 3408 appear to be from the same vessel, an internally glazed Surrey-Hampshire white ware which is tentatively assigned a later medieval or early post-medieval date (*c* 15th–17th centuries). Another context from the same feature produced sherds of glazed red earthenware of 18th century or later date.

Fragments of four clay tobacco pipes were recovered from the trackway ditches. This included a near-complete bowl with a fairly wide mouth and thin walls from trackway 2541. The base is plain but the initials 'P' and 'I' appear in relief either side of the base. This piece is of late 17th to early 18th century date. A stem fragment stamped with the initials 'OPH' in one half of a rectangle also came from the same context. The other two fragments came from trackway 3408. One, comprising just the base and a short section of the stem, bears the initials 'P' and 'I'.

Other artefacts include a small assemblage of late medieval to post-medieval ceramic building material and a range of common metal objects.

Animal bone *by Bethan Charles*

A small and poorly preserved assemblage of

Table 3.4   Quantification of Roman pottery by fabric

Fabric		No. of sherds	Weight (g)
ALHRE	Alice Holt reduced ware	55	363
CGSAM	Central Gaulish samian ware	13	31
CREAM	Roman cream sandy wares	2	6
DORBB1	Dorset Black Burnished ware fabric 1	2	23
GROG	Roman grog-tempered wares	2	128
GRSA	Roman grog-tempered sandy wares	4	186
GW	Roman grey wares	21	134
OXFRS	Oxfordshire colour-coated wares	2	8
OXFWHM	Oxfordshire white ware mortaria	1	35
OXID	Roman oxidised wares	5	11
SAM	Samian ware	1	1
WSLIP	Roman white-slipped oxidised ware	2	59
WW	Roman white wares	9	69
	Total	119	1054

Table 3.5 Animal bone from Iron Age and later contexts

Phase	Cattle	Horse	Dog	Unident.	Total
Middle to late Iron Age	-	-	-	114	114
Iron Age?	2	-	-	-	2
Romano-British	3	-	1	17	21
Post-medieval	3	2	-	19	24
Unphased	22	3	-	165	190

animal bone was recovered from Iron Age, Romano-British and post-medieval contexts (Table 3.5). None of the bone from certain Iron Age contexts could be identified to species, although two fragments of cattle bone were recovered from possible Iron Age ditch 3015. Cattle and dog were the only identified species from the Romano-British period. The cattle bones include a metacarpal that has been chopped, probably for marrow extraction.

Chapter 4: Moores Farm

THE ARCHAEOLOGICAL SEQUENCE

Introduction

Stripping of the site revealed a variable natural geology, consisting of gravel and sand overlain in places by silty deposits representing either loess or alluvium (Lobb and Rose 1996, 7). Two clay-filled palaeochannels crossed the site on SW-NE and WSW-ENE alignments, and the approximate extent of these is shown on Figure 1.4, using information from the evaluation trenches and the 1999 watching brief. The date of these palaeochannels is unclear, although early Iron Age material was recovered from the surface of the southern channel within Area 12 (see below). Most of the archaeological features were located in the zone between the two palaeochannels, with very few present in Areas 1–6 further to the north. The datable features represent four discrete phases of activity, in the early Mesolithic, middle Neolithic, middle Bronze Age and early Iron Age respectively. Many other pits and postholes contained no datable finds and could not be phased. Most features contained fills of silty clay; fills will only be described where they differ markedly from this norm.

Mesolithic

Two irregular hollows or tree throw holes located 55m apart within the northern half of Area 16 contained early Mesolithic flintwork (Fig. 4.1). Hollow 2429 measured 2.00 x 0.63m in plan and 0.22m deep, and produced 54 pieces of worked flint. Hollow 2697 measured 1.00 x 0.58m in plan and 0.13m deep, and contained 19 pieces of worked flint and flecks of charcoal. In addition to these two features, a number of residual or unstratified pieces of Mesolithic flintwork were also recovered, many of which had weathered out of the subsoil within the central part of Area 16 (context 2851; see Cramp below).

Middle Neolithic

Activity during the middle Neolithic was again focussed on the northern half of Area 16. An irregular pit or hollow (2967) and a posthole (2900) both contained pottery in the Impressed Ware tradition (Fig. 4.1). A few residual sherds of Neolithic pottery were also recovered from later features scattered across Area 16 (see Morris below).

Pit 2967 was only partially exposed beneath a sealing layer of alluvium, but measured at least

1.75m in diameter and 0.45m in depth. It contained five pieces of worked flint and 600g of Neolithic pottery, including large fragments of two Mortlake style bowls. One sherd of probable middle Bronze Age pottery was also recovered, however, which may indicate a degree of disturbance to the feature. A horse tooth fragment could also be intrusive as evidence for horses in Neolithic Britain is extremely sparse (see Charles below).

Lying 85m to the south, posthole 2900 was 0.70m in diameter and 0.42m deep, with a distinct post-pipe (0.32m in diameter and 0.40m deep). The fills of the post-pipe contained charcoal, 83g of probable Fengate style pottery and a single flint flake.

Late Neolithic to early Bronze Age

Although no features of this period were recorded, some activity on the site is indicated by residual sherds of pottery found in later deposits. Four sherds of Beaker pottery (late Neolithic/early Bronze Age) were recovered from Areas 12 and 16, and several sherds of early Bronze Age pottery, including fragments of two Biconical Urns, came from Area 16 (see Morris below).

Middle to late Bronze Age

During the middle Bronze Age, a field system was laid out across the area between the two palaeochannels (Fig. 4.2). Contemporary occupation within the field system was concentrated in Area 16, taking the form of a loose scatter of pits, postholes and two possible ovens. In addition, 11 middle Bronze Age waterholes were distributed around the periphery of the main occupation area and in the south-western part of the field system. Conclusive evidence for late Bronze Age activity was scant, although unstratified fragments of two late Bronze Age-type ovoid jars were recovered (see Morris below).

Field system

Although the full extent of the field system was not uncovered, it does not appear to have had a regular coaxial layout. Rather, it consisted of fields of varying sizes and forms, demarcated by both straight and curving ditches (Figs 4.2–6). While the ditches were on varying alignments, the predominant orientation of the system as a whole was broadly N–S/E–W. The irregular layout of the fields suggests that they may have been developed in an organic, piecemeal fashion. Certainly, there is

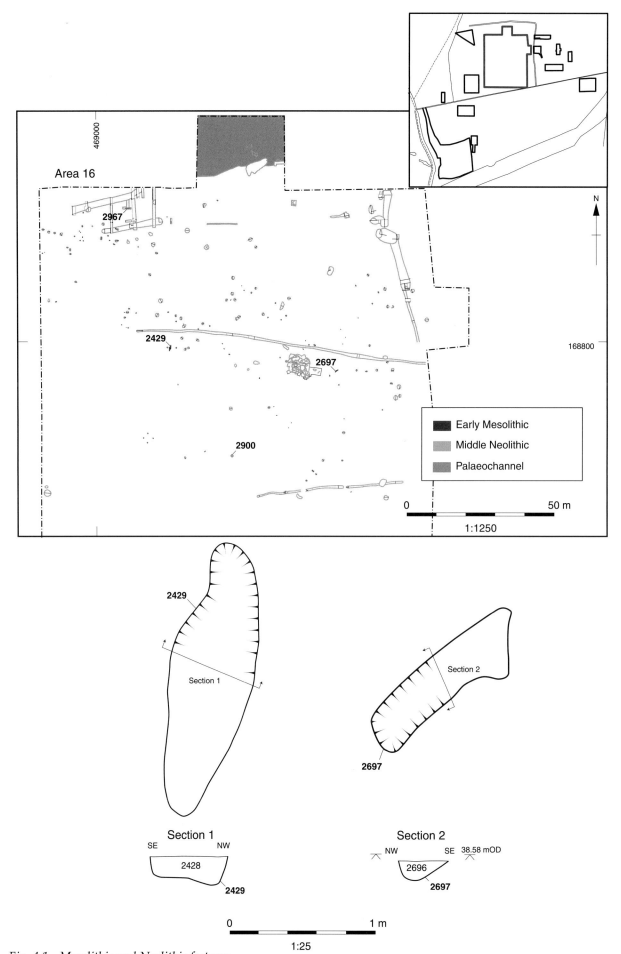

Area 16

469000

168800

2967

2429

2697

2900

Early Mesolithic
Middle Neolithic
Palaeochannel

N

0   50 m

1:1250

2429

Section 1

Section 2

2697

Section 1

SE   NW

2428

2429

Section 2

NW   SE   38.58 mOD

2696

2697

0   1 m

1:25

Fig. 4.1   Mesolithic and Neolithic features

evidence for maintenance and alteration of field system over time, as a number of the boundary ditches had been recut or realigned. For example, 1382 was recut as 1384 (Fig. 4.5); 1474 was cut by 1472 (Fig. 4.6); 2041 was recut twice; and 2117 was recut as 2199 (Fig. 4.3). Another feature of the field system was the presence of paired parallel ditches. Parallel ditches 710 and 712/717 were set only 0.30–0.50m apart (Fig. 4.3), and may have lain either side of a bank or hedge, a phenomenon attested in other Bronze Age field systems in the region (Yates 1999, 165–6). Two other pairs of parallel ditches that may form part of the field system (5209 and 5220; 5309 and 5311) had a wider spacing of *c* 2.00m and could either represent banked/hedged boundaries or narrow trackways (Fig. 4.2).

The ditches forming the field system were up to 0.81m deep and generally no more than 1.50m wide, with U-shaped profiles. They typically had pale, silty fills laid down by natural processes. Finds from the ditches were generally sparse, consisting of modest amounts of pottery, fired clay,

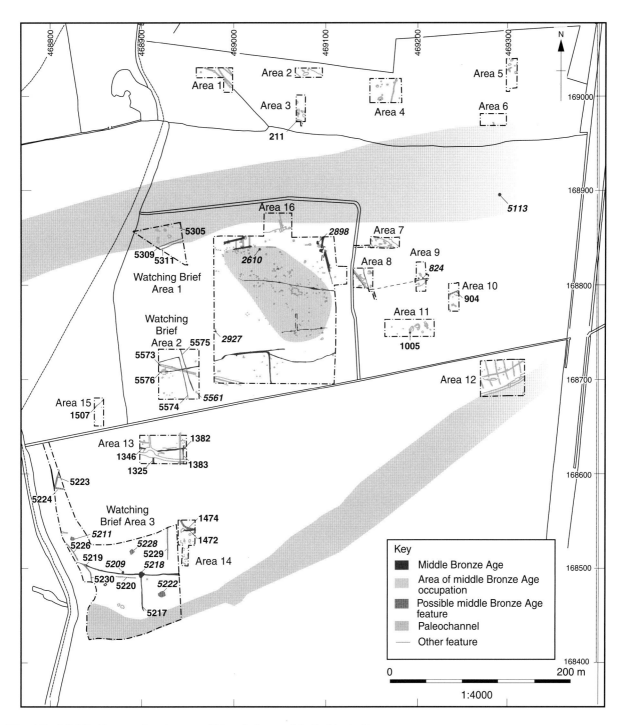

Fig. 4.2   Middle Bronze Age features. Waterholes are labelled in italics

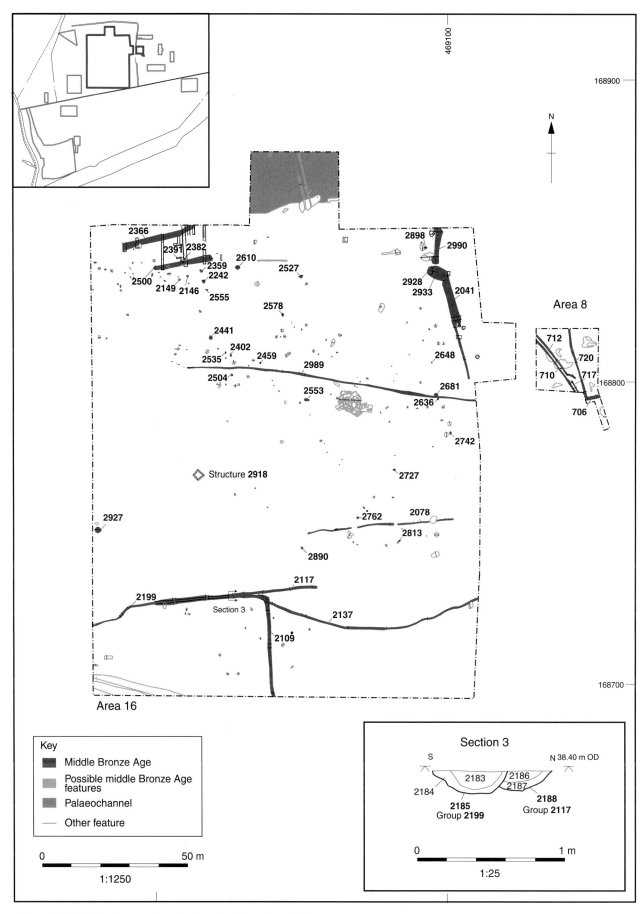

Fig. 4.3   Middle Bronze Age features in Areas 8 and 16

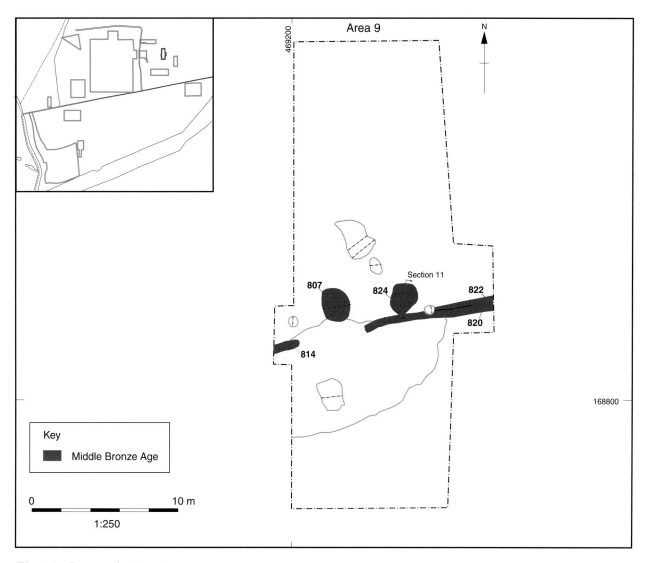

Fig. 4.4   Features in Area 9

worked flint and animal bone, with most finds unsurprisingly occurring close to the main area of contemporary occupation in Area 16 (Table 4.1). Dating evidence is provided by fragments of middle Bronze Age pottery from nine of the ditches, in some cases from the primary fills. Early Iron Age pottery was also recovered from some of the ditches, but only from upper fills, often being associated with alluvial deposits laid down when the ditches were already largely infilled (see below). There is thus no evidence that the field system continued to be actively maintained beyond the middle Bronze Age. The ditches from Areas 3, 10 and 15 and Watching Brief Areas 1 and 3 produced no datable finds, and are only tentatively ascribed to the field system.

Settlement features: pits, postholes and 'ovens'

Middle Bronze Age settlement was focused on Area 16, in a roughly NW-SE aligned swathe of dispersed features, including 20 pits, 7 postholes and 2 possible ovens (Fig. 4.3). Activity was sparse elsewhere, with single pits in Areas 9 and 11 (Figs 4.2 and 4.4), and a pair of postholes in Area 14 (Fig. 4.6).

Pits

The pits can be divided into two broad form categories: concave or bowl-shaped pits (Type 1), and pits with steep or sheer sides and a flat base (Type 2) (Table 4.2; Fig. 4.7). There were 10 bowl-shaped pits, most of which measured between 0.57–1.90m in diameter and 0.07–0.52m deep. Two larger examples, 2928 and (cutting this) 2933 were present in the northeast corner of the area, measuring up to 3m in diameter and 0.66–0.76m deep. It is possible that these larger features were actually shallow waterholes (see below). The 10 flat-based pits ranged from 0.42–1.20m in diameter and 0.11–0.45m deep. One of these (2402) appeared to have a stakehole (2413; 0.04m diameter) driven through its fill and base (Fig. 4.7). There is no clear spatial patterning in the distribution of the two pit types. Pits in both categories typically produced only small quantities of pottery (<150g), occasionally accompanied by pieces of fired clay, worked flint or animal bone. Three of the bowl-shaped pits stood out

Table 4.1 Summary of field system ditches

Feature	Dating evidence
706	Continuation of 814/820
710	1 sherd later prehistoric pottery
712/717	1 sherd later prehistoric pottery
720	Return of 706
814/820	1 sherd MBA pottery, 1 sherd later prehistoric pottery. Recut of 822
1325	Phased by alignment
1346	5 sherds later prehistoric pottery. Continuation of 1382 or 1384
1382	Cut by 1384
1383	8 sherds later prehistoric pottery. Cuts 1382, cut by 1384
1384	3 sherds later prehistoric pottery from primary fill; 13 sherds later prehistoric pottery and 1 sherd Roman pottery from top fill. Recut of 1382
1472	1 sherd BA pottery, 4 sherds later prehistoric pottery
1474	Cut by 1472
2041	1 sherd EBA pottery, 32 sherds MBA pottery, 4 sherds later prehistoric pottery

Table 4.1 (continued)

Feature	Dating evidence
2078	9 sherds MBA pottery
2109	2 sherds MBA pottery, 8 sherds later prehistoric pottery and 1 sherd Roman pottery, all from upper fill. Cuts 2117 and
2137	
2117	1 sherd MBA pottery
2137	1 sherd MBA pottery, 6 sherds later prehistoric pottery, 11 sherds post-medieval pottery from ditch surface. Cut by 2109 and 2119
2199/5576	1 sherd MBA pottery and 8 sherds later prehistoric pottery. Cuts 2117 and 2137
2366	1 sherd EBA pottery, 2 sherds MBA pottery, 23 sherds later prehistoric pottery
2391	5 sherds MBA pottery
2500	12 sherds MBA pottery, 10 sherds later prehistoric pottery
2989	7 sherds later prehistoric pottery
5573	Return of 5574
5574	3 sherds later prehistoric pottery. Cut by 5576
5575	Cut by 5576, parallel with 5574

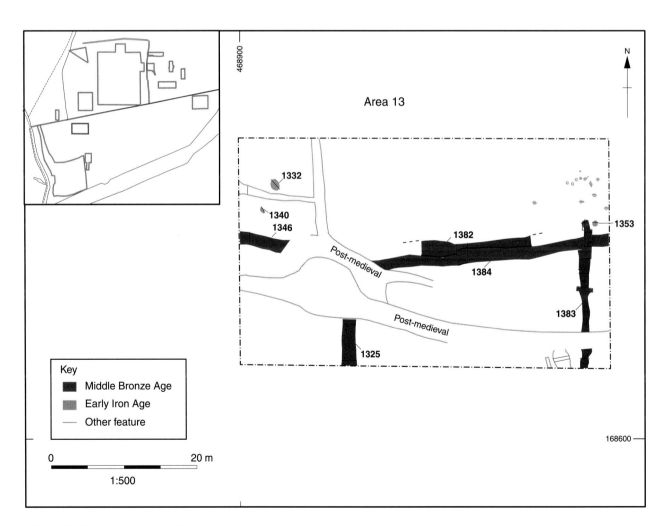

Fig. 4.5 Features in Area 13

for having more unusual deposits. Pit 807 (Fig. 4.4) contained 12 worked fragments of red deer antler in its upper fill, along with 22g of pottery and 2 flint flakes. Pit 2441 (Fig. 4.7) had unusually dark, charcoal-rich fills, containing burnt flint, fired clay

and 190g of pottery. An environmental sample from this pit produced occasional cereal grains (wheat and barley). Pit 2681 contained 1.1kg of pottery in its lower fill, most of which belonged to a single bucket urn; this was sealed by an upper fill of sterile soil.

Table 4.2 Summary of middle Bronze Age pits

Feature	Type	Diameter (m)	Depth (m)	Finds
807	1	1.90	0.28	Pottery, flint, antler fragments
1005	1	0.65	0.16	Pottery
2146	2	1.20	0.15	Pottery, flint, animal bone
2149	2	0.83	0.22	Pottery, flint
2382	2	0.90	0.45	Pottery, flint
2402	2	0.86	0.30	Pottery, flint
2441	1	1.50	0.44	Pottery, fired clay, flint
2504	1	0.80	0.52	Pottery, flint
2527	1	1.30	0.22	Pottery
2535	2	0.52	0.27	Pottery

Table 4.2 (continued)

Feature	Type	Diameter (m)	Depth (m)	Finds
2553	1	1.88	0.34	Pottery, flint
2555	2	0.66	0.11	Pottery
2636	1	0.57	0.29	Pottery
2681	1	1.25	0.26	Pottery
2727	2	0.73	0.17	Pottery
2742	2	0.88	0.53	Pottery, flint
2762	2	0.42	0.24	Pottery
2890	2	0.64	0.12	Pottery, flint, quern fragment
2928	4	1.12	0.76	Pottery
2933	4	2.00	0.66	Pottery, animal bone

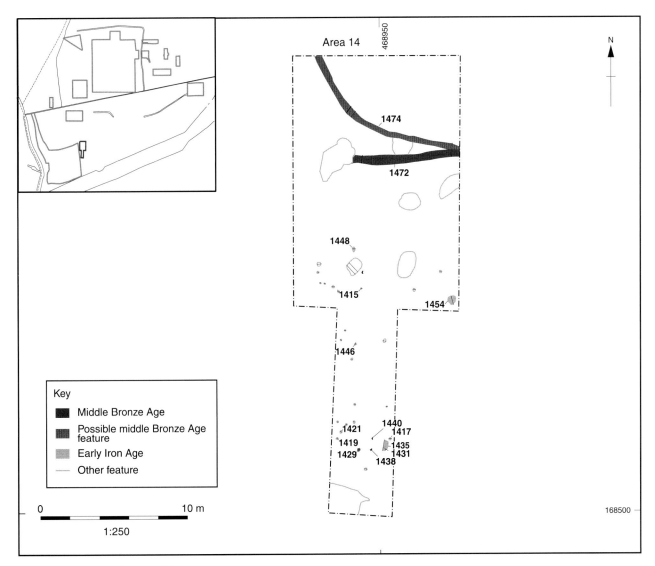

Fig. 4.6   Features in Area 14

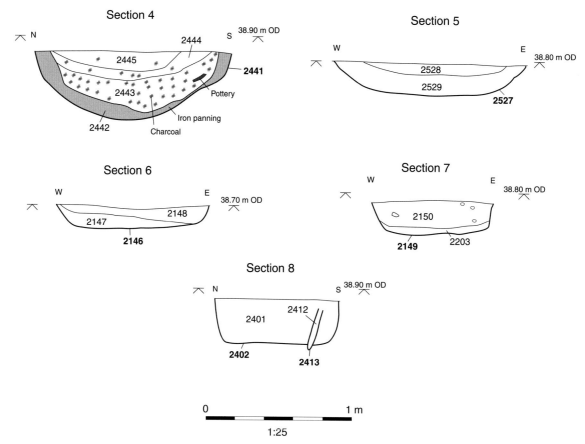

Fig. 4.7   Sections of middle Bronze Age pits

Postholes

The postholes were widely scattered, and measured between 0.14–0.44m in diameter and 0.11–0.22m deep (1305, 1438, 1440, 2459, 2578, 2648 and 2813). Most cannot be attributed to any structures. However, postholes 1438 and 1440 in Trench 14 might have been associated with undated posthole 1429, forming three corners of a four-post structure, measuring 1.30 x 1.30m (Fig. 4.6). Finds were very scarce, with none of the postholes containing more than 30g of pottery.

'Ovens'

A pair of shallow features (2242 and 2359) placed 4m apart in the north-western part of Area 16 appear to have had a specialised function (Figs 4.3 and 4.8). In both cases, numerous stakeholes had been driven through the primary silts in the base of the feature. These pits cannot be paralleled at other sites in the local area. However, finds of charcoal and fired clay from the features suggest a possible function as ovens, with the stakes perhaps supporting a superstructure of clay, earth or turf. In neither case do the stakeholes form any clear pattern, and it is possible that more than one phase of construction is represented.

Feature 2242 was roughly oval in plan, measuring 1.35m in diameter and 0.26m deep, with the sides sloping gently onto a flat base (Figs 4.8-9).

Thirteen stakeholes (2993), 0.04–0.07m in diameter and 0.04–0.10m deep, had been driven through the primary fill of the feature (2313) and were sealed by the upper fill (2243). Both fills were composed of dark grey-brown silty clay with frequent charcoal inclusions, and contained fragments of amorphous fired clay (230g in total) and middle Bronze Age pottery. Four pieces of horse bone were also recovered from the upper fill.

Feature 2359 was similar in size, measuring 1.38 x 1.02m in diameter and up to 0.33m in depth, but had a more irregular profile, being deepest at its western end (Figs 4.8 and 4.10). Nineteen stakeholes were present (2396), measuring 0.03–0.08m in diameter and 0.02–0.10m in depth. Again, these seem to have been driven through the primary fill (2395) but were sealed by the upper fill (2360). The two fills were similar to those within feature 2242, and again contained frequent charcoal inclusions. A few fragments of middle Bronze Age pottery were recovered from both deposits, with small fragments of possible fired clay oven furniture also found in the lower fill.

Waterholes

Eleven features were identified as waterholes, located around the edge of the main middle Bronze Age settlement area and in the south-west corner of

60

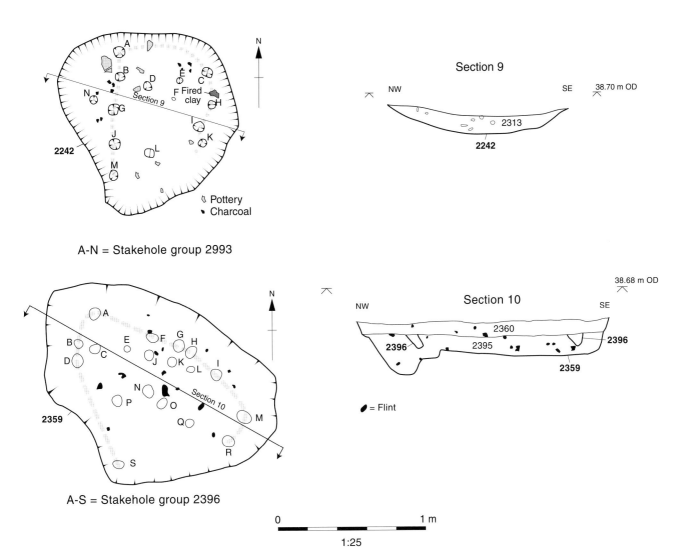

Fig. 4.8   Plans and sections of middle Bronze Age 'ovens'

the site (Fig. 4.2). These were up to 5.00m in diameter and 1.12m deep, and generally appear to have filled though natural processes of silting and erosion. In contrast to Green Park, none of the waterholes from Moores Farm were ramped, and none showed any evidence for *in situ* timber revetment structures. This is unlikely to be due to factors of preservation, as most of the waterholes had waterlogged lower fills. The waterholes typically contained few finds, with those in the southwestern part of the site producing no cultural material of any kind, making their ascription to the later Bronze Age tentative. Where finds did occur, the emphasis seems to have been on the deposition of animal remains rather than artefacts, with a butchered horse skeleton placed in waterhole 5113 and pig and deer bone in waterhole 2610.

Waterhole 824

Waterhole 824 was 2.17 x 1.84m in size and 1.02m deep, with an irregular, partly undercut profile (Fig. 4.11). It contained a primary erosion deposit of gravel (835) overlain by three fills of silty clay

(825–7), each of which contained a single sherd of middle Bronze Age pottery. Pollen analysis suggests that grassland/pasture was dominant around the waterhole, with aquatic plants such as duckweed growing within the feature itself (see Scaife below).

Waterhole 2610

Waterhole 2610 was 1.54m in diameter and 0.96m deep, with steep sides and a fairly flat base. It contained an initial gravel erosion fill and five subsequent silting deposits. A small assemblage of pig and red deer bone, all from immature animals, was recovered from the lower and middle fills of the feature. The middle and upper fills contained a few fragments of middle Bronze Age pottery.

Waterhole 2898

Waterhole 2898 was 1.10m in diameter and was excavated to a depth of 0.68m before work was abandoned due to standing water. The lowest of the exposed fills consisted of grey clay, which was sealed by a black silty deposit containing high

61

Fig. 4.9   Middle Bronze Age 'oven' 2242, facing south. Scale: 0.5m

Fig. 4.10   Middle Bronze Age 'oven' 2359, facing south. Scale: 0.5m

Section 11

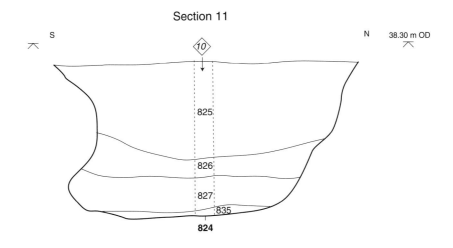

Section 12

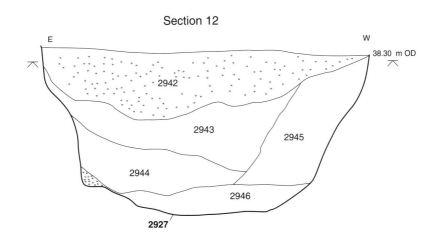

Section 13

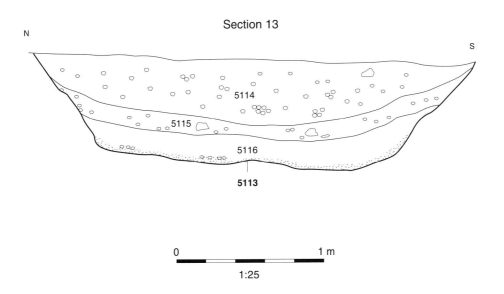

0   1 m

1:25

Fig. 4.11   Sections of middle Bronze Age waterholes

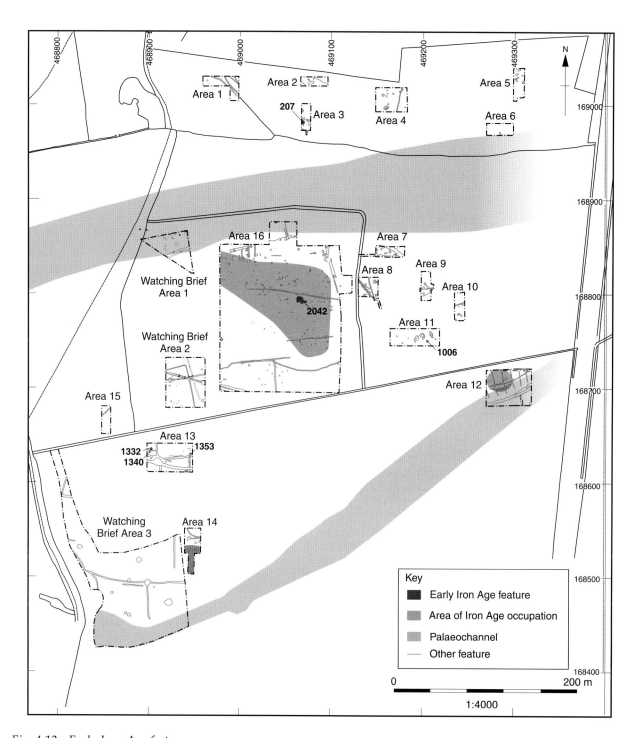

Fig. 4.12   Early Iron Age features

Table 4.3   Radiocarbon dates from early Iron Age pit group 2042. Dates calibrated using OxCal v3.10 (Bronk Ramsey 1995; 2001) and atmospheric data from Reimer et al. (2004)

Feature	Context	Laboratory number	Material	$\delta^{13}C$ (‰)	Uncalibrated date (BP)	Calibrated date (1 σ)	Calibrated date (2 σ)
2042	2043	OxA-17416	Charred grain, *Hordeum vulgare*	23.25	2458 ± 25 BP	750–410 cal BC	760–410 cal BC
2042	2065	OxA-17417	Charred grain, *Hordeum vulgare*	25.90	2447 ± 25 BP	740–410 cal BC	760–400 cal BC

frequencies of burnt flint and charcoal. The upper fills contained 48g of middle Bronze Age pottery.

Waterhole 2927

Waterhole 2927 was 2.23m in diameter and 1.12m deep, with a bowl-shaped profile (Fig. 4.11). A primary fill of grey clay (2946) was overlain by three layers of silty clay, which appear to have slumped into the feature from all sides of the cut (2943–5). The uppermost fill (2942) contained a high proportion of gravel. Small amounts of middle Bronze Age pottery were recovered from the upper three fills.

Waterhole 5113

Waterhole 5113 was an apparently isolated feature investigated during the 1999 watching brief (Fig. 4.11). It was 3.45 x 3.00m in size and 0.93m deep, and contained three layers of silty clay (5114–6). The primary fill contained a partial horse skeleton, which appears to have been butchered and placed within the waterhole in a semi-articulated state (see Charles below). The uppermost fill produced 21g of middle Bronze Age pottery.

Waterholes 5209, 5211, 5218, 5222 and 5228

These five waterholes, measuring 4–5m in diameter, formed a cluster within Watching Brief Area 3. Waterholes 5209 and 5211 were both 0.95m deep, and had a series of grey silty clay fills. Waterholes 5218, 5222 and 5228 were not fully excavated, but appeared to contain similar fill sequences. None of the waterholes produced any datable finds, although two showed a relationship to field system ditches of probable later Bronze Age date. Waterhole 5209 cut ditch 5219, and waterhole 5218 was located at the intersection of ditches 5201, 5217 and 5219, although its stratigraphic relationship to these features could not be established.

Waterhole 5561

Located in Watching Brief Area 2, waterhole 5561 was 2.80m in diameter and 0.82m deep, with a bowl-shaped profile. It contained an initial gravel-rich erosion deposit, overlain by six layers of clay. No finds were recovered.

Early Iron Age

Following the marked reduction in activity during the late Bronze Age, the site was resettled in the early Iron Age. Occupation again focussed on Area 16, where a concentrated cluster of pits (pit group 2042) was surrounded by a more dispersed swathe of pits and postholes. Activity on a smaller scale was found in Areas 12, 13 and 14, along with single pits in Areas 3 and 11 (Fig. 4.12).

Main settlement area

Group 2042 was a dense cluster of 54 pits, many intercutting, placed within a shallow hollow and extending across an area of 9 x 7m (Figs 4.13–15).

The individual pits were up to 1.50m in diameter and 0.95m deep, and generally had moderate to steep sides and a flat base. The pit fills were often dark with frequent charcoal inclusions. The function of the pits is unclear; certainly, they do not closely resemble the cylindrical or bell-shaped storage pits known from Iron Age sites elsewhere in southern England. The intense intercutting made it difficult to elucidate the stratigraphy of the group. In some cases individual layers were recorded as infilling more than one pit, although it is not clear whether this shows that the features were infilled simultaneously or simply reflects problems in distinguishing the fills of different pits.

Collectively, the pits within group 2042 produced 9.5 kg of early Iron Age pottery, representing more than half of the assemblage from the site. The largest quantities came from pit 2169 (1.9kg) and layer 2043/2065 (3.8kg), a dark deposit recorded as forming the upper fill of several pits in the north-west quadrant of the group, including 2131 and 2282. In both cases the pottery included large sherds of fineware and coarseware vessels. Other finds from the pit group included small amounts of animal bone and fragments of a fired clay triangular loomweight or oven brick. Environmental samples from layer 2043/2065 produced a few charred grains of barley and wheat. The barley grains

Table 4.4 Summary of early Iron Age pits, excluding pit group 2042

Feature	Type	Diameter (m)	Depth (m)	Finds
207	1	2.90	0.44	Pottery, animal bone
1006	1	1.10	0.30	Pottery, flint
1237	1	1.10	0.40	Pottery, fired clay, flint, animal bone
1267	2	0.80	0.18	Pottery, fired clay
1332	1	1.46	0.27	Pottery, fired clay, flint
1353	1	1.00	0.40	Pottery, fired clay, animal bone
1435	2	0.95	0.25	Pottery, fired clay, flint
1448	1	0.50	0.08	Pottery, fired clay
1454	1	1.20	0.15	Pottery, fired clay
2144	1	1.20	0.30	Pottery
2318	2	0.82	0.08	Pottery, flint
2340	1	0.80	0.06	Pottery, fired clay, flint
2393	1	0.60	0.08	Pottery, animal bone
2451	2	0.43	0.16	Pottery
2492	2	1.12	0.26	Pottery, flint
2494	2	0.75	0.14	Pottery, fired clay
2525	2	0.44	0.28	Pottery
2551	1	0.71	0.31	Pottery
2552	1	0.56	0.14	Pottery, fired clay
2618	2	0.58	0.23	Pottery, flint
2621	2	0.54	0.14	Pottery, flint
2640	1	1.07	0.28	Pottery
2642	2	0.70	0.18	Pottery
2831	2	0.51	0.20	Pottery, fired clay, quern fragment
2836	2	0.60	0.13	Pottery, fired clay

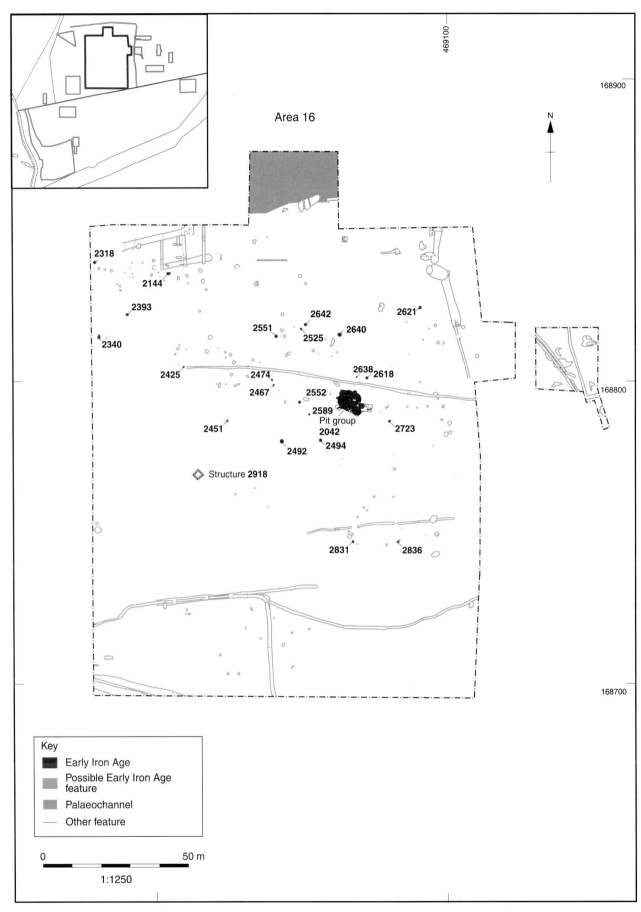

Fig. 4.13   Early Iron Age features in Area 16

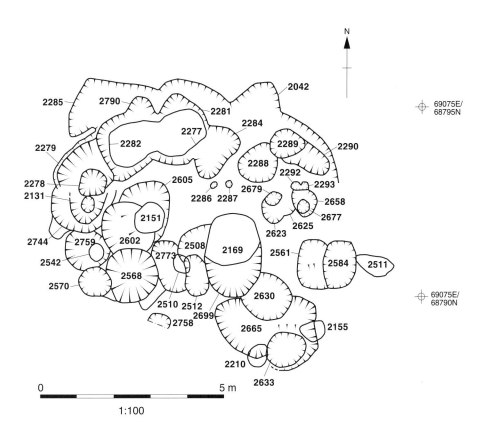

Fig. 4.14   Pit group 2042

Fig. 4.15   Early Iron Age pit group 2042, facing south. Scale: 1m

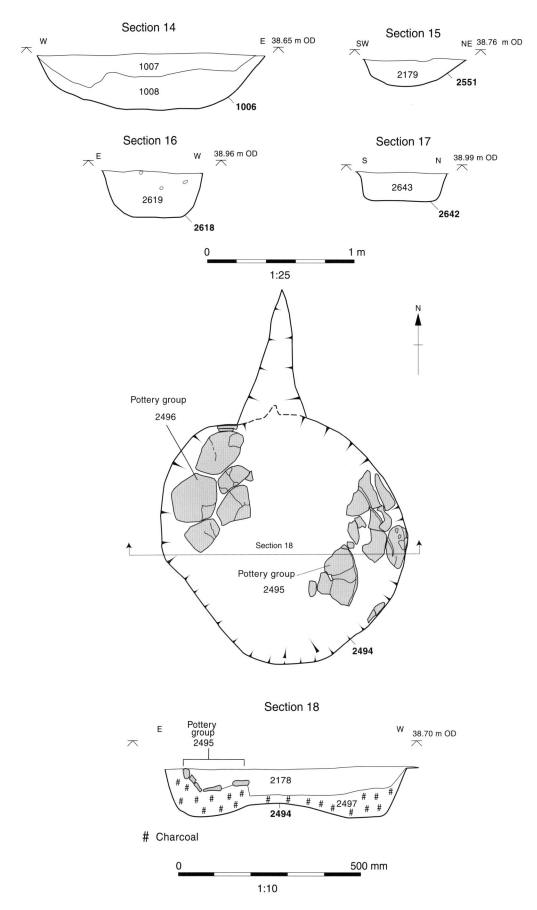

Fig. 4.16   Sections of early Iron Age pits

provided two radiocarbon determinations of 760–410 cal BC (OxA-17416: 2458 ± 25 BP) and 760–400 cal BC (OxA-17417: 2447 ± 25 BP) respectively (Table 4.3).

A further 16 shallow pits and 6 postholes were scattered across the main zone of settlement within Area 16 (Fig. 4.13). Following the same typology as used for the middle Bronze Age pits (see above), 6 of the pits were bowl-shaped, measuring up to 1.2m in diameter and 0.31m deep, and 10 were flat-based, measuring up to 1.12m in diameter and 0.28m deep (Table 4.4). The pits generally produced modest quantities of pottery (<350g) and other finds. Two of the flat-based pits contained significantly greater amounts of pottery, however. Pit 2494, located 12m to the south-west of pit group 2042 (Fig. 4.16), had a lower, sandy fill with frequent charcoal inclusions (2497) that was overlain by 2.2kg of pottery in two discrete clusters of sherds (2495 and 2496), before the pit was back-filled (2178). Pit 2836, located at the southern edge of the occupation swathe, had a single dark fill containing 1.0kg of pottery.

The postholes in Area 16 measured 0.10–0.34m in diameter and 0.14–0.35m deep. They were dispersed across the settlement area and did not form any clear structures, although 2467 and 2474 formed a pair placed 1.5m apart.

Other areas of occupation

A cluster of shallow pits and postholes was located at the northern edge of the southern palaeochannel in Area 12 (Fig. 4.17). Two pits (1237 and 1267) and four postholes (1241, 1247, 1257 and 1269) produced early Iron Age pottery. Further pottery and fragments of triangular fired clay loomweights or oven bricks were recovered from the surface of the palaeochannel (context 1271).

Within Area 13, two bowl-shaped pits (1332 and 1353) and a hearth (1340) were present (Fig. 4.5). Both pits had sterile lower fills and charcoal-rich upper fills containing pottery and fired clay. Hearth 1340 consisted of a sub-circular spread of burnt clay and charcoal, 0.50m in diameter, which produced a few sherds of pottery. A small quantity of early Iron Age pottery was also recovered from alluvial deposits sealing the Bronze Age field system ditches in this area.

Occupation in Area 14 took the form of a loose cluster of postholes (1415, 1417, 1419, 1421, 1431 and 1446) and shallow pits (1435, 1448 and 1454) (Fig. 4.6). The postholes ranged from 0.27–0.38m in diameter and 0.10–0.30m deep; none can be attributed to any recognisable structures. A number of the pits and postholes in this area contained a significant frequency of charcoal and/or fired clay

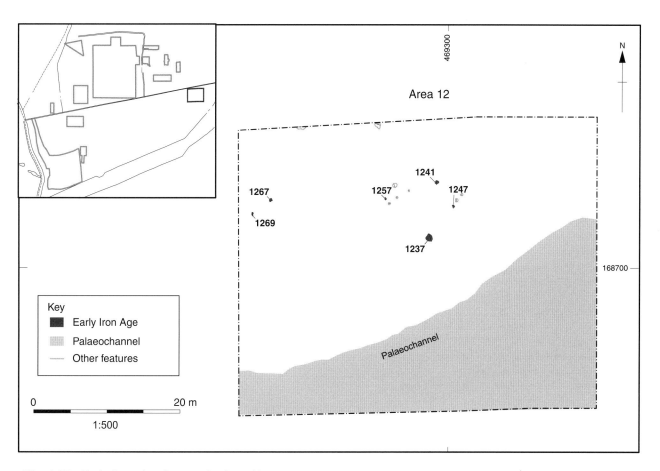

Fig. 4.17   Early Iron Age features in Area 12

inclusions, suggesting that either hearths or ovens or a burned down building lay in the vicinity.

Unphased prehistoric features

A number of pits and postholes scattered across the site produced no dating evidence. Most of the postholes could not be attributed to any recognisable structures. An exception was four-post structure 2918, located in isolation in the south-western part of Area 16 and measuring 2.20 x 2.20m (Figs 4.3 and 4.13). The individual postholes were up to 0.32m in diameter and 0.10m in depth, and contained no finds. The structure is likely to have been associated with either the middle Bronze Age or early Iron Age occupation of the site. Similar four-post structures are a common feature of later prehistoric settlements across the region, and are traditionally interpreted as raised granaries or storehouses (Gent 1983).

Later activity and alluvial layers

Alluvial clay or silt layers predating the modern subsoil sealed several of the middle Bronze Age and early Iron Age features, notably in Areas 12 and 13 and the northern part of Area 16. This indicates that the site was subject to flooding at some point from the later prehistoric period onwards. Some of the alluvial layers sealing the Bronze Age field system ditches contained sherds of probable early Iron Age pottery, especially in Area 13, hinting that the onset of wetter conditions may already have begun in the early to mid 1st millennium BC. This Iron Age pottery could be residual, however; at Green Park 1 similar alluvial layers sealed features of Roman date (Robinson 1992). Other than a few small, stray sherds of Roman pottery, there is no evidence for subsequent human activity on the site predating the post-medieval agricultural use of the area.

ARTEFACTS

Flint *by Kate Cramp and Hugo Anderson-Whymark*

Introduction

A total of 392 struck flints and 1407 pieces of burnt flint weighing 11.02kg were recovered (Table 4.5). The assemblage can be divided into two groups, which will be dealt with separately in this report. The first group comprises the material from tree throw holes 2429 and 2697 and subsoil layer 2851, which dates to the earlier Mesolithic. The second group comprises the remainder of the assemblage, recovered in a low-density scatter across the site. This is composed of Neolithic and Bronze Age flintwork combined with a residual Mesolithic element.

Methodology

The methodology for the recording and analysis of the assemblage as a whole followed that used for the Green Park 3 assemblage (see Chapter 2). In addition, technological, metrical and refitting analyses were selectively performed on the Mesolithic assemblages recovered from tree throw holes 2429 and 2697 and alluvial subsoil layer 2851. The technological analysis involved recording diagnostic attributes including butt type, termination type, probable hammer-mode, and the extent and position of dorsal cortex. The presence or absence of platform edge abrasion and dorsal blade scars were also recorded. To compensate for the considerable number of broken pieces, the metrical analysis was performed on all artefacts within the sample. This required taking the maximum length, breadth and width measurements of a specimen, in relation to the perpendicular provided by the striking platform. The intention was to enable the dating of the material to be refined, and to permit a more detailed characterisation of the reduction sequence.

Condition

The majority of the struck flint is in a fresh condition. Post-depositional edge damage is limited both in degree and distribution, and tends to be confined to the more vulnerable flake edges. On the basis of the condition, it is conceivable that the majority of the material has been recovered from *in situ* or minimally disturbed contexts. A few flints displayed a heavier degree of post-depositional damage; others were rolled. These generally occurred as residual material in later contexts.

Almost without exception, the material is uncorticated. Where cortication is present it is generally light, occurring as a blue-white mottled patina on the surface of flints. A total of 77 flints exhibit a light brown iron staining. This staining frequently occurs on flints considered to be of Mesolithic date, with 61.6% of the material from the Mesolithic tree throw holes being iron stained.

Raw material

The raw material consists of a locally available river gravel flint, which contains few thermal fractures and is probably of a good flaking quality. The cortex is generally thin and abraded, and varies in colour from light cream to mid buff. The interior of the flint is relatively fine-grained, usually brown or orange-brown in colour, and contains the occasional lighter-coloured cherty inclusion. The raw material used for the Mesolithic artefacts is a particularly good quality gravel flint, possessing a thin, rolled, creamy-coloured cortex.

A single flake of Bullhead flint was recorded from early Iron Age posthole 1237. Bullhead flint occurs in the Bullhead Bed at the base of the Reading Beds (Dewey and Bromehead 1915; Shepherd 1972, 114) and may also occur in the local river gravels in small quantities. The nearest outcrop of the Reading

Table 4.5 Worked flint

Category	Mesolithic contexts	Residual Mesolithic	Neolithic contexts	Other	Total
Flake	39	13	2	172	226
Blade-like flake	8	1	-	7	16
Blade	22	3	1	13	39
Bladelet	4	-	-	1	5
Rejuvenation flake tablet	-	-	-	1	1
Rejuvenation flake: core face/edge	1	-	-	-	1
Rejuvenation flake (other)	-	-	-	1	1
Chip	-	-	-	5	5
Irregular waste	2	1	2	9	14
Single platform flake core	1	-	-	4	5
Multi-platform flake core		2	-	3	5
Single platform blade core	1	2	-	-	3
Core on a flake	1	-	1	6	8
Unclassifiable/fragmentary core	1	-	-	-	1
Tested nodule	-	-	-	17	17
Retouched flake	4	3	-	11	18
Notch	1	-	-	1	2
Piercer	2	-	-	-	2
Serrated flake	-	-	-	2	2
End scraper	-	1	-	5	6
Side scraper	-	-	-	1	1
End and side scraper	-	-	-	4	4
Disc scraper	-	-	-	1	1
Scraper on a non-flake blank	-	-	-	1	1
Other scraper	1	-	-	2	3
Micro burin	1	-	-	-	1
Microlith	2	-	-	-	2
Oblique arrowhead	-	-	-	1	1
Unclassifiable/other arrowhead	-	-	-	1	1
Total	91	26	6	269	392

The table has header spanning: "Mesolithic contexts" over first column, "Remaining assemblage" spanning Residual Mesolithic / Neolithic contexts / Other, and "Total".

Beds is 2km to the north-east of the site. No artefacts of chalk flint manufacture were convincingly identified in the assemblage; given the quantity of non-cortical flakes recovered, it is possible that this source is under-represented.

The reliance on local gravel flint at this site parallels the raw material use at Green Park 3, where the assemblage dated broadly to the later Neolithic and Bronze Age, and appeared to be composed entirely of artefacts manufactured from a local flint type (see Chapter 2). Similarly, at Green Park 2 the flint was predominantly from a derived source, with a few pieces of Bullhead flint also present (Bradley 2004). It was noted that the later Neolithic assemblage contained a better quality local flint than the later Bronze Age assemblage. The Green Park 1 excavations revealed a more distinct chronological difference in the selection of raw material. In the Neolithic there was a preference for chalk flint sources, while the late Bronze Age assemblage was mainly of local gravel flint with only 36% chalk flint (Bradley and Brown 1992). The Moores Farm assemblage appears to bear out this general pattern of the declining importance of good quality flint over time. This can be seen most clearly when the Neolithic/Bronze Age assemblage is compared with the Mesolithic component, the latter containing flint of a better knapping quality.

The Mesolithic assemblage *by Kate Cramp*

The Mesolithic assemblage consists of 91 flints (Table 4.6). The majority of these were from tree throw holes 2429 (context 2428) and 2697 (context 2696), which contained 54 and 19 pieces respectively. The remaining 18 flints had weathered out of the subsoil in the central part of Area 16 (context 2851).

Assemblage composition

Although flakes form the largest category of debitage, the collection as a whole contains a considerable number of blades and blade-like pieces (37.4%) (eg Fig. 4.30.1–3). This figure is securely within the range predicted for blade-based Mesolithic assemblages (Ford 1987). Context 2696

Table 4.6 Worked flint from Mesolithic contexts

Category	Context 2428	2696	2851	Total
Flake	24	6	9	39
Blade-like flake	6	1	1	8
Blade	10	9	3	22
Bladelet	4	-	-	4
Irregular waste	1	1	-	2
Rejuvenation flake: core face/edge	1	-	-	1
Single platform flake core	1	-	-	1
Single platform blade core	-	-	1	1
Core on a flake	1	-	-	1
Unclassifiable/fragmentary core	-	-	1	1
Retouched flake	3	-	1	4
Flake from a scraper	-	-	1	1
Notch	1	-	-	1
Piercer	1	-	1	2
Microlith	-	2	-	2
Micro burin	1	-	-	1
Total	54	19	18	91

contained the highest proportion of blades at 47.4%, which is confirmed by the results of the metrical analysis for this material (see below).

Three cores, including a single platform flake core (context 2428), an incomplete single platform blade core, and a possible blade core fragment (both context 2851), were recovered. These weighed 50g, 35g and 74g respectively, producing an average weight of 53g for both complete and incomplete specimens. The flake core exhibited a number of blade-like removals. The cores/core fragments all displayed platform edge abrasion, indicative of a controlled reduction strategy aimed at the removal of flakes and blades of predetermined form. The single platform blade core was probably knapped using a soft-hammer percussor; in the case of the remaining cores, the hammer-mode was indeterminable. A single rejuvenation flake, removing an abraded platform edge, was recovered from context 2428. These cores and rejuvenations are representative of a blade producing industry, consistent with a Mesolithic date.

A single proximal microburin was recovered from context 2428 (Fig. 4.30.4), representing the initial stage of microlith manufacture (Inizan *et al.* 1992, 69). Another blade from this context had a notch near the bulb, and was apparently abandoned before the microburin removal was made (Fig. 4.30.5). Two broad-blade microliths were recovered from context 2696. The complete example (Fig. 4.30.6) is comparable to Jacobi's form 1b (Jacobi 1978, 68); the other was broken, perhaps during manufacture, and may be compared to Jacobi's form 1a.

In addition to the microliths, several other retouched pieces were recovered including two piercers, one notched piece, a retouched blade (Fig.

4.30.8) and a flake from a scraper. Four edge-retouched flakes were also recovered, exhibiting varying degrees of retouch. Macroscopically visible use-wear was detected on two of the retouched flakes, and a further 13 blades and flakes had apparently been utilised. Utilised pieces thus account for 16.5% of the assemblage, a figure that would undoubtedly increase with microscopic analysis.

Metrical and attribute analysis

The metrical analysis of the Mesolithic assemblage did not initially confirm the visual description of a blade-like industry when only intact pieces were considered (Fig. 4.18). Due to the relatively low numbers of intact pieces—resulting from possible microlith manufacture and/or the increased vulnerability of blades to pre- or post-depositional breakage—broken pieces were included in the analysis in order to reach a more representative sample. When these broken pieces were included, a more distinct clustering was noted along and above the 2:1 line (Fig. 4.18). This indicates that despite breakage, the incomplete pieces as a group were more blade-like than the intact pieces. The deliberate selection, and resultant breakage, of the longer, more slender blades during tool manufacture may explain this patterning. Microlith manufacture, in particular, would conceivably produce the observed pattern of breakage. Additionally, the longer pieces are likely to have been more vulnerable to breakage during knapping, use and deposition.

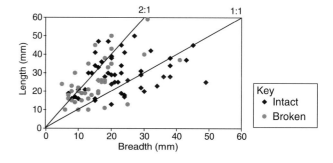

Fig. 4.18 Mesolithic flint assemblage: length/breadth ratio of broken and intact flints

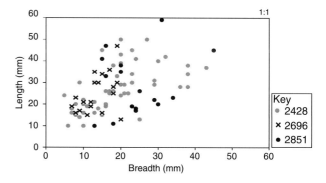

Fig. 4.19 Mesolithic flint assemblage: length/breadth ratio by context

The results of the metrical analysis for context 2696 (Fig. 4.19) revealed a more blade-like tendency than in either context 2428 or 2851. The flints from context 2851 appeared least blade-like, and included a noticeably higher proportion of squat flakes. This may suggest that the material from this alluvial subsoil layer incorporates some later prehistoric flintwork. Overall, however, with 22.2% blades and blade-like pieces context 2851 falls within the typical range of Mesolithic and earlier Neolithic mixed assemblages (Ford 1987).

When compared to the degree of breakage in the remaining assemblage, it is apparent that significantly more flints have been broken in the Mesolithic contexts (Fig. 4.20). Context 2428, for example, contained 53.7% broken artefacts (Fig. 4.21). Again, it is possible that the explanation for this patterning lies in the vulnerability of blades to breakage. However, the presence of a microburin and a notched blade from context 2428, representing the early stages of microlith manufacture (Inizan *et al.* 1992, 69), suggests a stage of activity which would result in the breakage of blades.

Technologically, the material from Moores Farm is typical of a Mesolithic industry, including a high incidence of platform edge abrasion (29.7%; Fig. 4.22) and the use of soft-hammer percussion. Context 2696 contained the highest percentage of flints with platform edge abrasion (36.8%), a feature that may be related to the more blade-like form of many of the pieces within this assemblage. With the exception of the material from this context, a correlation between a blade-like propensity and the

presence of platform edge abrasion was not noted for the assemblage as a whole (Fig. 4.23). It can be seen that both abraded and non-abraded flints form a general spread with a slight clustering around the 2:1 line. An analysis of butt-types reveals that, whilst plain butts were the most common type, linear and punctiform platforms were well represented across the assemblages (Fig. 4.24), being particularly abundant in context 2696.

Figure 4.25 demonstrates the close association between punctiform and linear butt-types and a blade-like morphology, compared to the range of size exhibited by pieces with plain platforms. Whilst

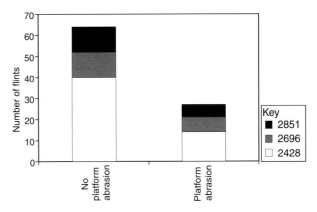

Fig. 4.22   Mesolithic flint assemblage: platform edge abrasion by context

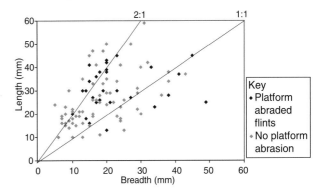

Fig. 4.23   Mesolithic flint assemblage: length/breadth ratio of flints with and without platform edge abrasion

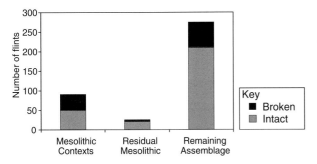

Fig. 4.20   Proportion of broken and intact flints

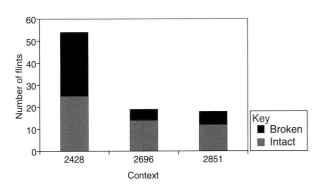

Fig. 4.21   Mesolithic flint assemblage: proportion of broken and intact flints by context

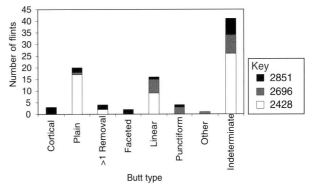

Fig. 4.24   Mesolithic flint assemblage: butt types by context

no direct correlation was noted between platform edge abrasion and morphology (Fig. 4.23), it appears that these attributes are indirectly related through butt-type. A total of 43.5% of plain butts had been abraded, compared to 75% of linear butts and 100% of punctiform butts. Platform edge abrasion thus appears to influence butt form, and hence the final shape of the removal. The more laminar form of pieces with linear and punctiform butts reflects attempts to produce blades through careful platform preparation and controlled percussion.

Hammer-mode was inferred using the morphology of the bulb of percussion. Four pieces (all from

context 2851) possessed lipped, diffuse bulbs and were probably struck using a soft-hammer percussor, such as an antler hammer (Fig. 4.26). Thirty pieces, which exhibited defined and prominent bulbs, were probably struck using a hard hammer. The majority of the flakes had been removed using a percussor of an indeterminate nature or could not be assessed due to breakage. It may tentatively be concluded that the material represents a mixed hammer-mode, with the possible predominance of hard-hammer percussion. The low numbers of hinge and step terminations, which are often associated with hard hammer reduction, in comparison to feather terminations (Fig. 4.27) implies that flakes struck using a soft-hammer percussor are under-represented in the analysis as a result of the difficulty of identification.

The overwhelming majority of flakes and blades (63.7%) are non-cortical (Fig. 4.28). Context 2696 contained the highest percentage of non-cortical removals, at 89.5%. Very few flakes retaining more than 25% dorsal cortex were identified, and only one entirely cortical flake was recovered. A similar pattern is evident from an analysis of flake type (Fig. 4.29). The various categories of secondary removal (side-trimming, distal-trimming and miscellaneous trimming) together provide 28.6% of the total, of which side-trimming flakes were the most frequently occurring sub-type.

The under-representation of flakes retaining

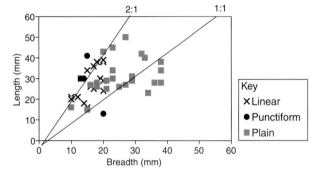

Fig. 4.25 Mesolithic flint assemblage: length, breadth and butt type

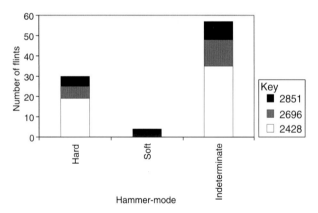

Fig. 4.26 Mesolithic flint assemblage: hammer mode by context

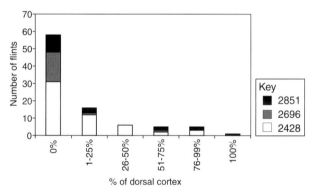

Fig. 4.28 Mesolithic flint assemblage: dorsal cortex extent by context

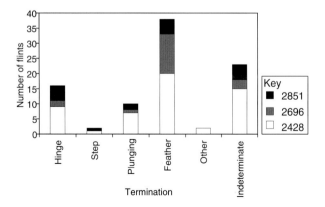

Fig. 4.27 Mesolithic flint assemblage: termination type by context

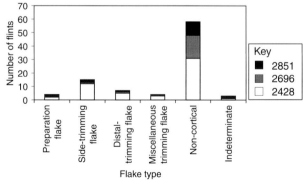

Fig. 4.29 Mesolithic flint assemblage: flake type by context

dorsal cortex, and in particular of wholly cortical flakes, implies that cores were at least partially prepared elsewhere. The predominance of non-cortical pieces suggests that, rather than general knapping waste, the groups of Mesolithic flintwork represent selected elements of the range of debitage produced in the course of a knapping episode. These pieces may have been preferred by virtue of their suitability for use and/or for secondary reworking as part of microlith manufacture.

Two refitting flakes were recovered, both from context 2428 (Fig. 4.30.9). A third flake may have been struck from the same core, but would not refit. These flakes are undiagnostic, and may date from the Mesolithic to Bronze Age. Contexts 2428 and 2696 both contained several small groups of flakes, from two to four pieces, that were identified as related groups on the basis of similarities in flint type. It is possible that these pieces were struck from the same core, although no refits were found to confirm this.

Discussion

The presence of earlier Mesolithic flint work at Moores Farm, both as a general spread across the site and in higher quantities within two tree throw holes, is significant. Excavations 200m north of the site at Pingewood produced a very small number of artefacts dating to the earlier Mesolithic, which included a microburin and scrapers (Care 1985, 33–5). Otherwise, few early Mesolithic findspots are known in the area, although a number of sites have been located in the Middle Kennet Valley (Lobb and Rose 1996, 74), and a substantial assemblage of Mesolithic flintwork was recovered from Park Farm, Binfield, 16km to the east (Ford and Roberts 1995). The large-scale excavations at Green Park 1 and 2 produced no evidence for Mesolithic activity (Bradley and Brown 1992; Bradley 2004), although a few pieces of probable Mesolithic or early Neolithic flintwork were recovered from Green Park 3 (see Chapter 2).

The assemblage from context 2696 appears to be the most technologically coherent. This feature contained both of the two broad-blade microliths, and the debitage component exhibited the most blade-like propensity. Although context 2428 contained two refitting flakes, the assemblage does not represent the full range of debitage produced in the course of a knapping event. The paucity of cortical flakes implies that the waste flakes produced during the decortication stage of the knapping sequence were deposited elsewhere, perhaps at the immediate source of the raw material. The absence of spalls may reflect sampling strategies or a collection bias, but again implies that the material was not deposited in the context of a knapping event.

Conversely, the percentage and range of retouched and utilised pieces in the assemblage indicates that the flints were deposited following various tool-using activities, and as such probably represent a selection of knapping products that were formed into a tool-kit. The range of retouched forms implies that a series of different tasks were performed, and that the site was not a specialised activity area. The relatively frequent occurrence of side-trimming flakes in the assemblage may reflect the preferential selection of naturally backed pieces for utilisation. Possible evidence of microlith manufacture, including a microburin and a notched blade, may suggest that tool-kits were being supplemented or maintained at the site. In the context of this interpretation, the cores may have been transported as raw material for the replenishment of the tool-kit, as needed. This could explain the presence of the two refitting flakes from context 2428.

The Mesolithic material from Moores Farm represents a low-density concentration, particularly when compared to the much larger quantity of flints recovered from occupation sites in the Middle Kennet Valley such as Thatcham (Healy *et al.* 1992) and Wawcott (Froom 1972; 1976). Unlike Area A/M at Binfield (Ford and Roberts 1995), where the pattern of distribution appeared to represent numerous superimposed concentrations over a wide area, the Mesolithic flints from Moores Farm were concentrated in three contexts in close proximity. These concentrations should be viewed against a general background spread of residual Mesolithic material (see below).

It is probable that the flintwork was deposited in the context of short term or temporary occupation. The assemblage appears to contain a notable earlier Mesolithic component; no diagnostic pieces of later date are present. It is possible, therefore, that the flints were deposited in one episode of activity over a relatively short period. The flints may have been cached or discarded in hollows following a brief stopover, for example, in the course of which tool-kits were renewed and a range of activities performed. Although it cannot be ruled out, there is no clear evidence to suggest that the material represents superimposed deposits resulting from the revisiting of the site. Similarly, the limited quantity of material and its discrete concentration strongly implies a small-scale, off-site activity area rather than a riverside base-camp.

The remaining assemblage by Kate Cramp and Hugo Anderson-Whymark

The remaining assemblage is composed of 301 flints (Table 4.5). Six pieces were recovered from middle Neolithic contexts, with the remainder being recovered from middle Bronze Age or early Iron Age features or as unstratified material. The flintwork is thinly distributed across the site; only four features produced more than 10 pieces, all dating to the middle Bronze Age (pits 2146, 2441 and 2742 and 'oven' 2359). Most of the material dates broadly to the Neolithic and Bronze Age, combined with a residual Mesolithic element. Given the low density of the material, it will be discussed as one assemblage, with separate reference to residual Mesolithic flints where appropriate.

The flakes are generally small, although some are of relatively broad dimensions. A mixture of hard and soft percussion appears to have been used. Blades, bladelets and blade-like flakes were less numerous than flakes (8.8%). This is significantly lower than the percentages for the Mesolithic contexts, and reflects the later prehistoric date of much of the material. Several fine soft-hammer blades were nonetheless present in the assemblage. A number of these exhibit dorsal blade scars and platform edge abrasion, and appear to belong to a Mesolithic blade industry.

Twelve pieces of irregular waste were identified, most of which represent attempted flake removals that were struck or had shattered down thermal fractures. Only five spalls were present in the assemblage; this is a disproportionately low figure, and is probably the result of excavation methods rather than the absence of microdebitage *per se*. Consequently, it cannot be certain whether the paucity of spalls is a true reflection of the original composition of the assemblage.

A range of formal core types were recovered, including four single platform flake cores, five multi-platform flake cores (eg Fig. 4.30.10), two single-platform blade cores and seven cores on flakes. The complete specimens weighed between 9g and 174g, with an average weight of 39.7g. The flake cores generally lacked much platform preparation and were aimed at expedient flake production rather than controlled blade production. The majority can be broadly attributed to industries of the later Neolithic or Bronze Age, although most probably date towards the later end of this range. Two of the single-platform blade cores exhibit a series of unidirectional blade removals and platform edge abrasion, and are probably of Mesolithic date. Both have been manufactured from a good quality gravel flint.

Tested nodules, defined as partially worked cores exhibiting a limited number of removals, occurred frequently within the assemblage, with 17 examples (48.6% of all core types). The majority consisted of relatively small gravel flint nodules, often in a frost-shattered condition, from which two or three flake removals had been taken. It is likely that the first few preparatory removals were designed to assess the knapping suitability of these pieces, which were subsequently abandoned when thermal fractures were encountered.

A total of 34 retouched pieces were present in the assemblage, providing 11.5% of the total. The most commonly occurring type within this group was the edge-retouched flake. A total of 14 were recovered, exhibiting varying degrees of retouch. Most, however, were characterised by slight abrupt retouch along one of the lateral margins. An edge-retouched blade from the subsoil in Area 4 is probably of early Mesolithic date, and has two notches that may have been related to microlith manufacture.

A total of 15 scrapers were recovered. The majority were end scrapers and end and side scrapers, although one disc scraper (Fig. 4.30.11) was present and a possible fragment of an early Bronze Age thumbnail scraper (Fig. 4.30.12) was also identified. The upper fill of middle Bronze Age waterhole 2610 contained a flake that had been struck from a scraper manufactured on a non-flake blank. As a group, scrapers form 44.1% of the retouched component and 5.1% of the total assemblage from the site. This constitutes an unusually high proportion, and may indicate that hide preparation was an important activity on site.

Two arrowheads were recovered as unstratified finds from Area 16. These comprised a later Neolithic oblique arrowhead (Fig. 4.30.13) and an undiagnostic fragment of a finely retouched arrowhead (Fig. 4.30.14). The latter may be part of a leaf, oblique or barbed and tanged form, and can only be broadly dated between the early Neolithic and early Bronze Age. The assemblage also contained two incomplete serrated flakes, recovered from an early Iron Age pit (Fig. 4.30.15) and undated tree throw hole 2656. Again, these artefacts may date from the Mesolithic to the Bronze Age.

Compared to the material from the Mesolithic contexts, a high proportion of the remaining assemblage exhibited evidence of burning. A total of 27 flints (9%) had been burnt, whilst only three flints (3.3%) in the Mesolithic assemblages displayed heat damage.

Discussion

Much of the remaining assemblage has been redeposited; no large, potentially *in situ* groups were detected. Most of the material, with the exception of the later Neolithic oblique arrowhead, can only be dated broadly to the Neolithic and Bronze Age. There is also undoubtedly some residual Mesolithic flintwork, represented by some of the fine blades and possibly some of the scrapers. The low density of material across numerous contexts would suggest that this material represents a background spread, rather than an occupation or working area. Nonetheless, the high proportion of scrapers within the assemblage may suggest a focus on hide preparation or similar activities.

Catalogue of illustrated flint (Fig. 4.30)

Mesolithic assemblage

1   Blade. Alluvial layer 2851
2   Blade. Tree throw hole 2429, context 2428
3   Blade. Tree throw hole 2429, context 2428
4   Microburin. Tree throw hole 2429, context 2428
5   Notch. Tree throw hole 2429, context 2428
6   Microlith, Jacobi type 1b. Tree throw hole 2697, context 2696
7   Microlith, Jacobi type 1a. Tree throw hole 2697, context 2696
8   Retouched blade. Tree throw hole 2429, context 2428
9   Refitting flakes. Tree throw hole 2429, context 2428

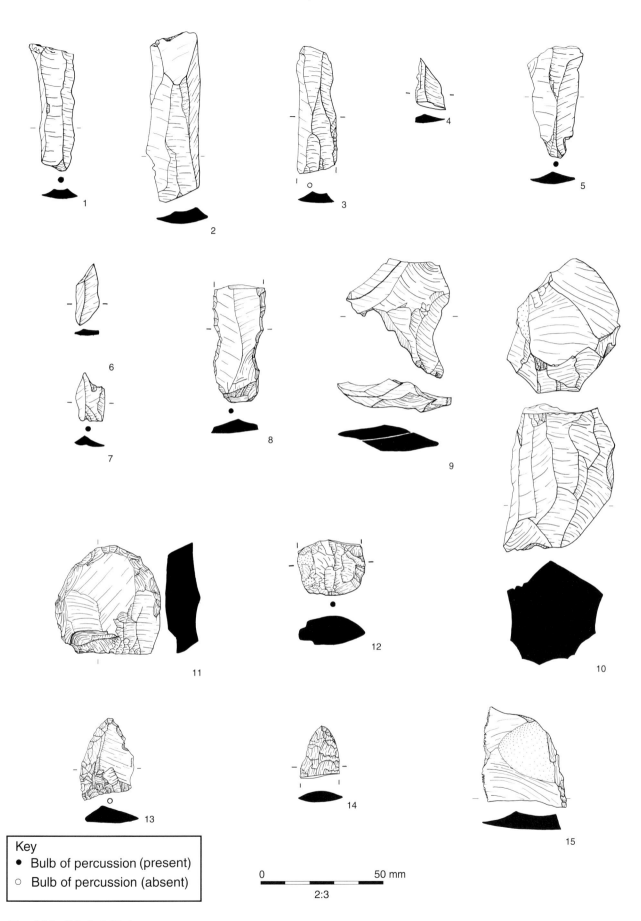

Key
● Bulb of percussion (present)
○ Bulb of percussion (absent)

0   50 mm
2:3

Fig. 4.30   Worked flint

Remaining assemblage

10 Multiplatform flake core. SF 31. Early Iron Age pit group 2042, layer 2044
11 Disc scraper. SF 6. Subsoil, Area 13 (context 1304)
12 Possible thumbnail scraper. Early Bronze Age? Early Iron Age posthole 1237, context 1238
13 Oblique arrowhead. Later Neolithic. SF 9. Subsoil, Area 16 (context 2001)
14 Unclassifiable arrowhead. SF 25. Unstratified, Area 16 (context 2172)
15 Serrated flake. Early Iron Age pit group 2042, pit 2508, context 2509

Neolithic and early Bronze Age pottery
by Sandy Budden and Elaine L Morris

Introduction

The assemblage of Neolithic and early Bronze Age pottery totals 238 sherds (1000g; Table 4.7). Owing to the small size of the assemblage individual vessels have been characterised, where sufficient evidence exists. The assemblage divides into four chronological groups. Most prominent of these is the Neolithic material, which is dominated by Peterborough, or Impressed, wares (Gibson 2002, 78–82). Late Neolithic/early Bronze Age pottery includes Beaker material and is the smallest group. Early Bronze Age sherds are also rare. The undiagnostic 'Indeterminate' group is made up of sherds that cannot be confidently assigned to any of the above groups, but which are clearly earlier prehistoric based on fabric. The methodology used in this analysis follows the guidelines of the Prehistoric Ceramics Research Group (PCRG 1997). All sherds have been subject to both macroscopic inspection and microscopic inspection at x20 magnification and have been assigned to each chronological group based on a combination of fabric, form, surface treatments and decorative characteristics. Seven fabric groups have been identified and these are described below.

Table 4.7 Quantification of Neolithic and early Bronze Age pottery by pottery date

Pottery date	No. of sherds	Weight (g)	No. of rim sherds	No. of base sherds
Neolithic	209	763	9	9
Neolithic/early Bronze Age	6	13	1	-
Early Bronze Age	11	115	3	-
Indeterminate	12	109	1	-
Total	238	1000	14	9

Fabrics

Analysis revealed three broad fabric groups based on the dominant inclusion present: flint, grog and

quartz. Each of these groups becomes further subdivided by identification of variations of size, density and combinations of inclusions and the presence of varied clay matrices, making a total of 11 fabrics (Table 4.8). Of these by far the most dominant fabric type is F1 which is associated with all the Neolithic Impressed Wares, in particular the pots identified as Mortlake bowls, and is a fabric typical of this pottery type (Cleal 1995, 189). Fabric F2 varies most notably from F1 in its clay matrix of rounded rather than angular quartz and is associated with a possible Fengate Ware base and a decorated Fengate body sherd. Of particular interest is fabric Q2 which appears just once as a Mortlake rim. Angular-quartz-bearing fabrics in the Mortlake sub-style are particularly noted in Wales (Gibson 1995, 33) and a known phenomenon in the Oxfordshire region. It is interesting that the same apparent Mortlake sub-style present in the Moores Farm assemblage occurs in two such contrasting fabrics with clear differences in the execution of decoration and firing relating to these fabric types. This could well suggest the work of two different potters. Fabric F4, with 70% flint temper in what otherwise appears to be a Beaker sherd, is another interesting anomaly within this assemblage as flint in this quantity is not a tempering practise common to Beaker vessels. All the other fabrics in this small assemblage fall into appropriate classifications for the periods that they represent and there is nothing to suggest anything other than local origins for the pottery assemblage as a whole.

Flint-tempered group

F1: An orange through to dark red and black fabric, the latter caused by an unoxidised firing atmosphere but also by refiring. Common (25%) inclusions of poorly sorted angular flint range in size from 0.25 to 6mm. Of this flint 15% ranges from 0.25 to 1mm while 10% is between 2 and 7mm and is particularly poorly sorted. Some of the flint in this fabric group is flint core and appears degraded possibly from refiring and ensuing decomposition following deposition. The clay matrix of this fabric contains very common (30%), angular and subangular, fine quartz and rare (2%) pieces of red iron, both of which are very well sorted. The fabric is hard with a well-compacted surface despite the flint inclusions. The fracture is laminated.

F2: Well oxidized, orange fabric with common (25%) inclusions of poorly sorted angular flint, ranging from 0.25 to 4mm in size. Of this flint 10% ranges from 0.25 to 1mm, while 15% is between 1 and 4mm, with the vast majority of inclusions lying in the 2mm range. The sorting of these larger inclusions is very poor. The clay matrix of this fabric contains moderate (10%), rounded, fine quartz. The fabric feels soft to medium with a rough texture and has a hackly fracture.

F3: A highly oxidized, orange to red fabric with

common (20%) inclusions of poorly sorted, multi-faceted, angular, calcined flint with a grey crackled appearance, 0.5 to 7mm across. This fabric is particularly characterized by the irregular, multi-faceted flint on the exterior surface. The clay matrix contains common (20%), angular, medium to fine, well sorted, quartz and 3–5% poorly-sorted, well-rounded red iron. The fabric is soft to medium with a very rough surface texture and hackly fracture.

F4: An oxidized exterior surface but otherwise unoxidised fabric, black with some buff colouring. Inclusions are an unusually abundant (70%) amount of poorly sorted angular, calcined flint, 1–2mm across. The high density of the inclusions makes identification of the clay matrix impossible without resorting to petrological analysis. The fabric is of medium hardness with a rough texture and hackly fracture.

Grog-tempered group

G1: A highly oxidised orange and buff fabric with moderate (10%), moderately sorted, angular grog, 2–3mm across. Also present is sparse (5%) angular, very poorly sorted flint ranging from 0.5 to 3mm. The clay matrix contains abundant (40%), very fine, rounded quartz. The fabric is soft, feels powdery and has a hackly fracturing surface.

G2: A highly oxidised, orange fabric with moderate (10%), well-sorted, angular grog measuring 1–2mm across. The grog is hard to detect and 10% is suggested as a reasonable quantity present. Also present is sparse (7%), moderately sorted, angular flint, 0.5–1mm in size. Rare (1%), well rounded, red iron generally 1mm in size is a characteristic of this fabric. The clay matrix contains common (20%), fine rounded quartz. This is a fine, dense, medium to hard-fired fabric with a surprisingly rough surface texture and a smooth fracturing surface.

G3: A black, unoxidised, fabric with moderate (15%), moderately sorted, angular, grey grog ranging from 0.5 to 2mm. It is probable that the grog content is not of the same fabric as the sherds examined. The clay matrix includes common (20%), fine, well-sorted, rounded quartz. G3 is of medium hardness with a soapy texture and has a hackly fracture.

G4: An orange, iron rich, oxidised fabric with very common (30%), poorly sorted, angular grog that appears to be the same or very similar to the fabric of the sherds examined. The grog ranges from 1–4mm in size. The clay matrix includes abundant (40%), well-rounded, fine to medium, quartz with red iron also present. This fabric is soft, feels powdery, with a very slightly grainy surface texture and a smooth to hackly fracture.

G5: A red, orange and black fabric with oxidised exterior surfaces and both oxidised and unoxidised interior surfaces. The majority of G5 sherds appear well tempered with grog but firing conditions of this fabric makes it hard to suggest precise amounts. Moderate (10%) to common (25%) moderately sorted, angular grog ranging from 1–2mm in size is, therefore, the suggested description. Sparse (7%), well sorted, calcined, angular flint, 1–4mm in size, is also present. The well-sorted and angular nature of this flint suggests its use as a deliberate tempering agent despite the low percentage present. The clay matrix contains very common (30%), fine, rounded quartz with iron also present. This fabric is hard, particularly on exterior surfaces, with a smooth texture and has a laminated fracture.

Quartz/quartzite-bearing group

Q1: A buff/black fabric generally showing unoxidised firing conditions but with oxidised exterior surfaces. Q1 has sparse (7%), poorly sorted, angular quartz ranging in size from 2–4mm. Given the low

Table 4.8 Quantification of Neolithic and early Bronze Age pottery by fabric

Fabric	Neolithic No.	Weight (g)	Neolithic/early Bronze Age No.	Weight (g)	Early Bronze Age No.	Weight (g)	Indeterminate No.	Weight (g)	Total No.	Weight (g)
F1	195	667	0	0	0	0	1	3	196	670
F2	4	21	1	5	0	0	1	6	6	32
F3	9	70	0	0	0	0	0	0	9	70
F4	0	0	1	4	0	0	0	0	1	4
G1	0	0	0	0	3	89	0	0	3	89
G2	0	0	1	1	0	0	0	0	1	1
G3	0	0	0	0	3	4	2	9	5	13
G4	0	0	3	3	5	22	0	0	8	25
G5	0	0	0	0	0	0	7	50	7	50
Q1	0	0	0	0	0	0	1	41	1	41
Q2	1	5	0	0	0	0	0	0	1	5
Total	209	763	6	13	11	115	12	109	238	1000

frequency of these large quartz inclusions it is difficult to place them as deliberate temper. However, the clay matrix also contains moderate (10%), rounded fine naturally-occurring quartz, and is likely to be the same matrix as in fabric F1 which suggests that the large quartz fragments are possibly temper. The fabric is soft with a rough, soapy feel and hackly breaking surface. The general appearance is of a highly laminated fabric.

Q2: A black, unoxidised, laminated fabric with sparse (5%), moderately sorted, angular quartzite ranging in size from 0.5 to 2mm. As with Q1 the low percentage of quartz present makes it difficult to determine if this is a deliberate tempering agent. The clay matrix of Q2 contains common (20%), rounded, well-sorted, naturally occurring quartz with black iron also present. The fabric is hard, especially on the exterior surface, with a smooth texture and a rough fracturing surface.

Neolithic pottery

Neolithic pottery makes up the majority of the assemblage (Table 4.8). The mean sherd weight is only 3.7g, which indicates the fragmented condition of the vessels. The pottery belongs to the Mortlake and Fengate sub-styles of Impressed Wares, dating to the middle Neolithic, c 3500–2800 cal BC (Barclay 2002, 90). In terms of fabric the Neolithic material is dominated by F1 (Table 4.8) which is characteristic of Neolithic Impressed wares (Cleal 1995, 185–94). One vessel in this fabric appears to have been subjected to processes of reburning after use as a cooking pot. Each identified vessel is described below.

Vessel 1 (Fig. 4.31.1): Recovered from Neolithic hollow 2967 (context 2969). No rim sherds are present. There are three slightly rounded basal sherds and 123 body sherds, mostly of a reasonable size, averaging 30mm across. Despite the absence of a rim the numerous sherds, decoration type and fabric all combine to define this as a single globular Mortlake bowl. The quantity of sherds, combined with an average wall thickness of 10mm, allows the suggestion that this bowl may be somewhat larger than Vessel 2 described below. Decoration covers the exterior of the pot, with the exception of the basal sherds, and takes the classic form of bird or small mammal bone impressions (Gibson 2002, 79) accompanied by a small amount of twisted cord decoration. Fabric F1 has been used for the manufacture of this pot.

Vessel 2 (Fig. 4.31.2): Recovered from the same context as Vessel 1. The morphology, and impressed whipped cord, 'maggot' decoration, which is particularly crisp, indicates that this is a second Mortlake bowl. The available rim sherds, c 6% present, reveal a diameter of 160–180mm suggesting it had been a medium-size pot for this sub-style (Barclay 2002,

91). The construction of the rim is particularly clear allowing for an accurate description of the manufacturing process. The basic rim had been formed and then small coils were added internally and externally in order to embellish the rim morphology and create a better platform for the impressed decoration. Based on wall thickness measurements and fragmentation, this is probably a smaller vessel than Vessel 1. The sherds from Vessel 2 include all of the reburnt sherds within the F1 fabric description. There is some evidence of both sooting and residues associated with this vessel which suggest an association with food preparation. However, the very dark nature of the sherds indicates that this alone cannot account for the refired appearance of this vessel. What is certain is that Vessel 2 was not in close association with Vessel 1 when it was reburnt, because there is no corresponding evidence of burning on Vessel 1. This suggests that the reburning may have occurred prior to deposition in hollow 2967.

Vessel 3: Represented by a single, small basal sherd which is flat externally and slightly rounded internally. Again, it is constructed in fabric F1 and was recovered from the same context as Vessels 1 and 2. The construction of the base leads to the suggestion that this may belong to a Fengate vessel.

Vessel 4 (Fig 4.32.3–4): The sherds ascribed to this vessel include a base sherd and a decorated body sherd. The base sherd (Fig. 4.32.3) was recovered from middle Bronze Age ditch 2041, and has a rounded interior and flat exterior, with a base diameter of 80–100mm. The F2 fabric with its highly laminated structure and firing characterise this as a Neolithic sherd, most likely a Fengate style base. The decorated body sherd (Fig. 4.32.4) was recovered from middle Bronze Age pit 2441, 80m to the west. The decoration takes the form of tiny bird or mammal bone impressions. Despite the different contexts of final deposition, the two sherds share many distinctly similar characteristics. The possibility that they are from two vessels of the same style cannot be ruled out, but the favoured interpretation is that they represent a single vessel and that this anomaly may reflect redeposition occurring on the site.

Vessel 5 (Fig. 4.32.5): This unstratified sherd is very definitely characterised as a Mortlake vessel through reference to rim morphology and the very clear whipped cord, maggot decoration. This vessel was manufactured in fabric Q2 and fired in an unoxidising atmosphere making an almost entirely black fabric.

Vessel 6: This consists of four body sherds from Neolithic posthole 2900, dated by their manufacture in fabric F3. One is a very small base sherd with a flat exterior and slightly curved interior. In the absence of any other significant featured sherds it is not possible to do more than suggest that these sherds may belong to another Fengate vessel.

The final four sherds in the Neolithic group add weight to the argument for extensive redeposition amongst the Neolithic material. All are plain body sherds. Three sherds in fabric F1 and bearing all the same characteristics as Vessel 1 were found in middle Bronze Age contexts (ditch 2078, posthole 2890 and fill 2943 of waterhole 2927). Either these sherds represent other vessels exhibiting identical characteristics to Vessel 1 or we are seeing evidence of redeposition of sherds belonging to Vessel 1. The final sherd is also in fabric F1, and has the same reburnt characteristics as Pot 2, but was found in early Iron Age tree throw hole 2336.

Late Neolithic/early Bronze Age pottery

This period is scantily represented within the assemblage and is somewhat problematic in nature. There are just four possible vessels, only one of which, Vessel 7, is characterised through reference to a featured sherd.

Vessel 7 (Fig. 4.32.6): Represented by two joining rim sherds, counted as one for quantification purposes. The rim is slightly incurving with a squared off, flattened lip, and has a diameter of *c* 120mm. This is a very fine pot manufactured in fabric G2, which contains grog, flint and sand, and appears to be very similar in character to the G21 fabric at Field Farm, Burghfield (Mepham 1992a, 40). This combination of tempering materials is not a common fabric for Beaker vessels but is noted by Cleal (1995, 188) to represent 8% of Beaker fabrics in the Wessex region. The vessel fits well into Boast's (1995, 72) characterisation of Beakers found in settlement contexts in that its very fine, but plain, surface is untreated apart from limited smoothing. The sherds were recovered from early Iron Age pit 1267, indicating redeposition.

The remaining sherds in this group are all problematic to one extent or another. One unstratified plain body sherd from Area 16 exhibits Beaker characteristics in terms of its general appearance but is manufactured in fabric F4, which consists of 70% of angular flint. This is unusual for a Beaker vessel but not unheard of (Mepham 1992a, 42; Cleal 1995). It shows evidence for burnt food residues on the interior surface. Three highly abraded fragments from middle Bronze Age posthole 2813 are in a grog-tempered fabric which displays typical Beaker characteristics. A final sherd from middle Bronze Age ditch 2500 is again established as Beaker only on the grounds of general characteristics.

Early Bronze Age pottery

This is a slightly more substantial group than the late Neolithic/early Bronze Age group.

Vessel 8 (Fig. 4.32.7): This consists of two joining, plain rim sherds of a neutral-profile vessel with a rim diameter of *c* 220mm. The grog-tempered fabric, G1, and general rim form characterise this as of Early Bronze Age origin. It was recovered from posthole 2531.

Vessel 9: This is very similar in character to Vessel 8, manufactured in the same G1 fabric, and was recovered from the same context. However, the wall thickness of the rim is 2–3mm greater than that of Vessel 8, and the rim morphology is of a slightly different character. In addition, the rim of Vessel 8 has no surface treatment while that of Vessel 9 is noticeably smoothed on its interior surface.

A further plain body sherd in fabric G1 was recovered from posthole 2890 and could derive from either of the above vessels; wall thickness and surface treatment suggest a close link with Vessel 9. This is one of the few sherds in this assemblage with evidence of burnt food residue. It may be that this sherd represents a third vessel in this fabric group, or simply disturbance and redeposition of sherds.

Vessel 10 (Fig. 4.32.8): This is a small, bevelled rim sherd, found in middle Bronze Age pit 2144. Its fabric, G3, and morphology suggest the possibility that this rim is part of a Biconical Urn although no precise parallel has been found.

Vessel 11 (Fig. 4.32.9): This is a single decorated body sherd manufactured in fabric G4. The orientation and nature of the applied cordon with impressed finger decoration suggests a horseshoe handle of a Biconical Urn more in keeping, perhaps, with the later Ardleigh style (Brown 1995, 127) than those found on Wessex horseshoe-handled urns (Gibson 2002, 100).

Four further sherds also manufactured in fabric G4 share many similar characteristics to Pot 11 but were found in a number of different contexts, again leaving us to wonder whether we have a number of similar vessels or one vessel that has been subject to redeposition.

Indeterminate pottery

This group of pottery consists of sherds that cannot be confidently assigned to any of the three preceding chronological groups. It is also not possible to confidently identify individual vessels. Significant within this group is a small, plain rim sherd in fabric F1, recovered from middle Bronze Age ditch 2109. There is also a striking group of sherds manufactured in fabric G5 and sharing firing and surface treatment characteristics which result in a highly distinctive 'leathery' texture and dark brown colour. All but one of the sherds also share a wall thickness of 7–9mm. Each sherd in this group was, however, found in a different context, with no

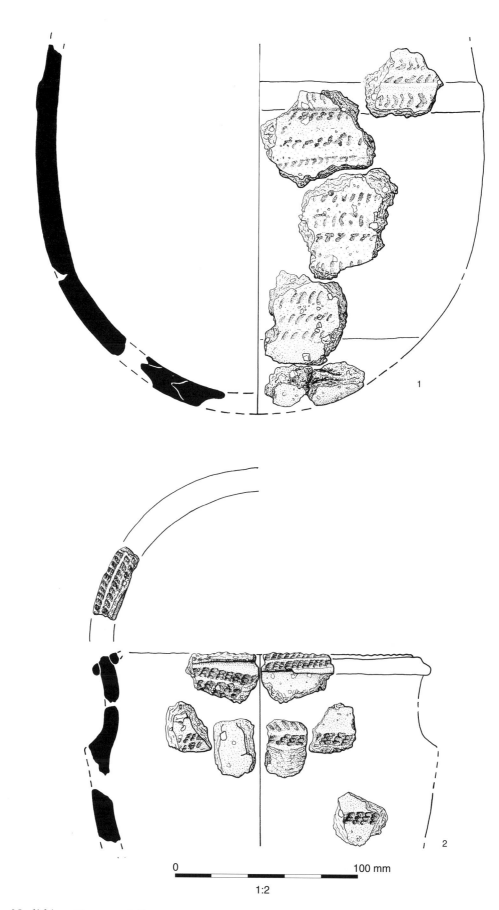

Fig. 4.31   Neolithic pottery, nos 1–2

apparent relationship across the site. These sherds represent either the repetitive use of particular manufacturing strategies to produce a number of very similar vessels, or yet again these sherds are linked to the apparently highly disturbed nature of the earlier prehistoric archaeology at Moores Farm. Cleal and Raymond (1990, 120) suggest that sherds of the same fabric occurring widely scattered across a site cannot be used to chart the movement of individual pots. Perhaps, however, this is only the case if we are unprepared to accept that sherds exhibiting strong technological signature traits, as with the G5 fabric group, may just as well represent one pot as several.

Discussion

With reference to each of the pottery groups within this assemblage there appears to be considerable evidence of disturbance of early prehistoric deposits across the site. The only other explanation for so many technologically similar sherds deriving from separate contexts would be a very low presence of sherds originating from more vessels across the site than have been suggested in this report. This, however, seems an unlikely scenario for two reasons. Firstly, this would seem not to

account for the multi-periodicity of the phenomenon. Secondly, in the case of the G5 fabric group, it assumes that pots were being made on a scale of production that is perhaps more suited to later prehistoric periods. The nature of this disturbance is not necessarily caused by the same factors across the whole assemblage. The digging of pits in the later Bronze and Iron Age may account for some of this disturbance, for example the Beaker rim found in an early Iron Age pit, but it seems unlikely that this is should be regarded as the sole cause of redeposition, particularly in the case of the G5 fabric group. Given the known intricacies of Impressed Wares in relation to social, and possibly ritual, activity in earlier prehistory (Barclay *et al.* 1996, 5; Thomas 1991, 89–125; Cleal 1984, 146–50), and as a new technology, careful consideration should be given to the many possible reasons for deliberate movement of pottery sherds to different parts of the site.

This kind of action is perhaps underlined by the refiring of Vessel 2 at some time in its biography. This may be incidental, for example, accidental refiring within a hearth, which given the evidence of sooting and residues associated with it seems a reasonable supposition. However, it could just as easily be linked to similar complex actions such as

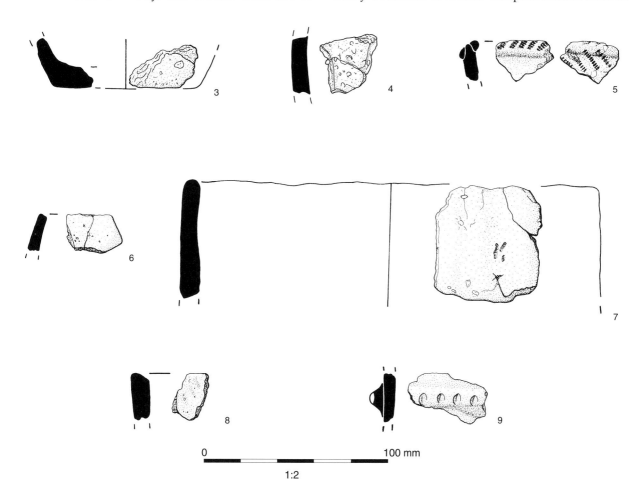

Fig. 4.32   Neolithic and early Bronze Age pottery, nos 3–9

those outlined by Barclay *et al.* (1996, 8) with regard to tree felling in earlier prehistory in the Oxford region or to other forms of ritual behaviour (Barclay *et al.* 1996, 5; Thomas 1991, 89–125; Cleal 1984, 146–50).

Catalogue of illustrated pottery

1   Mortlake Bowl; fabric F1; decorated with bird/mammal bone and twisted cord impressions; smoothed interior and exterior surfaces; oxidised exterior and unoxidised interior. Neolithic hollow 2967, context 2968.

2   Mortlake Bowl; 6% of c 160–180mm diameter present; fabric F1; whipped cord 'maggot' decoration; very well smoothed (polished) interior surfaces and smoothed with grass on upper exterior; some oxidisation but mostly unoxidised firing conditions plus refiring of this fabric. Neolithic hollow 2967, context 2968.

3   Fengate base sherd, rounded interior with flat exterior; 5% of c 80-100mm diameter present; fabric F2; interior and exterior smoothed with grass; oxidised firing throughout. Middle Bronze Age ditch 2041, context 2053.

4   Decorated body sherd, possibly same vessel as no. 3; fabric F2; decorated with mammal or bird bone impressions; interior smoothed, exterior smoothed with grass; oxidised. Middle Bronze Age pit 2441, context 2243.

5   Mortlake vessel; <5% present; fabric Q2; decorated with impressed whipped cord 'maggots' lying diagonally across the rim; smoothed exterior; unoxidised. Unstratified (context 2851).

6   Plain Beaker rim; 7% of c 120mm diameter present; fabric G2; smoothed interior and exterior; oxidised. Early Iron Age pit 1267, context 1268.

7   Plain early Bronze Age rim; 5% of c 220mm diameter present; fabric G1; oxidised. Middle Bronze Age posthole 2531, context 2530.

8   Biconical Urn rim; <5% present; fabric G3; smoothed/burnished all over; oxidised. Middle Bronze Age pit 2144, context 2145.

9   Biconical Urn decorated body sherd; applied and impressed cordon; fabric G4; interior and exterior smoothed with grass; oxidised. Middle Bronze Age ditch 2041, context 2081.

Middle and late Bronze Age pottery
by Elaine L Morris

A total of 610 sherds (4046g) of middle Bronze Age pottery was recovered (Table 4.9). All of the pottery is flint-tempered. Identifiable vessel forms include the typical range of globular, bucket and barrel urns of this date. In addition, there are two vessels which probably date to the late Bronze Age.

Methodology

The current recommended guidelines for the study of later prehistoric pottery were followed (PCRG 1997), with the addition of codes to describe sherd thickness as follows: code 1, <5mm; 2, 5–<7mm; 3, 7–<9mm; 4, 9–<11mm; 5, 11–<13mm; 6, 13–<15mm; 7, 15–<17mm; and 8, 17–<19mm. The establishment of 2mm thickness codes provides a practical means of using the data to examine the frequency of wall thickness variability by fabric. Each sherd was examined by eye, and some also by using a binocular microscope at 10x power, to determine the size and density of temper and the presence of quartz sand in the clay matrix.

Condition of the assemblage

The general condition of the assemblage is moderately poor, with a mean sherd weight of 6.6g. This is a clear indication of the degree of fragmentation. This aspect is given additional emphasis when the number of sherds without one or both surfaces present, ie sherd flakes, is quantified (Table 4.10). Nevertheless, there are several featured sherds present including rims, shoulders, bases and decorated examples which provide evidence of the variety of vessels used at this settlement. Some of the sherds have been affected by iron staining, not

Table 4.9 Quantification of middle to late Bronze Age pottery by fabric

Fabric	No. of sherds	Weight (g)	Mean sherd weight (g)	% by number	% by weight
F6	297	2189	7.4	48.7	54.1
F7	93	622	6.7	15.2	15.4
F8	22	113	5.1	3.6	2.8
F9	93	751	8.1	15.2	18.6
F10	101	362	3.6	16.6	8.9
F11	4	9	2.2	0.7	0.2
Total	610	4046	6.6	100	100

Table 4.10 Middle to late Bronze Age pottery, quantification of sherds from each fabric type that have one or both surfaces missing

Fabric	No. of sherds	% by fabric type
F6	71	23.9
F7	47	50.5
F8	9	40.9
F9	35	37.6
F10	22	21.8
F11	1	25.0
Total	185	100

only on the surfaces but also throughout the fabric of the sherds. This is a common occurrence amongst prehistoric pottery from the Lower Kennet Valley and can be compensated for during identification and definition of fabric types.

Fabrics

Six fabric types were defined for this assemblage of flint-tempered pottery (Table 4.9). There are two coarseware fabrics (F6 and F7), two which could be classified as intermediate to coarsewares (F8 and F9) and two which are distinctively finewares (F10 and F11). This range of fabrics is typical of middle Bronze Age pottery from central southern England as described by Ellison (1980). Very similar, if not identical, fabrics have been identified on other sites with middle Bronze Age pottery in the Lower Kennet Valley at Field Farm, Burghfield (Mepham 1992a) and Shortheath Lane, Sulhamstead (Mepham 1992c). Re-examination of the fabric reference collection from Green Park 1 has shown that the fabrics associated with decorated sherds from middle Bronze Age urns (Hall 1992, fig. 51, 206, 211, 212) are also the same types of fabric as F6 and F7, described below, with a significant density of large, angular, crushed burnt flint temper in a relatively clean clay matrix. Woodward has indicated that the range of fabrics from Shortheath Lane in particular is typical of the Lower Thames Valley (1992, 77).

The Moores Farm fabrics had no specific inclusions to indicate that the resources used to make the fabrics were other than local in origin. However, it is important to indicate that the clay matrices in these fabrics do not display any iron oxide inclusions of a specific geological nature, a fact which contrasts significantly with the types of clays used to make late Bronze Age pottery in this area.

F6 (coarseware): A common to abundant amount (25–40% concentration) of very angular to angular, moderately sorted, crushed, calcined flint temper measuring ≤7mm across with the majority of pieces ≤3mm; principal characteristics are a distinctive harshness to both surfaces and the presence of all size ranges of inclusions, especially pieces ≤0.2mm across in an only slightly sandy clay matrix containing subrounded, medium to fine quartz grains ≤0.5mm across in rare to sparse concentrations (1–3%) with many sherds often displaying very fine to silt-grade size quartz of ≤0.2mm across, creating a nearly quartz-free clay matrix.

F7 (coarseware): A common to very common amount (20–30%) of poorly sorted, very angular to angular, crushed calcined flint temper measuring ≤8mm across with the majority measuring ≤4mm and very few fragments ≤0.5mm in a sandy clay matrix containing a sparse to moderate amount (7–10%) of subrounded quartz grains, measuring ≤0.5mm across with the majority ≤0.2mm. The paucity of flint fragments less than 0.5mm and the

resultant absence of harshness to the surfaces of sherds distinguishes this fabric from fabric F6.

F8 (intermediate): A sparse to moderate amount (7–15%) of very angular to angular, moderately sorted, crushed, calcined flint temper measuring ≤3mm across in a very fine to fine sandy clay matrix with a moderate amount of quartz grains measuring ≤0.2mm across so that it clearly twinkles in well-lit condition when viewed at 10x power. This fabric could be described as a less dense version of F6.

F9 (intermediate/coarseware): An abundant amount (40–50%) of very angular to angular, well-sorted, crushed, calcined flint temper measuring ≤3mm across but majority ≤2mm in an only very slightly very fine sandy-silty clay matrix with rare to sparse quartz grains measuring ≤0.125mm across. A well-processed fabric but not as much preparation effort as for F10 (see below). The infrequency of very fine quartz may be a result of the considerable amount of temper. This fabric visually appears to be similar in texture and, therefore, manufacturing process to middle Iron Age flint-tempered 'saucepan pot' fabrics from central southern England.

F10 (fineware): An abundant amount (40–50%) of very angular to angular, very well-sorted, crushed, calcined flint temper measuring <2mm across with the majority <1mm; quartz sand grains not visible at 10x power. A very distinctive fabric with a sieved temper, almost like 'flint dust' in appearance, resulting from an extraordinary amount of pounding. A considerable amount of effort was invested to make this fabric type.

F11 (fineware): A moderate to common amount (15–20%) of very angular to angular, crushed, calcined flint temper measuring ≤2mm across with the majority <1mm across in an only very slightly silty clay matrix with microscopically visible quartz grains.

Forms

The classic types of middle Bronze Age Deverel-Rimbury urns were identified in the assemblage, as well as two examples of ovoid vessels which may bridge the transition from middle to late Bronze Age pottery repertoires (Table 4.11). While there is a clear correlation between the fineware fabric F10

Table 4.11 Middle to late Bronze Age pottery, quantification of vessel forms

Form	No. of vessels
Barrel/bucket urns	121
Globular urns	29
Late Bronze Age jars	2

and the very distinctive globular urn type, there is considerable variation amongst the fabric types used for making the coarser bucket and barrel urns.

Two rims (Figs 4.33.5 and 4.34.17) are typical of the externally expanded, thickened, flattened rims found on barrel urns (Gibson 2002, fig. 51.5). No examples of barrel urns were found at Field Farm (Butterworth and Lobb 1992) but a similar rim was found on a Lower Thames Valley type 5 sub-biconical cordoned vessel from Shortheath Lane, Sulhamstead (Woodward 1992, 76–7, fig. 24.2). Further afield another can be seen on an urn from Ashford Common, Sunbury, Middlesex (Barrett 1973, fig. 1.2). Bucket urns, however, are a more common type in middle Bronze Age assemblages in this region, and Moores Farm is no exception. At least seven different bucket urns were identified from rims alone, and these include the simple upright, vertical-sided, thick-walled vessel type with rounded rims, one of which is girthed with a plain applied cordon for lifting (Fig. 4.35.20), or slightly flattened examples and some which may be inclined towards the top (Figs 4.33.10, 4.34.13 and 4.35.21–2). Other examples have distinctive hooked rims, one of which bears an attached knob (Fig. 4.34.18–19). Complete examples of knobbed vessels display four opposing knobs and are considered to be functional appendages for lifting, rather than decorative, and therefore similar to plain, applied cordons. Fragments of a very similar, plain bucket urn with knob-like lug was found at Knight's Farm, Burghfield (Bradley *et al.* 1980, fig. 32.39) associated with a radiocarbon date of 1750–1200 cal BC (BM-1594).

What is most unusual about the Moores Farm assemblage is the frequency of fineware, globular urns compared to coarseware barrel and bucket urns. The featured sherds from probably six different globular urns have been identified in this assemblage, including three represented by the upper parts of vessels (Figs 4.33.1 and 4.33.3–4), two specifically by decoration (Figs 4.33.8 and 4.34.16), and one by the angled hip of an urn (Fig. 4.35.23). One of the undecorated globular urns has the slight hint of an attached knob or lug below the neck zone (Fig. 4.33.4). In addition, there are numerous plain but burnished, thin-walled body sherds made from fabrics F10 and F11 which must have derived from globular urns similar to these diagnostic examples. No other published site in the immediate area has this frequency of globular urns relative to other urn types.

One coarseware body sherd from an F6 fabric vessel (thickness code 5; oxidised throughout; pit 807) was perforated prior to firing from the exterior into the interior, creating a 4mm diameter hole. The presence of prefiring, through-the-wall perforations is a common characteristic of coarseware urns of middle Bronze Age date, and is thought to provide a method for securing soft covers as lids on vessels, as the holes often occur just below the rim.

Two unstratified vessels are ovoid jars, and most likely to date to the late rather than the middle Bronze Age. One is made from the moderately tempered fabric F8 and has medium-thick walls (Fig. 4.33.6), while the other is also made from this fabric and has thin walls (Fig. 4.35.24). Both examles were fired in unoxidising conditions.

The range of vessel forms from Moores Farm demonstrates the smooth transition from the middle Bronze Age to those profile characteristics of the earliest of the late Bronze Age plain assemblage types. The hooked rim, ovoid jars of the post-Deverel Rimbury late Bronze Age period certainly derive from the hooked rim bucket urns of the middle Bronze Age, as do the straight-sided upright rim vessels of the post-Deverel-Rimbury late Bronze Age which reflect the very similar straight-walled bucket urns with uniform vertical body to rim profiles. What is most distinctive about the pottery of the late Bronze Age, however, is the subsequent development of the distinctive shouldered jar—a truly new vessel profile. While it would be comforting to suggest that biconical bowls derive from globular urns due to the dropped girth angle profile on many globular urns, this characteristic is not a common one in the Berkshire region. Therefore, while the burnished biconical bowl may have had the same or a similar function as the highly burnished globular urn, there is an apparent gap in time between these urns and the new bowls. This gap needs to be examined more carefully to positively confirm its presence.

Decoration and surface treatment

One of the most distinctive aspects of middle Bronze Age pottery is the presence of fingertip- and fingernail-impressed decoration on applied cordons, and also fingertip impressions straight onto the body of the vessel (Table 4.12). The Moores Farm assemblage contains two examples of fingertip impressions directly on the wall (Figs 4.33.7 and 4.33.11), and four examples of both fingertip and fingernail impressions onto cordons (Figs 4.33.2, 4.33.9 and 4.34.14–15). There are possibly two variations amongst the impressed decoration examples: (1) broad, flat fingertip decoration applied into the wall and onto broad cordons and (2) narrow fingernail impressions only on a narrow cordon. This suggests that there may be two different potters creating the same general

Table 4.12 Middle to late Bronze Age pottery, quantification of decoration types

Decoration type	No. of vessels
Fingertip impressions	2
Applied cordon	2
Applied cordon and fingertip impressions	3
Applied cordon and fingernail impressions	1
Tooled lines	2
Fingernail impressions on LBA jar	1

decorative effect on these urns, these personal impressions constituting 'signatures' (Tomalin 1995). In addition, one of the late Bronze Age-type ovoid jars (Fig. 4.33.6) is decorated with fingernail impressions along the bevelled rim.

Applied cordons were likely to have been primarily for functional use, supporting the vessel walls of large, thick-walled urns or acting as horizontal lifting bands. There are two examples of undecorated, applied cordons in the assemblage (Figs 4.34.12 and 4.35.20). Two similar examples were recovered at Weir Bank Stud Farm, Bray (Cleal 1995, figs 21.21 and 21.25).

The tooled parallel lines on globular urns (Figs 4.33.8 and 4.34.16) are quite distinct for this area. Obvious parallels were not identified in a search of the literature. For example, there are no decorated examples amongst the globular urns from Bray (Cleal 1995, figs 19–21). The vessels are made with extraordinarily well-processed flint temper, and they are thin-walled and burnished to a high degree on at least one if not both surfaces. They are uniformly dark grey to black in colour, and when decorated they display what appear to be tooled parallel strands of some material, similar in appearance to necklaces and located on the neck zone of the vessels.

In addition, most of the sherds from vessels made in fabric F7 also appear to have been smoothed on both surfaces when leather-hard, prior to firing. This is unusual because the fabric is quite coarse with frequent large flint inclusions, and the smoothing of the surface tends to conceal or at least partially hide the flint inclusions. This smoothing effect is commonly found amongst the urns from Shortheath Lane, Sulhamstead (Lobb 1992, 75), and the phrase 'slip on exterior surface' has been used to describe many middle Bronze Age urns from Middlesex (Barrett 1973) and may be a similar effect. This smoothing or slipped effect is thus characteristic of Middle and Lower Thames Valley urns and demonstrates that some special effort was applied to these particular coarseware vessels. The fabric coarseness may have been necessary to take the weight of the thick walled large urns but the context of vessel use and regional identity may have required a more finished appearance to the vessels. It is important to emphasise that this effect is observed on vessels recovered from settlement as well as funerary contexts.

Evidence for use

There are four plain body sherds which display evidence for use in the form of burnt residues on the interior surface, one decorated body sherd (Fig. 4.33.11) which has soot captured in the fingertip decoration and one rim sherd (Fig. 4.34.18) with soot on the exterior surface. These all are derived from coarseware urns in fabrics F6 and F7, which were used as cooking pots. The presence of burnishing on both surfaces of the fineware sherds

suggests that these fancy vessels were used for the serving of liquids. A programme of lipid residue analysis of middle Bronze Age urns should be encouraged to determine what kinds of foods were cooked in these vessels, and the carbonised residues could provide samples for AMS radiocarbon dating of these last meals.

Discussion

Why are there two variations of each class of fabric—two coarse, two intermediate, and two fine? This question is worth exploring from three perspectives to determine which appears to have the greater validity based on the evidence at hand.

Chronology: The middle Bronze Age activity at Moores Farm may represent a 400-year period of inhabitation, during which time different clays were selected for pot making. The procedures for making and adding temper are likely to have changed over such a long time span (20 generations of potters may have lived and died within this period). Even if the period of inhabitation was not long-term, several generations of potters would have been represented. While apprenticeships would have been expected during the middle Bronze Age, with an older potter teaching a younger potter the normal methods and expectations of potting for this community, subtle variations could have developed. The ceramic evidence does not favour long-term occupation due to the limited variation in fabric types, but this interpretation needs comparative investigation with other middle Bronze Age settlement assemblages where several phases of occupation phasing are strongly represented.

Technology: It may be that the two different fabrics in each class represent a change in technology, perhaps stemming from the recognition that certain materials were better for pottery production than others. This can be supported by the nature of fragmentation if, for example, the rate of disintegration for F7, which had poor cohesion of vessel walls compared unfavourably with F6, which had better cohesion (Table 4.10).

Society: It is worth considering the effect of different residency patterns (matrilocal/patrilocal) and pottery production as a possible explanation. If an extended family was in residence at this site, including an older woman potter and her daughter or daughter-in-law who came from a settlement nearby, the older woman could have 'trained' her daughter or the newcomer daughter-in-law to the ways of the community/family. She may have allowed elements of non-conformity to enter, if middle Bronze Age society at this time was not a repressive, controlling society. Therefore, different clay beds could have been used and slightly different procedures for tempering fabrics allowed—as long as the general concepts of coarse, medium and fine, crushed calcined flint-tempered wares were followed along with Middle-Lower Thames valley-style vessel forming, surface treatment and firing standards.

This social aspect of pottery production is particularly evident if two sherds are examined. Two decorated sherds (Fig. 4.34.14–15) are identical 'concept' sherds: they are coarseware fabrics, they are both from thicker-walled vessels which appear to be straight-sided urns of very similar thickness and each vessel was decorated with an applied cordon and then impressed with decoration. However, they are also very different sherds. One was made from fabric F6 and the other from fabric F7; one was smoothed and wiped on the interior (despite the presence of large, sharp flint grits) and the other was not; and one was fired in an unoxidising atmosphere while the other was irregularly oxidised. Furthermore, the impressed decoration of each is executed in a different manner: one (Fig. 4.34.14) was fingertip impressed with the full end of the finger resulting in fewer impressions on the cordon and the other (Fig. 4.34.15) was fingernail impressed with a higher density of crescent-shaped and oval impressions. Are these potters' signatures? The key which links these two sherds is that both were found in the same layer and both are nearly the same sherd weight. As they were clearly selected for specific deposition into the eastern terminus of ditch 2500, this strongly suggests that they represent some kind of relationship—a relationship of similarity and difference.

Can we recognise different hands in the preparation of middle Bronze Age urns? A methodology needs to be developed to identify individual potters' products, and one possible approach would be to study the entire array of fingertip and fingernail decorated pottery from several vessels in a small area of landscape such as the Burghfield environs.

Catalogue of illustrated pottery (Figs 4.33–5)

1. Globular urn, rim; 5% of c 220mm diameter present; fabric F10; burnished exterior; unoxidised firing throughout; thickness code 3. Middle Bronze Age ditch 2041, context 2058.

2. Decorated urn, body sherd; fabric F7; applied cordon, fingertip impressed decoration on straight vessel wall; thickness code 4; oxidised on exterior, unoxidised core and interior. Middle Bronze Age ditch 2078, context 2072.

3. Globular urn, rim; 11% of c 140mm; angled, shoulder sherd also present; fabric F10; thickness code 2; burnished on both surfaces; unoxidised throughout. Middle Bronze Age ditch 2391, context 2125.

4. Globular urn, rim; 30% of 140mm; flat base, 30% of 100mm diameter present; fabric F10; thickness code 1; burnished on both surfaces; the start of a knob or lug attachment visible on the neck to body zone; faint traces of possible shallow parallel lines on lower neck

zone; unoxidised throughout to an unusual pale grey colour. Middle Bronze Age ditch 2391, context 2125.

5. Barrel urn, rim; <5% present; fabric F7; thickness code 5; oxidised exterior, unoxidised core and interior. Unstratified, Area 16 (context 2127).

6. Ovoid jar, decorated rim; <5% present; fabric F8; thickness code 3; fingernail impressed decoration on top, inner edge of rim; unoxidised throughout. Unstratified, Area 16 (context 2130).

7. Decorated urn, body sherd; fabric F6; thickness code 5; fingertip impressed decoration on straight vessel wall; unoxidised throughout. Middle Bronze Age pit 2146, context 2148.

8. Globular urn, body sherds; fabric F10; thickness code 2; at least six, parallel, tooled lines creating a curved effect; burnished on both surfaces; unoxidised throughout. Middle Bronze Age pit 2146, context 2148.

9. Decorated urn, body sherd; fabric F7; thickness codes 4–5; applied cordon, fingertip impressed; oxidised on both surfaces, unoxidized core. Unstratified, Area 16 (context 2173).

10. Bucket urn, rim; <5% present; fabric F9; thickness code 5; irregularly fired exterior, unoxidised core and interior. Middle Bronze Age posthole 2636, context 2177.

11. Decorated urn, body sherd; fabric F7; thickness codes 4–5; smoothed exterior; fingertip impressed decoration on straight vessel wall; unoxidised throughout; sooted on exterior. Middle Bronze Age ditch 2500, context 2181.

12. ?Bucket urn, lower portion; 100% of 120mm diameter base; fabric F9; thickness code 3; applied cordon around girth; irregularly fired exterior, unoxidised core and interior. Middle Bronze Age ditch 2500, context 2262.

13. Bucket urn, rim; 5% of c 200mm; fabric F7; thickness code 4; smoothed on both surfaces; unoxidised throughout. Middle Bronze Age ditch 2500, context 2303.

14. Decorated urn, body sherd; fabric F7; thickness code 5; applied cordon, fingertip impressed; smoothed and wiped on interior; unoxidised throughout. Middle Bronze Age ditch 2500, context 2322.

15. Decorated urn, body sherd, fabric F6; thickness codes 4–5; applied cordon, fingernail impressed; irregularly fired exterior, unoxidised core and interior. Middle Bronze Age ditch 2500, context 2322.

16. Globular urn, decorated sherds; fabric F10; thickness codes 2–3; four parallel, tooled lines; smoothed on both surfaces; irregularly fired exterior, unoxidised core and interior. Middle Bronze Age ditch 2366, context 2353.

17. Barrel urn, rim; <5% present; fabric F7; thickness code 4; smoothed exterior, smoothed and wiped interior;

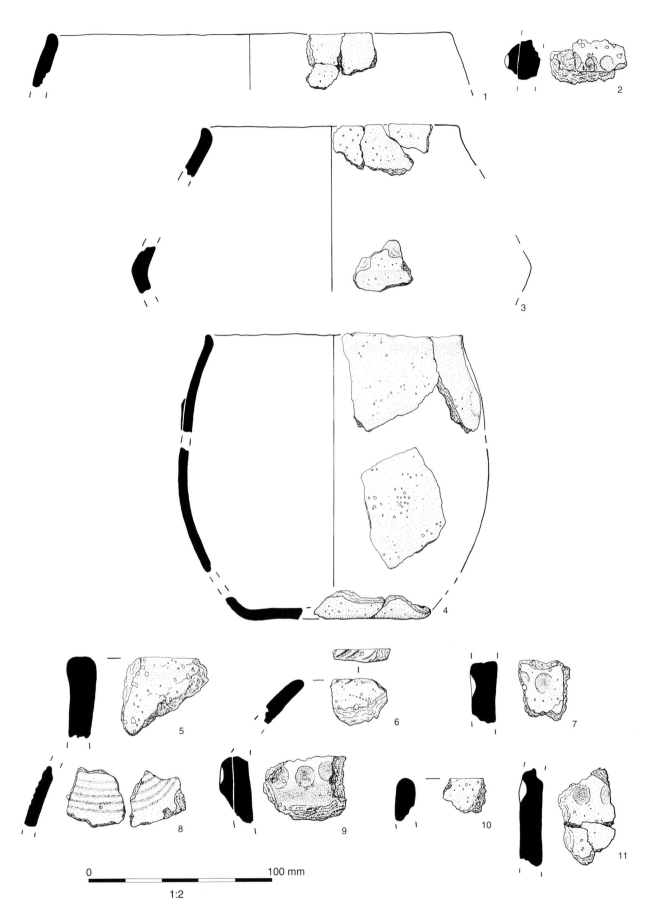

Fig. 4.33 Middle Bronze Age pottery, nos 1–11

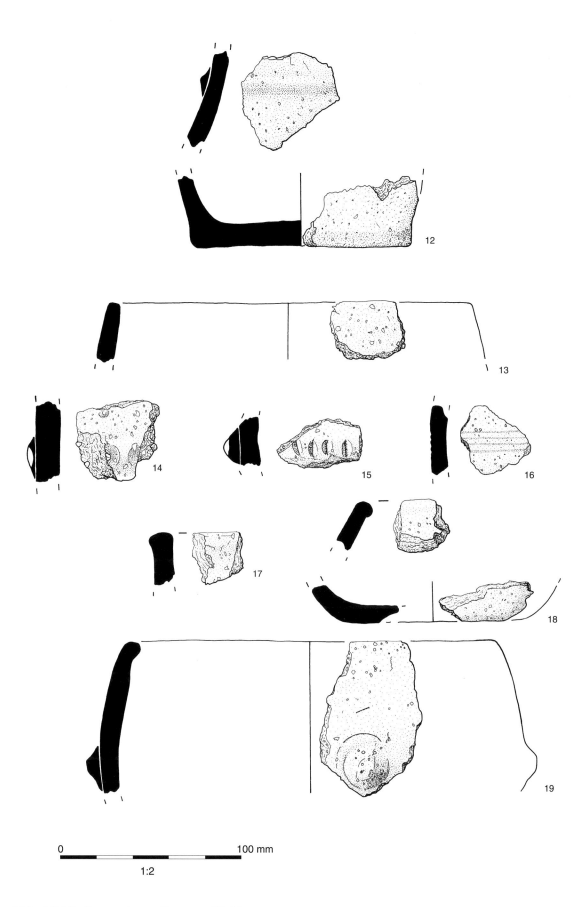

0   100 mm

1:2

Fig. 4.34 Middle Bronze Age pottery, nos 12–19

oxidised exterior, unoxidised core and interior. Middle Bronze Age ditch 2500, context 2375.

18. Bucket urn; <5% present; flat base, 12% of 100mm diameter present; fabric F6; thickness codes 3–4; unoxidised throughout; sooted on rim exterior. Middle Bronze Age pit 2382, context 2380.

19. Bucket urn, rim; 5% of 200mm diameter present; fabric F6; thickness codes 3-4; knob at girth; irregu-

larly fired exterior, unoxidised core and interior; Middle Bronze Age pit 2441, context 2443.

20. Bucket urn; 35% of 180mm rim diameter present; flat base, 35% of 180mm diameter present; fabric F6; thickness codes 4–5; 5% of undecorated, applied cordon at girth present; mainly oxidised exterior, unoxidised core and interior. Middle Bronze Age pit 2681, context 2682.

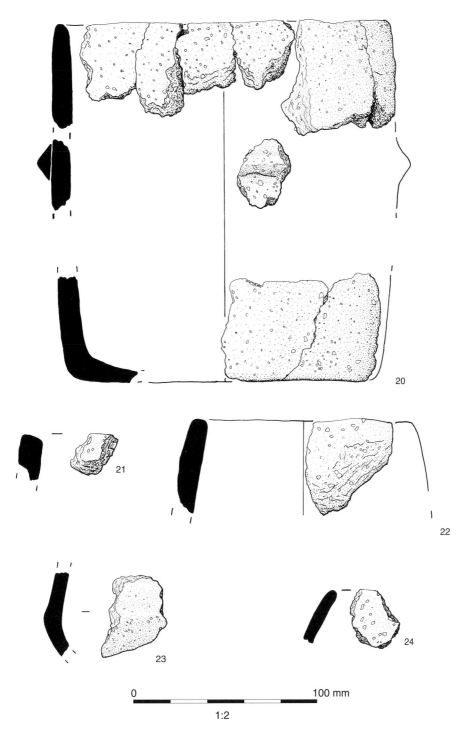

0   100 mm

1:2

Fig. 4.35 Middle Bronze Age pottery, nos 20–24

21. Bucket urn, rim; <5% present; fabric F7; thickness code 5; smoothed both surfaces; unoxidised throughout. Middle Bronze Age pit 2742, context 2743.

22. Bucket urn, rim; 11% of 120mm diameter present; fabric F8; thickness codes 4–5; irregularly fired exterior, unoxidised core and interior. Area 16, unstratified (context 2851).

23. Globular urn, angled sherd; fabric F10; thickness code 3; smoothed exterior, burnished interior; unoxidised throughout. Middle Bronze Age pit 2933, context 2935.

24. Ovoid jar, rim; <5% present; fabric F8; thickness code 2; unoxidised throughout. Unstratified (context 5082).

Early Iron Age pottery *by Kayt Brown*

The excavations produced a total of 1829 sherds (18,230g) of early Iron Age pottery (Table 4.13). A large proportion of the assemblage was recovered from pit fills, primarily from intercutting pit group 2042. The assemblage was recorded following PCRG (1997) guidelines.

Condition of assemblage

The mean sherd weight (MSW) of 10g for the entire assemblage conceals considerable variation in the condition of the material. The material from pits has a MSW of 10.5 g, compared to only 3.9g for that from postholes. Some particularly well-preserved groups of pottery were recovered from intercutting pit group 2042, notably the material from pit 2151 (26 sherds, MSW 26.2g). No inter-feature sherd joins were noted.

Table 4.13 Quantification of early Iron Age pottery by fabric

Fabric group	No. sherds	Weight (g)	% sherds	% weight
A1	3	27	0.2	0.2
A2	31	148	1.8	0.8
AP2	161	1729	9.4	9.7
APM1	103	439	6.0	2.5
BF2	5	32	0.3	0.2
PFA1	220	1101	12.8	6.2
PFA2	1194	14,386	69.5	80.5
Fabric total	1717	17,862	100.0	100.0
Indeterminate	112	368	-	-
Total	1829	18,230	-	-

Fabrics

Although 26 fabrics were initially identified, a number of these contained varying proportions of the same inclusions, and probably represent a single basic fabric. The fabrics have thus been amalgamated into the 8 broad fabric groups described below; a full breakdown of the original 26 fabrics is available in the archive.

The large majority of the pottery (80.5% by weight) was made in a coarse fabric containing flint, iron oxide and quartz sand in varying proportions (PFA2). Occasionally crushed calcined flint also appears to have been added, particularly to the underside of bases. A number of sherds in this fabric also contain gravel or pebbles, some quite substantial, suggesting poor preparation of the clay prior to manufacture. This iron-rich fabric was very distinctive and clearly different from the middle Bronze Age fabrics at this site. A second coarseware fabric (BF2), represented by only five sherds, contained glauconitic inclusions. This could indicate a source in Greensand deposits, the nearest of which lie 25–35km from the site, although glauconitic sand can also be found in some of the local Reading beds (Morris and Mepham 1995, 79). The finewares show a greater degree of variation, including a number of fine sand and silty fabrics, along with a finer version of the main coarseware fabric (PFA1). A number of small fragments could not be identified to a specific fabric and were assigned to a general 'indeterminate' group.

Coarsewares

PFA2: Coarse, flint tempered; rare to moderate sub-angular flint <3mm, moderately sorted; sparse to moderate rounded iron oxides <1mm; moderate sub-rounded, moderately-sorted quartz grains, <1mm. Occasionally sherds contain very coarse (>5mm) gravel inclusions or additional crushed calcined flint (<3mm).

BF2: Glauconitic fabric; common sub-rounded glauconite and quartz grains <1mm in clay matrix; sparse sub-angular flint <3mm (occasionally >3mm); sparse iron oxides <1mm.

Finewares

A1: Fine, slightly micaceous sandy fabric; fine, common, rounded quartz grains <0.25mm; sparse iron oxides <2mm; mica.

A2: Sandy, micaceous; moderate rounded quartz grains <0.5mm; sparse iron oxides <2mm, mica.

AP2: Moderately fine; moderate poorly-sorted quarz grains <1mm; sparse to moderate iron oxides <3mm; rare sub-angular flint <1mm.

APM1: Very fine, alluvial clay fabric; microscopic quartz, mica, rare flint <2mm, linear strands carbonaceous material <3mm, iron oxides <2mm.

PFA1: Finer version of PFA2; rare sub-angular flint <2mm (occasionally <5mm); sparse iron oxides <1mm, sparse to moderate sub-rounded quartz grains <0.5mm.

Table 4.14 *Early Iron Age pottery, correlation of fabric group and vessel class by rim count*

| Vessel type | Coarsewares | | | Finewares | | Total |
	PFA2	BF2	AP2	APM1	PFA1	
Shouldered jars	19	-	2	-	-	21
Barrel-shaped jars	-	-	-	-	1	1
Bucket-shaped jars	1	-	1	-	-	2
Slack-shouldered jars	4	-	-	-	3	7
Tripartite angled jars	1	-	-	-	-	1
Uncertain jar/bowl forms	1	-	-	1	2	4
Uncertain bowl forms	-	-	3	1	8	12
Carinated bowl	-	-	2	-	5	7
Hemispherical/curving-sided bowl	-	-	-	-	1	1
Bipartite jar/bowl	-	-	-	1	-	1
Uncertain/unidentifiable forms	3	1	-	-	1	5
Total	29	1	8	3	21	62

Vessel forms, decoration and use wear

There is a clear distinction in the assemblage between coarseware jars on the one hand and fineware bowls and jars on the other (Table 4.14). The coarseware jars are shouldered, mainly with short upright or slightly everted rims, though occasionally with quite flared rims (Figs 4.36. 1–2, 4.37.8 and 4.38.16). The rims are either rounded or, most commonly, squared or flattened. Such vessels are frequently decorated with a row of fingertip impressions on the neck or shoulder, or both. A small number of slack-shouldered, bucket-shaped or barrel-shaped jars were also present within the assemblage. Several bases were pinched out, and some had flint-gritted undersides. Although this latter characteristic is usually regarded as a late Bronze Age phenomenon, it continued into the early Iron Age in this region.

The fineware bowls are carinated, often with long necks and flaring rims. A number of long-necked 'furrowed' bowls were present, ornamented with shallow-tooled horizontal lines (Figs 4.37.9 and 4.37.11–12). One long-necked bowl displayed incised oblique lines on the shoulder (Fig. 4.36.6), similar to an example from Potterne, Wiltshire (Gingell and Morris 2000, fig. 47.12). One fineware bowl or jar has a bipartite profile

(Fig. 4.38.17). Most fineware vessels had flat bases, although one omphalos base was recovered, probably from a bowl.

The occurrence of decorative techniques by fabric type is shown by Table 4.15. Fingertip or fingernail decoration occurs principally on coarseware jars, with only two examples on fineware jars. Burnishing is largely restricted to finewares, and furrowing and incised decoration is restricted to bowls in fabric PFA1.

Evidence for vessel use was only visible as carbonised deposits on the exterior of some coarseware jar sherds. This may indicate that the primary function of such jars was food preparation.

Chronology and comparisons with other sites in the region

Independent dating evidence is provided by two radiocarbon determinations from upper layer 2043/2065 within pit group 2042 (OxA-17416 and OxA-17417). These produced dates of 760–410 cal BC and 760–400 cal BC respectively (Table 4.3), confirming the early Iron Age date of the pottery from this deposit (Fig. 4.36.1–6). The pottery from the pit group shows a combination of coarse, shouldered jars, often ornamented with fingertip and fingernail impressions, and fine, carinated bowls

Table 4.15 *Early Iron Age pottery, correlation of fabric group and decoration type by number of vessels*

| | Coarsewares | | | | Finewares | | | Total |
	PFA2	BF2	A1	A2	APM1	PFA1	AP2	
Burnished	5	-	1	1	4	18	3	32
Furrowed	-	-	-	-	-	5	-	5
Incised lines	-	-	-	-	-	-	-	-
Fingertip/fingernail	25	1	-	-	-	1	1	28
Total	30	1	1	1	4	24	4	65

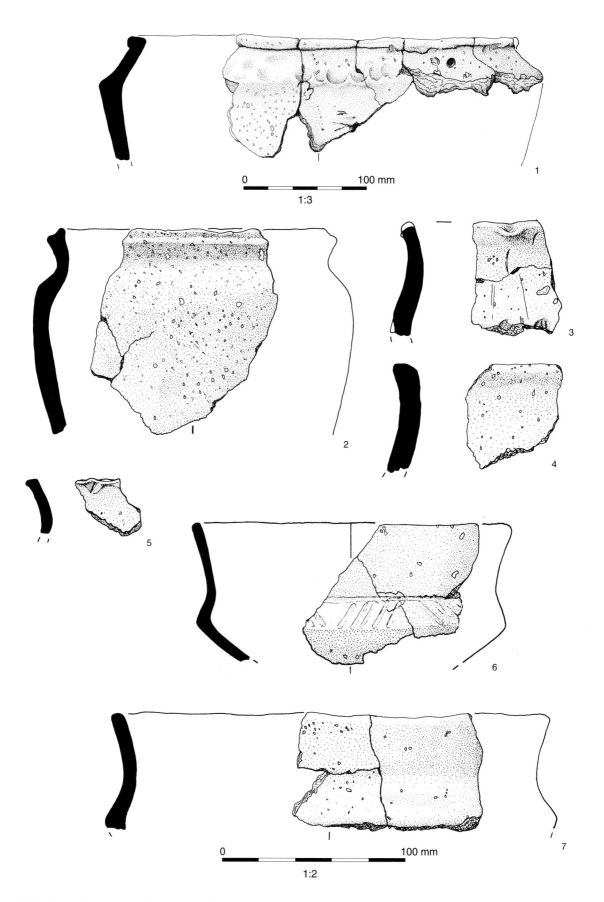

Fig. 4.36   Early Iron Age pottery, nos 1–7

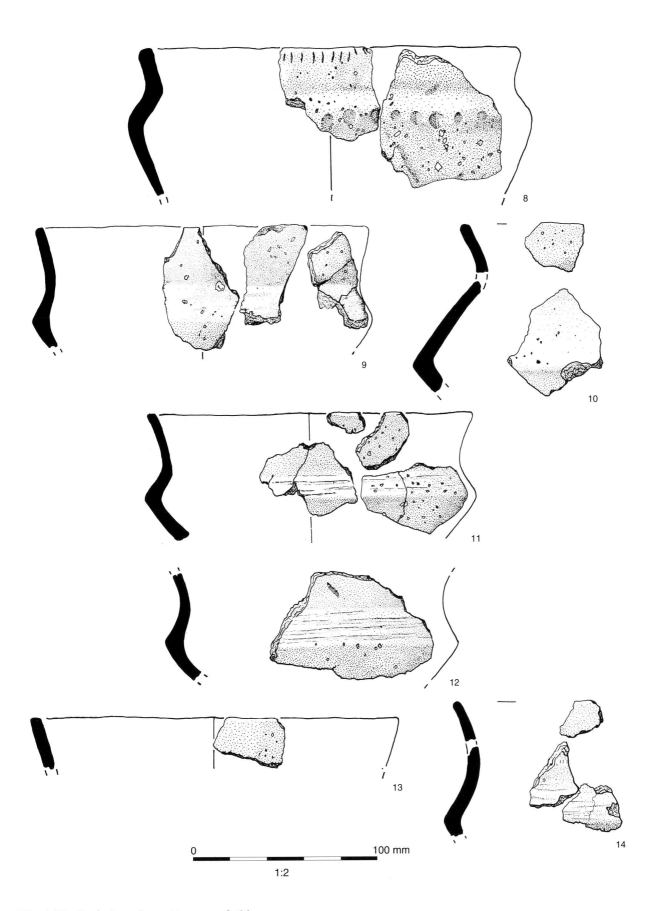

Fig. 4.37   Early Iron Age pottery, nos 8–14

and jars, often with linear tooled decoration. The assemblage can be attributed to the All Cannings Cross ceramic style, the distribution of which extended from Wessex into the Kennet Valley (Cunliffe 2005). Current understanding suggests that this style can be divided into two chronological groups, distinguished mainly by the form and decoration of fineware vessels. The early All Cannings Cross group, dating to around the late Bronze Age to early Iron Age transition, is characterised by bipartite bowls and large, decorated jars with rounded shoulders and everted rims (*ibid.*, fig. A2), while the later group (or All Cannings Cross-Meon Hill group) is characterised by long-necked bowls with flaring rims (*ibid.*, fig. A8). The Moores Farm assemblage, with its long-necked rather than biconical bowls, clearly belongs to this later group. Evidence from stratified deposits at Potterne, Wiltshire, has suggested that the shift from biconical bowls to long-necked bowls occurred around 700 BC (Gingell and Morris 2000), in line with the radiocarbon dates from Moores Farm.

The Moores Farm pottery appears to be later in date than the post-Deverel-Rimbury (PDR) assemblages from Green Park. At Green Park 2 and 3,

only plain ware PDR pottery of the late Bronze Age was found. At Green Park 1, a small element of decorated ware PDR pottery of late Bronze Age/early Iron Age date was recovered, but the presence of a decorated jar with early All Cannings Cross parallels and the absence of long-necked or furrowed bowls indicates an earlier date than the Moores Farm assemblage. Elsewhere in the Kennet Valley, decorated ware assemblages have been found at Knight's Farm (Lobb *et al.* 1980), Field Farm (Mepham 1992a) and Wickhams Field (Laidlaw 1996b), all in Burghfield parish, and at Theale Ballast Hole (Piggott 1938), Dunston Park, Thatcham (Morris and Mepham 1995) and Hartshill Copse, Upper Bucklebury (Morris 2006). The pottery from Knight's Farm Subsite 1 is a classic early All Cannings Cross assemblage, with decorated biconical bowls but no long-necked or furrowed bowls, again suggesting an earlier date than Moores Farm. This can be accommodated by the radiocarbon evidence from the site, with one large group of pottery from a pit being associated with two dates of 1060–590 cal BC (Har-1011) and 810–430 cal BC (Har-1012) respectively. Sites that show greater similarities to the Moores Farm

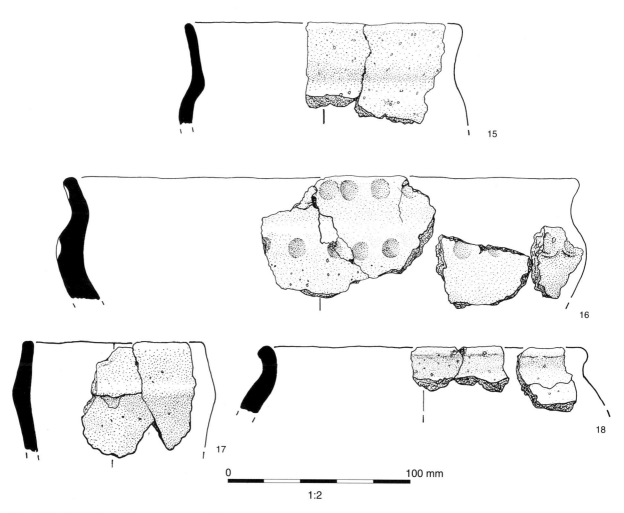

Fig. 4.38   Early Iron Age pottery, nos 15–18

assemblage, and could perhaps have been broadly contemporary, include Dunston Park, Field Farm and Wickhams Field. At Dunston Park, furrowed bowls and a possible long-necked bowl are present, and the assemblage was suggested on stylistic grounds to date to around the 7th century BC (Morris and Mepham 1995, 84). Long-necked furrowed bowls are also present at Field Farm and Wickhams Field.

Catalogue of illustrated pottery (Figs 4.36–8)

Pottery from pit group 2042

1 Shouldered jar. Fabric group PFA2. Pit 2131, context 2043/2065

2 High-shouldered jar with faint groove on rim. Fabric group PFA2. Pit 2131, context 2043/2065

3 Long-necked jar/bowl with fingertip impressions on rim top and shoulder. Fabric group PFA2. Pit 2131, context 2043/2065

4 Long-necked jar/bowl. Fabric group PFA2. Pit 2131, context 2043/2065

5 Long necked bowl with fingertip impressions on rim. Fabric group PFA1. Pit 2131, context 2043/2065

6 Long-necked tripartite bowl with incised/burnished oblique lines on shoulder. Fabric group PFA1. Pit 2131, context 2043/2065

7 Long-necked bowl. Fabric group PFA1. Pit 2151, context 2204

8 Shouldered jar with fingernail impressions on rim front and fingertip impressions on shoulder. Fabric group PFA2. Pit 2169, context 2207

9 Tripartite 'furrowed' bowl with shallow tooled lines on shoulder. Fabric group PFA1. Pit 2169, contexts 2182 and 2207

   Long-necked tripartite bowl. Fabric group AP2. Pit 2169, context 2171

11 Tripartite 'furrowed' bowl with shallow tooled lines on shoulder. Fabric group PFA1. Pit 2665, context 2664

12 Tripartite 'furrowed' bowl with shallow tooled lines on shoulder. Fabric group APM1. Pit 2699, context 2698

13 Long-necked bowl rim, burnished external surface. Fabric group PFA1. Layer 2044

14 Tripartite bowl with burnished lines on shoulder. Fabric group PFA1. Layer 2414

15 Long-necked bowl. Fabric group PFA1. Layer 2414

Pottery from other features

16 Shouldered bowl/jar with fingertip impressions on rim front and shoulder. Fabric group PFA2. Pit 2494, context 2495

17 Bowl/jar rim. Fabric group APM1. Pit 2836, context 2174

18 Bowl/jar rim with rounded shoulder. Fabric group AP2. Pit 2318, context 2122

Fired clay *by Sandy Budden*

A small assemblage of fired clay weighing 2531g was recovered. Almost all of this had an iron-rich matrix containing quartz sand; full details of the fabrics are available in the archive. Middle Bronze Age contexts produced only a small quantity of fired clay (178 fragments, 378g). Most of this consisted of amorphous fragments, although possible oven 2359 produced some pieces with flat surfaces that might represent fragments of oven furniture. A greater quantity of fired clay was recovered from early Iron Age contexts (668 fragments, 1897g), again mostly amorphous; almost half (900g) came from hearth 1340. The only recognisable objects were triangular loomweights or oven bricks (Poole 1991, 380; 1995) with pierced corners, in sandy fabrics. Fragments of one or two of these objects were recovered from layer 1271, and one further fragment came from pit group 2042 (context 2157).

Querns *by Ruth Shaffrey*

Ten quern fragments were recovered, of which four are fragments from the main lower stones of saddle querns, three are probably upper stones or rubbers, and three are too small to be diagnostic. Two of the objects were recovered from middle Bronze Age contexts and two from early Iron Age contexts, with the remainder being unstratified (Table 4.16).

Sarsen was the most common quern material, accounting for half of the fragments recovered. This included one of the middle Bronze Age querns and both of the early Iron Age querns. One of the latter (context 2043) still had evidence of the pecking used to dress the grinding surface. Sarsen would have been widely available in the local area, and was commonly exploited for quern manufacture in later prehistory (see Shaffrey, Chapter 2). The other middle Bronze Age quern fragment was made of friable, heavily iron-stained sandstone, probably from the local Tertiary sandstone. A rubber fragment in the same material was recovered from the alluvium. Other unstratified finds included two Greensand quern or rubber fragments. Lower Greensand was not available locally, the nearest sources being 25–35km away in Oxfordshire or Surrey. Despite this, Greensand saddle querns are not uncommon in the local area, with examples recovered from later Bronze Age contexts at Green Park 1 and 2 (Jennings 1992, 94; Roe 2004).

Table 4.16 Saddle querns and rubbers

Feature	Context	Phase	Stone type	Description	Measurements
Ditch 2041	2754	Middle Bronze Age	Medium to very coarse, poorly sorted ferruginous sandstone	Probable quern fragment with one smooth surface but no edges	60mm thick x 90mm x 50mm
Pit 2890	2891	Middle Bronze Age	Fine- to medium-grained sarsen	Possible quern fragment with one flat surface which is slightly worn	65mm x 55mm x 82mm
Pit group 2042	2043	Early Iron Age	Medium-grained quartz sarsen with lilac/pale blue siltstone inclusions	Small quern or rubber fragment with two flat surfaces, one worn smooth and originally pecked	45mm thick x 54mm x 70mm
Pit 2831	2832	Early Iron Age	Fine- to medium-grained, well-sorted, pure quartz sarsen	Probable quern fragment with two flat edges perpendicular to each other, one of which is worn smooth. Other edges are angular	37mm x 25mm x 27mm
Subsoil, Area 13	1304	Unphased	Very well-sorted, pure quartz sarsen	Probable rubber fragment with one grinding surface and one edge remaining.	*c* 45mm thick
Alluvium, Area 13	1338	Unphased	Dark, glauconitic Greensand	Possible rubber fragment with one flat surface worn smooth	50mm x 35mm x 45mm
Unstratified, Area 16	2166	Unphased	Fine-grained, well-sorted, almost quartizitic sandstone	Rubber or quern fragment with one worn, flat surface and one pecked curved surface	59mm x 34mm x 33mm
Alluvium, Area 16	2332	Unphased	Grey, fine-grained sarsen	Broken pebble which may have been utilised as a rubber	65mm x 51mm x 34mm
Alluvium, Area 16	2851	Unphased	Poorly sorted limonite cemented sandstone	Probable rubber fragment with one flat and worn surface with remaining edges angular	46mm x 35mm x 27mm
Alluvium, Area 16	2970	Unphased	Fine grained and well-sorted, pale green, slightly glauconitic Greensand	Quern fragment with one concave surface, which has been worn smooth. Other edges are also worn	

OSTEOLOGICAL AND ENVIRONMENTAL EVIDENCE

Animal bone *by Bethan Charles*

1120 fragments of bone were recovered, of which 598 were hand collected and 522 were recovered from sieved samples (Table 4.17). The bone was generally in poor condition, although the material from the middle Bronze Age waterholes was better preserved. The majority of the bones were from large animals and it is likely that smaller bones such as those from sheep have not survived.

Middle Neolithic

A badly fragmented horse tooth was retrieved from pit 2967. Horse remains are extremely rare from Neolithic contexts in Britain (Burleigh *et al.* 1991), and it is possible that this is an intrusive fragment, particularly as a sherd of middle Bronze Age pottery was also recovered from this feature.

Middle Bronze Age

Although horse was the most frequent species by fragment count, almost all of the horse bone came from the primary fill of waterhole 5113. The horse bone from this deposit almost certainly belongs to a single individual. Only part of the skeleton was recovered, including both radii and ulnas, metatarsals, scapulas, innominate bones, the left tibia and femur and the right metacarpal as well as vertebrae and rib bones. As the remains were recovered by machine during the watching brief, some bones might have been missed. The animal was male and over three and a half years of age. Some of the bones had butchery marks, including both the left and right innominate (pelvis) bones, four of the thoracic vertebrae (which had chop marks just off the sagittal plane) and two of the lumbar vertebrae (which had knife marks down the body and the transverse processes chopped off). It is possible that the animal was partially disarticulated, possibly for meat, before being placed in the waterhole.

Pig and red deer were the other most numerous species. Pit 807 contained 12 fragments of red deer

Table 4.17 Animal bone, numbers of fragments.

Phase	Cattle	Sheep	Hand-recovered bone Horse	Pig	Red deer	Unidentified	Sieved bone Pig	Frog/toad	Unidentified
Middle Neolithic	-	-	1*	-	-	1	-	-	-
Middle Bronze Age	4	5	59**	22	21	326	1	-	314
Early Iron Age	11	-	4	1	1	105	-	-	37
Unphased	4	-	-	-	-	33	-	170	-
Total	19	5	64	23	22	465	1	170	351

* = possibly intrusive. ** = 57 bones from a single skeleton

antler, which appeared to be waste from antler working. Otherwise, most of the red deer and pig bone came from waterhole 2610. All of the red deer fragments appeared to be from immature animals, and may have come from two or more individuals. The pig bones were also from immature animals. It is possible that the pig and deer bones from this waterhole represent a special deposit, although the fact that the remains were not complete suggests that they may simply be butchery refuse.

Early Iron Age

A few fragments of cattle, horse, pig and red deer bone were recovered. The majority of the bone came from pit group 2042.

Charred and waterlogged plant remains
by Ruth Pelling

A total of 34 samples were processed for the recovery of plant remains using bulk water flotation. The volume of deposit processed ranged from 20 to 40 litres and flots were collected onto a 250 mm mesh. Samples were scanned under a binocular microscope at x10 magnification. A summary of those samples in which seeds or chaff were noted is provided by Table 4.18; all date to either the middle

Bronze Age or early Iron Age. Waterlogged plant remains only occurred in middle Bronze Age waterhole 2927, consisting of occasional elder (*Sambucus nigra*) and a small Labiate seed. Charred seeds and chaff were very rarely present in the samples. Occasional poorly preserved grain was noted in five samples and included barley (*Hordeum vulgare*) and emmer or spelt wheat (*Triticum dicoccum/spelta*). No sample produced any more than five grains. Very occasional weed seeds were noted in two charred samples only. Charcoal was present in the majority of samples. Oak (*Quercus* sp.) was most abundant in both the middle Bronze Age and early Iron Age samples, with occasional samples containing small amounts of Pomoideae (apple/pear/hawthorn etc.). The early Iron Age samples additionally produced occasional sloe (*Prunus spinosa*) and hazel or alder (*Corylus/Alnus* sp.).

Pollen *by Robert G Scaife*

Introduction

Pollen analysis was carried out on the fills of middle Bronze Age waterholes 824 and 2927. Of these, only waterhole 824 (sample 10: see Fig. 4.11) contained sub-fossil pollen and spores in the grey humic sediments at the base of the feature. The assem-

Table 4.18 Charred and waterlogged plant remains

		Phase	MBA	MBA	MBA	EIA	EIA	EIA	EIA
		Sample	32	35	41	11	14	26	28
		Feature	Pit 2441	Ditch 2117	Water hole 2927	Pit 1353	Posthole 1419	Pit group 2042	Pit group 2042
		Context	2443	2187	2946	1354	1420	2043	2065
Charred	*Hordeum vulgare*	Barley grain	2	0	0	0	1	2	5
	Triticum spelta/dicoccum	Spelt/emmer wheat grain	1	0	0	0	0	2	0
	Indet	Indeterminate cereal grain	0	1	0	0	0	0	0
	Vicia/Lathyrus sp.	Vetch/vetchling	0	0	0	0	0	0	1
	Eleocharis palustris	Common spikerush	0	0	0	1	0	0	0
Waterlogged	Labiate	Small-seeded labiate	0	0	1	0	0	0	0
	Sambucus nigra	Elderberry	0	0	4	0	0	0	0

MBA = middle Bronze Age; EIA = early Iron Age

blages obtained provide information on the local environment and land use contemporary with the filling of this feature.

Methods and results

Monolith profile tins were used to obtain samples for pollen analysis. These profiles were later examined in the laboratory and were sub-sampled for pollen analysis at 50mm intervals. Standard techniques were used for the extraction of the pollen and spores (Moore and Webb 1978; Moore *et al.* 1991). Absolute pollen frequencies were calculated using added exotics (Stockmarr *Lycopodium* tablets) to known volumes (1–2ml) of sample. Sufficient pollen was present in the material to enable pollen counts of generally 300 grains per level (the pollen sum) to be made plus all extant marsh/aquatic taxa and spores of ferns. Data are presented in standard pollen diagram form (Fig. 4.39 with percentages calculated as follows:

Sum	= % total dry land pollen (tdlp)
Marsh/aquatic	= % tdlp+sum of marsh/aquatics
Spores	= % tdlp+sum of spores
Misc.	= % tdlp+sum of miscellaneous taxa

Taxonomy follows that of Moore and Webb (1978) and Stace (1991), modified according to Bennett *et al.* (1994).

Two local pollen assemblage zones (l.p.a.z.) have been recognised (Fig. 4.39). These, however, relate to the changing stratigraphy, depositional environment and pollen taphonomy of the waterhole sediment fills. Overall, the pollen spectra are dominated by herbs while trees and shrubs are poorly represented. Pollen was absent in soils above 0.55 m, due possibly to oxidation. The two pollen assemblage zones are characterised as follows:

l.p.a.z. 1 (0.91–0.73m). Basal, humic, grey silt. Absolute pollen frequencies are relatively high with values to 130,000 grains/ml. Poaceae are dominant (to 60%). Other taxa include Chenopodiaceae (to 10%), *Plantago lanceolata* (3%), cereal type (2%), Lactucoideae (increasing into zone 2) and a diverse range of herbs. Trees and shrubs comprise *Quercus* (6%) and *Corylus* type (to 9%) with sporadic occurrences and small numbers of other taxa. Marsh and aquatic taxa include Cyperaceae and *Lemna*.

l.p.a.z. 2 (0.73–0.55 m). Brown soil with transition into underlying grey silts of zone 1. Absolute pollen frequencies are substantially lower than l.p.a.z.1, with values down to 9000 grains/ml and absence in higher levels. Tree and shrub pollen remain consistent with herbs remaining dominant. There is a marked expansion of Lactucoideae (*Taraxacum* type to 51%). Poaceae remain relatively important but with declining values (to 20%) and *Plantago lanceolata* (8%). There is also some reduction in species diversity. Cyperaceae remain consistent but *Lemna* declines. *Pteridium aquilinum* expands progressively up the profile (to 60%).

Discussion

Pollen arriving in small catchments such as waterholes will most probably come largely from the very local area. Such complex taphonomy is likely to cause serious under-representation of pollen from even near-local and further regional sources. This may be the reason why there are only small amounts of tree and shrub pollen in these spectra, which overall show dominance of herbs of pasture suggesting preponderance of grassland locally.

As noted, the two pollen zones which are distinguished may be attributed to the stratigraphical variation which is evident. The lower humic sediments which represent accumulation in the waterhole contain well preserved pollen and spores. Given the small areal extent of this waterhole, the pollen catchment will have been of restricted extent, being derived principally from vegetation growing in and adjacent to the site and within the local area. As such, some useful information can be gained from the analysis. However, pollen zone 2 within the overlying brown soil, whilst containing pollen, displays marked evidence of differential pollen preservation and substantially smaller absolute pollen frequencies. This is evidenced by the rising percentages of Lactucoideae (dandelion types), a taxon with robust exine which is typically over-represented in poor pollen preserving environments where thinner walled grains have been destroyed. Thus, the pollen assemblages of zone 2 are skewed in favour of robust taxa. A further problem with the soils/sediments of zone 2 is the possible secondary origin of the fills.

As this feature was a waterhole, some evidence of aquatic and fringing vegetation might be expected. This is the case with duckweed (*Lemna*), which occurs on slow flowing water or stagnant ponds. Sedges (Cyperaceae), which are also present, may have fringed this pond with other rooting marginal aquatic plants such as bur reed/reedmace (*Typha/Sparganium*). Other taxa not differentiable to species may also relate to this habitat, for example, horsetail ferns (*Equisetum* eg *E. palustre*). The majority of taxa present are, however, attributed to dry land and are dominated by grasses (Poaceae), ribwort plantain (*Plantago lanceolata*) and goosefoots/oraches (Chenopodiaceae). The dominance of grasses with other herbs which occur sporadically suggests that grassland/pasture was dominant in the vicinity of the waterhole. Goosefoots/oraches are consistently present and these may also be indicative of nitrogen-enriched soils (livestock dung and urine) and disturbed

Fig. 4.39 (facing page)   Middle Bronze Age waterhole 824: percentage pollen diagram

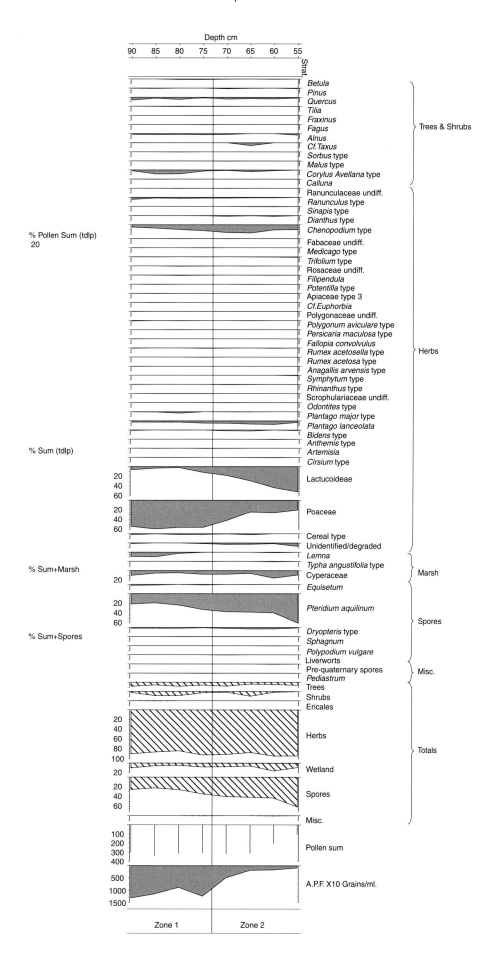

ground. Plants of the latter also include hoary or greater plantain (*Plantago media/major*) and weeds which are also associated with arable agriculture; knotgrass (*Polygonum aviculare*), bistorts/redshank (*Persicaria maculosa* type), black bindweed (*Fallopia convolvulus*) and mugwort (*Artemisia*). Whether these taxa relate to disturbed ground around the waterhole is not clear, since there is also some evidence of cereal/arable cultivation indicated by the small numbers of cereal pollen grains (wheat and barley type). The presence of cereal pollen, although definitely showing that arable agriculture was practised, is further complicated by the fact that the pollen may have derived indirectly from crop processing, with pollen trapped in the cereal heads liberated and dispersed during threshing and winnowing.

There are notably small numbers of tree and shrub pollen throughout. Oak (*Quercus*) and hazel (*Corylus*) are most consistent with only small numbers of other trees and shrubs. These include tree taxa which are normally under-represented in pollen spectra such as beech (*Fagus*), lime (*Tilia*), ash (*Fraxinus*) and yew (*Taxus*), and as such it is likely that these taxa may have been present occasionally in the local environment.

Chapter 5: The Middle to Late Bronze Age ceramic transition in the Lower Kennet Valley and beyond

by Elaine L Morris

INTRODUCTION

The most exciting discovery from the analysis of the later Bronze Age pottery recovered from the Green Park Phase 1–3 and Moores Farm sites has been the recognition that our perception of this ceramic period has been very categorised and surprisingly limited in its contribution to the study of past human behaviour. Previous analyses either suggested that there was a straightforward recognition of middle and late Bronze Age ceramic evidence or presented an accommodative description to cope with the variation observed. What has been missing from much of the archaeological field-work for this period in southern Britain has been any systematic use of radiocarbon dating to assist in the interpretation of the ceramic sequence; it is important that we link the ceramics, the occupation evidence and the outstanding metalwork evidence (Needham 1996). This paucity of absolute dating evidence for the pottery, and therefore the cemeteries and settlements, has continued despite the call thirty years ago for this to be conducted on a regular basis (Barrett and Bradley 1980, 252). The landscape project presented in this volume has demonstrated that the use of radiocarbon dating can transform our assumptions and provide a new way of looking at the later Bronze Age.

Ceramic periods tend to be represented by distinctive, 'best' examples displaying strong characteristics of recognisable vessel forms and decoration supported by broad trends in fabric recipes. Often in the general literature the same best vessels (Langmaid 1978, fig. 14) are repeated again (Darvill 1987, fig. 67) and again (Gibson 2002, fig. 51), ingraining the images of the perfect examples and period divisions in our minds. We describe and name these types, and expect others to follow our work by comparing their pots to these 'fossil types'. This trend results in straight-jacketing of the evidence and the reinforcement of periodisation of past behaviour, cutting it into distinct phases without exploring or explaining how people evolved their daily interactions and general social reproduction to get from one 'phase' to the next. It is as though one day a group of people are classifiable as middle Bronze Age urn users and the next morning they wake up and discover they have become late Bronze Age pot people. This method of classification and periodisation does nothing to help explain how or why what we see in the archaeological record, the residues of past human behav-

iour, changed. Even worse, it has restricted our exploration of the subtle variations which may have been taking place during one defined period by stopping us from seeing these variations because they do not fit the classic definition – we justify the variation by not accepting its presence until the overwhelming amount of evidence forces us to do so. This landscape project is one of those cases; it provides an opportunity to focus on the *transition* from the middle Bronze Age to the late Bronze Age, first in the area of the Kennet and Middle Thames Valleys, and then more widely in central southern England.

POTTERY TRADITIONS

The above introduction is undoubtedly unfair and overly critical of many researchers. The history of archaeology is one of classification and the structuring of material culture, monuments, settlements and landscapes in order to try and make sense of those fragments of information left to us. Many archaeologists are now reaching well beyond classification to investigate the differences in social organisation, lifeways and expression through deposition, vision and variation in the archaeological record of prehistoric Britain. This overview will attempt to do the same for the ceramic evidence from the later Bronze Age, the second half of the second millennium BC. But first it is necessary to present briefly the basic, traditional classification of the two main phases within this broad ceramic period.

Middle Bronze Age

The pottery forms classified as belonging to the middle Bronze Age in this area are known as Deverel-Rimbury barrel, bucket and globular urns. The middle Bronze Age in this particular area dates from the 16th to 17th centuries cal BC, based on radiocarbon dating of samples associated with metalwork (Needham 1996, 133–4, fig. 1), but the infrequency of determinations associated with ceramics is striking. Distinctive regional sub-divisions of barrel, bucket and globular urns for central Wessex, the Lower Thames Valley and Sussex have been detailed by Ellison (1975; 1978; Dacre and Ellison 1981, 173–4) and a general summary of middle Bronze Age pottery is provided here.

Barrel urns are always large and tall, with either a convex profile with the rim slightly smaller than the girth or a flared profile with the rim diameter slightly larger than the girth (Dacre and Ellison 1981, figs 10–13). The rims are distinguished by having a broad, flat top surface and a slight external protrusion or lip, as well as the occasional internal protrusion. Decoration consists of applied and fingertipped, horizontal, vertical or wavy cordons. This effect is often reinforced by fingertip impressions along the external rim lip. The vessels are invariably medium to thick-walled (*c* 8–14mm), can be up to 0.5m tall and range in capacity from *c* 7000–56,000cm^3 (Barrett 1980, fig. 2; Dacre and Ellison 1981, figs 10–13). It is likely that barrel urns were storage vessels due to their size and shape, and it is easy to imagine that the lip of the rims provided a means to secure a leather cover using rope or a broad, flat surface upon which to rest a wooden lid. However, more studies of vessel sizes by rim diameter correlated to visible residues and absorbed lipid analysis need to be conducted to confirm this assumption. The absence of any residue evidence on or in barrel urns would help to support this assumption of barrel urns as dry storage vessels.

Bucket urns are medium to thick-walled, straight-sided, slightly convex or slightly flared profile vessels which were made from coarse to intermediate-grained, heavily flint-tempered fabrics in much of central southern England. Wall thickness ranges from 8–18mm for published examples from the region. These vessels vary considerably in size from *c* 2000–40,000cm^3 (Barrett 1980, fig. 2). When decorated, which is usually the case for published examples from cemeteries, this consists of fingertip impressions (ibid., fig. 3.1–2), nailed or tooled slashes (ibid., fig. 4.2), plain raised or applied cordons, or cordons with fingertip impressions or slashes on the widest point of the vessel if convex or just above the middle of the vessel profile if neutral (ibid., figs 4.1 and 4.3; Lobb 1992, fig. 24.1). The applied and impressed cordons can be a combination of horseshoe-shaped with horizontal designs, either applied cordons or simply impressions (Barrett 1973, fig. 1.1; Dacre and Ellison 1981, fig. 19.E3). Fingertip impressions are also found on the top or inner surface of the rims of bucket urns (Lobb 1992, fig. 25.51–6). Four opposing, applied and often pinched knobs are another frequent feature on bucket urns. These may be decorative or functional, and they link these vessels to globular urns (Barrett 1973, figs 1.7–8, 1.10, 4.6, 5.6). There can be a horizontal row of impressions between the knobs. Several bucket urns have a single horizontal row of prefiring perforations just below the rim, which is regarded as a functional attribute for securing a cover (ibid., figs 1.13, 2.22, 4.1, 4.3; Lobb 1992, fig. 24.1). Bucket urns are usually far more common than barrel urns in cemetery and settlement assemblages, and have been interpreted as everyday and heavy-duty vessels (Ellison 1980).

Globular urns are, in contrast, usually made from extraordinarily well-processed flint-tempered fabrics in much of this region. The temper is well-sorted in character, which means that the size range of the angular flint chips is quite narrow, creating the effect of a sieved temper with chip sizes measuring 3mm and finer. The density of temper is extremely high, with usually between 25–50% of the fabric made of these inclusions. The vessels are far more graceful in shape, with the distinct effect of a thin-walled (3–8mm) upright plain rim falling down along a ski-slope neck onto a sloping to rounded, globular girth or distinctively hipped girth (Barrett 1973, fig. 2.15–16; Dacre and Ellison 1981, figs 14.D6, 14.D14, 14.D16, 15.D/E5–D/E7, 16–17, 20.F3). Globular urns range in size from *c* 3000–35,000cm^3 (Barrett 1980, fig. 2), and these are clearly the fineware vessels of the middle Bronze Age (Ellison 1980). The exterior surfaces are nearly always at least well-smoothed if not fully burnished. Decoration, however, is even more distinctive for these vessels and consists of tooled or incised simple horizontal linear or more complex geometric patterns located on the zone between the girth and the lower part of the neck. Tooling is created by simply pushing the surface of the pot inwards to a shallow depth while incising actually breaks the surface of the vessel and creates a sharp, rough, often deep edge to the impression; tooling is similar to burnishing while incising is like carving. The most common designs are composed of separate, repeated chevrons composed of many parallel sets of lines almost like combed, open triangles, or a panel of open triangles with infilled spaces of parallel diagonal lines between the triangles. Four opposing horizontally or vertically perforated lugs, pinched knobs like those on bucket urns, or bar handles (Sussex) are a very common characteristic of globular urns and the linear and geometric designs often incorporate these attachments within the decorative complex (Dacre and Ellison 1981, fig. 17.E30). Lugs, knobs and bar handles are usually located at the girth point. The balanced quartets of lugs or handles are likely to have been for suspension but usewear patterns are not mentioned in site reports. In the absence of published information about the use of these vessels for cooking, it is worth asking for what purpose the vessels were being suspended. Barrett (1980) has indicated that they were the most likely candidates to have been employed in the feasting activities of middle Bronze Age life.

Bases found on middle Bronze Age urns are simple, plain and flat in profile. There are often numerous extra pieces of flint chips embedded into the underside surface of these urns. Although the extra chips are the same range as those found in the vessels' fabric, the presence of base chips on all sizes and types of vessels (large, medium, small; barrel, bucket and globular) suggests that the technique is just as likely to be a period style characteristic as a functional attribute of manufacture. The absence of chips on some vessels suggests that it may be the potter's choice to add chips or not, but the choice may be determined by the weather since this effect could assist in the drying of the pot in damper conditions. These suggestions need to be tested by experimentation. Most importantly, the bases of urns are nearly always unelaborated in profile – they are just a basic basal angle with no frills.

The function of middle Bronze Age pottery appears to be related to the storage of agricultural produce (Drewett 1979; Tomalin 1992, 86), particularly for the large and medium-sized, thick-walled urns, while the fancy globular urns may have been used for feasting events. All types of urns are found on both settlements and in cemeteries. Barrett notes that as both types of site lie in close proximity it is important to emphasise that "those vessels which were selected to accompany the ashes of the dead were drawn directly from the domestic repertoire" (1980, 298), rather than having been made specifically for cremation burial. Often cemetery assemblages include vessels which have been repaired, as shown by major cracks straddled by pairs of post-firing drilled holes. One recent study of vessels from cemeteries has demonstrated that some urns were used for cooking and storage of foodstuffs prior to their selection for the storage of the dead (McNee 2000). Clearly much work on the absorbed lipid residues of middle Bronze Age pottery needs to be conducted to elaborate on this apparent trend, and the evidence should be correlated to vessel sizes, types and visible evidence of use, as well as subtle variations in both fabric recipes and the individuality of decoration. This research would increase our understanding of the potters, their products and the role of pots in the middle Bronze Age. Ellison indicated that the size of middle Bronze Age cremation cemeteries (most with between 10–25 burials) was strongly correlated to the size of the nearby settlements and is likely to reflect "separate kinship units of roughly equal size, each in use over a fairly limited period of time" (1980, 124). Little has been done to take this observation forward in recent years.

Late Bronze Age

In contrast, late Bronze Age pottery assemblages are composed of jars and bowls (Barrett 1980, 302–6). The late Bronze Age is currently accepted as beginning in the second half of the 12th century cal BC as a plain or predominantly undecorated phase which develops into a decorated phase by the 8th century cal BC (Needham 1996, fig. 1.134–7), having previously been thought to begin during the 10th century BC (Barrett 1980). However, as will be detailed below, radiocarbon dating of late Bronze Age pottery assemblages is still a rare occurrence.

The jars in particular are quite distinctive, with a variety of upright and slightly everted rims, distinct necks which may be short to medium in length and strong, pronounced and rounded shoulders falling to narrower bases. In addition, hooked-rim, neckless, convex-profile vessels are also recognised as being part of the late Bronze Age jar continuum while "others have straighter profiles" (Barrett 1980, 307, figs 5.8 and 5.16). Jars are closed forms with the height of the vessel always greater than the diameter of the opening. Protruding, slightly flared or splayed bases with spurs or expanded projections are a distinguishing characteristic of late Bronze Age jars, and the presence of added flint chips to the base underside is still an expected attribute. Jar fabrics can be coarse or fine in texture and finish (Class I and II; Barrett 1980) and in central southern England there is a gradual replacement of flint-tempered and shell-tempered fabrics with quartz sand fabrics (Barrett 1980; Raymond 1994). This process of change in fabric recipes appears to start with the use of sandy clay matrices into which the flint temper is added in contrast to middle Bronze Age fabrics which rarely have obviously sandy clay matrices. Burnishing can often be found on the exterior surface of finer fabric Class II jars.

For this overview only the beginning of the late Bronze Age will be presented. Jars were rarely decorated at this time, but when decoration occurred it consisted of fingertip or fingernail impressions on either the shoulder zone or the interior of the rim. Applied or raised cordons and knobs are no longer present. The combination of fingertip decoration of shouldered jars on both the exterior rim and the shoulder, as well as on an applied cordon midway down the neck (Barrett 1980, fig. 6) is a later development in the decorated phase of the late Bronze Age (c 8th century cal BC onwards) which is not under discussion here. Jars range in size from 1000–56,000cm^3 (Barrett 1980, fig. 2), and thus it is possible to see late Bronze Age jars evolving from middle Bronze Age bucket urns in particular. Rim diameters of Class I jars in larger assemblages are consistently smaller than those of middle Bronze Age urns (Barrett 1980, fig. 3).

What is special to the late Bronze Age ceramic repertoire, however, is the appearance of bowls. These are short, squat, open forms with the aperture greater than the height of the vessel. Bowl forms include a wide range of bipartite (shouldered or biconical), hemispherical and conical profiles with upright, everted and platform rims. The flared or splayed base type characteristic of late Bronze Age jars is also found on bowls. The fabrics can be coarse or fine in texture and in finish (Class III and IV; Barrett 1980). Flint-bearing fabrics were commonly used to make bowls, but quartz sand fabrics also were developed during the late Bronze Age. Initially, naturally sandy clays were used as the clay matrix into which flint temper was added, but subsequently the sandy clays were used without adding temper. This gradual change in fabric recipe is another principal characteristic of the full late Bronze Age ceramic tradition, since it was applied to both jars and bowls by the ninth century BC. Bowls are usually medium to thin-walled, range in size from 500–4000cm^3, and are often but not always burnished on the interior or both surfaces. At the beginning of the late Bronze Age decorated bowls are extremely rare. Very small bowls are often designated as cups, but these are quite rare in this plain assemblage phase of the late Bronze Age. It is clear from the small size of these vessels (the majority appear to have a capacity of <2000cm^3) that they are mainly individual, personal pots, although this evidence needs to be reassessed using the large assemblages which have been published during the past 20 years (eg Needham 1991; Needham and Spence 1996; Lawson 2000). Bowls expand the variety of visible shapes used in the late Bronze Age, and appear to be a complete contrast to the middle Bronze Age. This vessel type becomes more frequent during the course of the late Bronze Age.

In addition, very small bowls with rim diameters in the range of 8cm or less and capacities of less than 500cm^3 are interpreted as cups (Class V; Barrett 1980, 303, figs 5.2–3, 6.5; Gingell and Morris 2000, fig. 60.98–117) and even miniature vessels, which may be children's toys or apprenticeship attempts, are known (ibid., fig. 60.118–20).

Late Bronze Age pottery is thought to have developed in response to the increasing need for utensils or containers for feasts. The jars may have been used for storing, cooking and serving food, while the bowls may have been used for serving and eating from. It may well be that wooden bowls were used for the same purpose in the middle Bronze Age, but by the late Bronze Age this requirement was strongly expressed through the ceramic medium. There are no published examples of late Bronze Age assemblages describing evidence of use, although the presence of soot, carbonised residues and pitting of the interior surface is commonly noted (cf. Morris 2000a, 157). This absence of information is a considerable weakness in pottery analysis methodology which has been emphasised recently (Morris 2002), and a major research project using absorbed lipid residue analysis has now begun to explore the invisible evidence from several later prehistoric pottery assemblages (Copley *et al.* 2002).

What is undeniable is the sheer increase in the quantity of pots that were made and discarded during the late Bronze Age, and this is coupled with the appearance of the first ceramic-rich midden deposits (Gingell and Lawson 1984; 1985; Lawson 2000; McOmish 1996; Needham 1991; Needham and Spence 1996) and large, open settlements (such as Green Park 1 and 2) in central southern England.

Post-Deverel-Rimbury (PDR)

The above, apparently distinctive divisions of middle Bronze Age and late Bronze Age have been emphasised by the introduction of the phrase 'post-Deverel-Rimbury' (PDR) into the literature and its common adoption to replace the rather long-winded name 'plainware assemblage of the later Bronze Age'.

Labelling plainware late Bronze Age assemblages as post-Deverel-Rimbury has automatically closed down any consideration of the contemporaneity in production and use of middle Bronze Age with late Bronze Age, removed the possibility of distinctive assemblages which may fall between middle Bronze Age and late Bronze Age in their character, and discouraged the exploration of the changes from middle Bronze Age pottery to late Bronze Age pottery. Even the author of the term, John Barrett, admitted that it was not a very good term to use (1980, 306).

What do these transformations represent and can they inform us about the changes in society during the last 500 years of the second millennium BC? What were middle Bronze Age and late Bronze Age pots used for? Why were many middle Bronze Age urns so thick-walled despite the range of vessel sizes (some thick-walled urns are actually quite small)? How were middle Bronze Age and late Bronze Age vessels used and deposited, and in what kinds of sites and deposits have each been found? Are there sites where these types have been found together, and should we recognise the possibility of their contemporaneity of use? Or was the middle Bronze Age pottery curated over a long period of time? Are there assemblages of late Bronze Age pottery which can be viewed as not really late Bronze Age, as traditionally defined, but more like middle Bronze Age in their fabrics, forms and deposition? Are there regional variations in the change from middle Bronze Age to late Bronze Age which need to be explored?

Why was flint temper the only temper used to make middle Bronze Age urns and the principal temper used for later Bronze Age pottery generally? Why was so much coarse flint temper used for barrel and bucket urns, and in particular why was so much fine flint temper used to make globular urns? Flint, as many potters today will relate, is an extraordinarily difficult temper to create and to use (Cleal 1995, 191). The author has seen a famous flint-knapper work up quite a sweat trying to crush calcined flint with a metal hammer for use as temper. This was not an easy choice for later Bronze Age potters to make, but this temper was used consistently in Berkshire and Wessex (Cleal 1995, table 16.2) throughout the middle Bronze Age and the beginning of the late Bronze Age.

The application of fingertip decoration to both middle Bronze Age and late Bronze Age pots is a very personal marker, and must be a key indicator of what these pots meant to their makers and users. If so, why are there no fingertip impressions on globular urns? Are marks of personal identity less important than marks which represent the social unit on this particular pottery type? Many authors have stressed the productive investment associated with the making of globular urns, in the processing of the flint temper for the fabrics, finer walls and general care of vessel construction, surface treatment and complex decorative motifs.

Was there a longer period during the second half of the second millennium BC when these changes were taking place, rather than simply a single century as suggested previously? Both Barrett (1980) and Gingell (1980; 1992) have argued that there are regional variations in the date ranges for the middle Bronze Age and late Bronze Age, but this overview will show that there is a greater similarity within the region than once was suspected, and the time scale is even longer.

THE EVIDENCE: POTS AND DATES

This section will review the evidence which demonstrates that there is a range of pottery which is not typical of the late Bronze Age period as described above, and that the contemporaneity of middle Bronze Age and this non-Deverel-Rimbury/non-

late Bronze Age pottery is widespread and surprisingly common. There are a few available dates for some of the pottery, and these are compared to dates for middle Bronze Age urns and classic examples of late Bronze Age pottery to show that the results from this landscape project belong to a long and variable continuum of transition in central southern England (Table 5.1). It will be suggested that we recognise this transitional pottery in a positive manner and radiocarbon date deposits containing such examples, as well as deposits with solely middle Bronze Age pottery and those with just late Bronze Age pottery, in the whole of central southern England.

The Lower Kennet Valley

The Lower Kennet Valley will be investigated first in order to place the Moores Farm and Green Park 1–3 assemblages into context. There are several sites

Table 5.1   Radiocarbon dating of middle and late Bronze Age pottery in south-central England

County/site	Pottery type(s)	Radiocarbon sample	Radiocarbon date (BP)	Calibrated date (95% probability)
Berkshire				
Green Park 3	MBA	KIA-19180	3020 ± 35	1388–1130 cal BC
	MBA	KIA-19181	2995 ± 60	1395–1047 cal BC
	MBA and non-DR	KIA-19182	3070 ± 35	1412–1218 cal BC
	MBA and non-DR	KIA-19183	3150 ± 40	1518–1318 cal BC
Heron's House, Burghfield	MBA	HAR-2754	3060 ± 100	1550–1000 cal BC
Knight's Farm Subsite 3	MBA and non-DR	BM-1594	3195 ± 95	1750–1200 cal BC
Aldermaston Wharf	non-DR	BM-1592	3240 ± 135	1900–1100 cal BC
	non-DR and LBA ('plain')	BM-1590	3000 ± 40	1390–1110 cal BC
	non-DR and LBA ('plain')	BM-1591	2785 ± 35	1010–830 cal BC
Oxfordshire				
Eynsham Abbey	non-DR	OxA-7930	2895 ± 60	1310–910 cal BC
	non-DR	OxA-7931	2950 ± 40	1320–1030 cal BC
	non-DR	OxA-7932	2900 ± 55	1300–920 cal BC
	non-DR and LBA ('plain')	OxA-7928	2925 ± 35	1270–1010 cal BC
	non-DR and LBA ('plain')	OxA-7929	2915 ± 35	1260–1000 cal BC
Wiltshire				
Potterne	non-DR	HAR-6982	3130 ± 100	1630–1130 cal BC
	non-DR	HAR-8938	3000 ± 90	1460–990 cal BC
Hampshire				
Balksbury Camp	LBA ('plain')	HAR-442	2740 ± 170	1395–410 cal BC
	LBA ('plain')	HAR-5127	2800 ± 70	1160–820 cal BC
Sussex				
Black Patch	MBA and non-DR	HAR-2939	2780 ± 80	1130–800 cal BC
	MBA and non-DR	HAR-2940	3020 ± 70	1430–1040 cal BC
	MBA and non-DR	HAR-2941	2970 ± 70	1400–990 cal BC
	MBA and non-DR	HAR-3735	2970 ± 80	1410–970 cal BC
	MBA and non-DR	HAR-3736	3080 ± 70	1520–1120 cal BC
	MBA and non-DR	HAR-3737	2850 ± 70	1220–830 cal BC
Itford Hill	MBA (and 'LBA')	GrN-6167	2950 ± 35	1300–1010 cal BC

in this area which provided the basis for a definition of both plain and decorated late Bronze Age assemblages, including Aldermaston Wharf and Knights Farm sub-sites 1–4 (Bradley *et al.* 1980) which are located west of the Green Park complex. The Aldermaston assemblage contains very few decorated vessels but the forms include shouldered jars, both coarse and fine variants, a variety of bowl forms and some cups, making it a type site for the plain assemblage phase of the late Bronze Age (ibid., fig. 11, type series). In addition, however, there are several contexts where only ovoid-profile, often hooked rim jars and straight-sided jars were recovered. The latter include Pit 6 (ibid., fig. 12.18–24) with three ovoid jars, similar to Green Park 2 type 11, and three straight or slightly expanded 'flower pot' or conical-profile jars similar to some examples of the Green Park 1 type 7 vessels (Hall 1992, fig. 41). One radiocarbon determination from charcoal in Pit 6 produced a date of 1900–1100 cal BC (95% confidence, BM-1592, 3240±135 BP). A second feature, Pit 68, contained four illustrated vessels (ibid., fig. 14.67–70) including two fineware examples and two ovoid/straight-sided coarseware jars. Two radiocarbon determinations were established for grain from this pit, providing dates of 1390–1110 cal BC (95% confidence, BM-1590, 3000±40 BP) and 1010–830 cal BC (95% confidence, BM-1591, 2785±35 BP). Deverel-Rimbury pottery was not identified at Aldermaston. No dates were obtained for features containing the classic array of late Bronze Age plain assemblage pottery of shouldered jars and bowls despite 6849 sherds having been recovered from the site.

Knights Farm subsite 1 (Bradley *et al.* 1980, figs 34–6) is an outstanding example of a decorated assemblage of the late Bronze Age, but its late date places it beyond the scope of this overview. It has two radiocarbon dates from one pit rich with pottery, 2690±80 BP (HAR-1011) and 2550±80 BP (HAR1012), which support a later date. Subsites 2 and 4 (ibid., fig. 33), on the other hand, could easily have been contemporary with Aldermaston based on the range of forms and infrequency of decoration, with the exception of two Deverel-Rimbury sherds.

However, excavation of Knights Farm subsite 3 revealed two interesting small assemblages from pits. Feature 103 (ibid., fig. 32.39–42) contained a bucket urn with a knob associated with a straight-sided vessel with external slashes on the rim, an upright necked vessel with uncertain profile and a thick-walled, urn-like profile base. One sample from this feature produced a radiocarbon determination of 1750–1200 cal BC (95% confidence, BM-1594, 3195±95 BP) which is similar to the radiocarbon dating results from Green Park 3, where middle Bronze Age and non-Deverel-Rimbury pottery were also recovered together. Feature 249 contained sherds from another straight-sided vessel with fingertip impressions on the top/internal edge of the rim but a typically late

Bronze Age-style flared base (ibid., fig. 32.46), again similar to the Green Park types. Other features on this site have plain assemblage late Bronze Age pottery similar to Aldermaston. At Heron's House, Burghfield (Bradley and Richards 1980) another middle Bronze Age bucket urn with a pinched knob was recovered from a circular scoop containing charcoal with a radiocarbon determination of 1550–1000 cal BC (95% confidence; HAR-2754: 3060 ± 100 BP). The scoop had cut the upper fill of a ring ditch with a radiocarbon determination of 1500–1010 cal BC (95% confidence; HAR-2749: 3040 ± 90 BP).

These three were the only radiocarbon determinations for middle Bronze Age pottery in this area prior to the Green Park determinations. What is significant for this project is the association of middle Bronze Age and non-middle Bronze Age/non-late Bronze Age types of pottery, no matter how broad the suggested date range for the Knights Farm subsite 3 deposition. There are two other assemblages which demonstrate that there are extremely secure contexts where classic middle Bronze Age pottery is found with so-called late Bronze Age pottery that is not the full range expected of a plain assemblage group of the late Bronze Age. These sites are Pingewood (Johnston 1985) and Brimpton (Lobb 1990).

The most remarkable evidence for a clear transition period from the middle Bronze Age to the late Bronze Age was discovered at Pingewood, where over 10 kg of later Bronze Age pottery was recovered. Several features contained an array of sherds from both middle Bronze Age fingertip decorated bucket urns and straight-sided jars with fingertip impressions on the rim top, flower pot jars and ovoid jars, as well as a series of features with only the latter. The middle Bronze Age and non-middle Bronze Age pottery types are found in the same coarse flint-tempered fabrics with non-sandy clay matrices. In addition, some of the non-middle Bronze Age pottery from the site is made from flint-tempered fabrics with sandy clay matrices and there are two necked vessels, with thin walls made from a fineware fabric, which could be late Bronze Age Class II jars. Base types include both thick, plain ones from urns and splayed examples, again in the non-sandy fabric with coarse flint temper. Therefore, the "Deverel-Rimbury material is found in the same features and the same fabrics as the other pottery, and there is no *a priori* case for separating the two groups chronologically" (Bradley 1985, 27).

At Brimpton, a watching brief conducted in 1978–9 discovered a palaeochannel of the River Enborne, which had been cut by later Bronze Age features (Lobb 1990, Site A). Rescue conditions allowed for only partial recording of the features and limited recovery of finds. Just over 8 kg of pottery (284 sherds) was recovered from layers deposited in the river channel which sealed these features. Approximately 95% of the pottery is flint-tempered and consists of two main fabric groups, a very coarse and poorly-sorted group and a finer group with dense, well-sorted smaller temper. This pottery is predominantly from middle Bronze Age bucket urns, four of which are illustrated (ibid., fig. 2.3–6), with the finer fabrics used to make suspected globular urns (ibid., fig. 2.10–11). Additional types include a small tub with a knob, which may be another bucket urn (ibid., fig. 2.7), and a very large (42cm rim diameter, 32cm base diameter), thick-walled, expanded profile vessel with a rim shape very similar to many barrel urns, with a broad flat top and protruding exterior edge (ibid., fig. 2.1–2). In addition, there are a number of vertical-sided vessels, called possible jars, with flat and rounded rims (ibid., fig. 3.11–17) in the same fabrics which "would perhaps be better placed in the post-Deverel-Rimbury tradition and may suggest a date for the end of the Deverel-Rimbury period" (ibid., 47). The deposits also contained a bronze-working crucible, a Group 2 bronze side-looped socketed spearhead (which is common in the north Wiltshire, Berkshire and Oxfordshire area: Rowlands 1976, 51–2), a middle Bronze Age type bun-shaped clay weight and 69 identifiable animal bones including cattle, sheep/goat, red deer and pig. This range of material has been interpreted as representing dumps of domestic refuse into the palaeochannel from nearby occupation due to the lack of abrasion on the pottery and the good to moderate state of bone preservation. The jar-like pottery is identical to Green Park 2 R11 and R16, and this is therefore another example of the contemporaneous deposition of middle Bronze Age and non-middle Bronze Age pottery.

At Green Park 1 (Moore and Jennings 1992), Deverel-Rimbury through to plain and then decorated assemblage late Bronze Age pottery was described and illustrated, although a stratified sequence was not available. Bradley and Hall (1992) single out ovoid and straight-sided vessels, both plain and with decorated rims, applied bosses and fingertip impressed walls, as visually transitional in type, and they suggest a date of 11th century BC. However, the possibility that some of the occupation could be earlier in the second millennium BC should be explored. For example, the vessels illustrated from contexts 3515, 3585, 3631 and 3681 (ibid., fig. 49) could all be classified as transitional in type; there are no shouldered jars and only two possible bowls, while the rest are ovoid or straight-sided jars.

Other assemblages in this area which are dominated by similar ovoid profile and straight-profile vessels rather than shouldered jars and bowls and which have between 95–100% of the pottery made from flint-tempered fabrics are Field Farm (Mepham 1992a, fig. 19) and Anslow's Cottages (Mepham 1992b, fig. 42). At Field Farm there were also several middle Bronze Age cremations with urns, as well as features which contained more typical late Bronze Age pottery. Anslow's

Cottages had no evidence for middle Bronze Age activity, but the pottery was dominated by straight-walled and ovoid profile vessels as well as classic late Bronze Age pottery. The pottery from both of these sites is not presented contextually in the publications, but the occurrence of this material makes the archives of these sites worth re-examination.

In summary, the evidence from several sites in the Lower Kennet Valley shows that we can expect to find secure contexts containing middle Bronze Age pottery together with pottery which is similar to it but not exactly the same, having simple, straight or convex, ovoid or conical profiles in fabrics similar to middle Bronze Age urns, as well as vessels of this shape in fabrics that show a different selection of clays for pot-making while still demonstrating continuity in the addition of crushed burnt flint as temper. Knobs and applied cordons do not occur on these new vessels, but fingertipping is present on the tops and inner surface of the rims. The bases become more distinctive, with pinched or flared profiles, and the addition of flint grits to the bases can still be found. The walls of these non-middle Bronze Age vessels are never as thick as the majority of the bucket or barrel urns. Bowls do not usually occur in this phase of production, although one does appear at Green Park 3 in the middle fill (context 2687) of waterhole 2690, in association with middle Bronze Age pottery and other vessels which would not appear out of place within a late Bronze Age plain assemblage (Figs 2.17.6, 2.18.7–12 and 2.19.13–21). The primary fill of this waterhole produced two radiocarbon dates of 1412–1218 cal BC (KIA19182) and 1518–1318 cal BC (KIA19183) respectively.

The picture at present is thus not at all simple. The dating of this transition appears to focus on the 15th to 12th centuries cal BC. If this dating proves reliable in future, it appears to cover Period 5 of Needham's chronology for metalwork assemblages of the middle Bronze Age, including Taunton, Penard and the commencement of the Wilburton phase (1996, fig. 1). Ceramically, it spans not only the middle Bronze Age but also the post-Deverel-Rimbury phase, and therefore to refer to it as post-Deverel-Rimbury can no longer be appropriate. But is this phenomenon a limited, regional development which does not occur elsewhere in central southern England?

The Thames Valley: Berkshire, Oxfordshire, Surrey and Middlesex

Until recently, the Upper Thames Valley has been seen as a core area for middle Bronze Age activity but not for the late Bronze Age. Excavations at Eynsham Abbey, Oxfordshire revealed late Bronze Age activity in the area of an enclosure ditch (Barclay *et al.* 2001). The pottery assemblage is modest (414 sherds; *c* 4 kg) but very significant due to the range of vessel forms present and the direct dating of the burnt residues on five of the vessels.

Three basic rim forms were defined as straight, incurving and everted. Rounded-shoulder sherds are rare in the collection, and the bases are steep rounded, squared angle or expanded/pinched in profile. This typology resulted in four vessel types: straight-sided, with occasional circular indentations or perforations; rounded (ovoid, convex-profile) with incurving rims, with occasional circular indentations or perforations; slightly shouldered vessels; and round-shouldered jars. The four decorated vessels with oblique incised lines or fingernail impressions on the top of the rims are all straight-sided or ovoid types which do not find parallel forms in the Upper Thames Valley, but are most similar to those from sites within the Kennet Valley and Middle Thames, in particular Green Park 1 and Aldermaston Wharf. The knobbed vessel illustrated is likely to be of early-middle Bronze Age date because it has a grog-tempered fabric. Otherwise, there are no obvious sherds from middle Bronze Age urns. Only one positively identified bowl, which is burnished on both surfaces and may be quite large in size (ibid., P6), was recovered from the same layer and section of the enclosure ditch as a round-shouldered jar.

Six radiocarbon determinations were established for the assemblage, five from burnt residues on the interior of vessels and one from an articulated animal bone deposit. Three of these were from the middle fills of the enclosure ditch and three from a ground surface (ibid., table 16). The combined dates range from 1380–910 cal BC. While the pottery is recognised by the authors as a plain ware assemblage of late Bronze Age (1150–800 cal BC) tradition, it is also equally likely to "represent the transition from the middle to the late Bronze Age during the final centuries of the 2nd millennium cal BC (1150–950 cal BC), with a range of simple straight-sided or ovoid jars replacing the heavier Bucket Urns that are so typical of the local Deverel-Rimbury tradition" (ibid., 138). The less common round-shouldered jars, a decorated jar with slashed cordon on the neck, the bowl and a miniature vessel or cup are cited as examples of a possible second phase of occupation dating to the later part of the period (*c* 950–800 cal BC).

The Eynsham Abbey assemblage and radiocarbon determinations are the most important indication that the dates from the Green Park deposits are inherently reliable, ceramically. This assemblage has virtually no examples of middle Bronze Age pottery and therefore the range of dates from the early 14th to 10th centuries cal BC overlap significantly with those from Green Park. Similarly, much of the pottery from Green Park is like that from Eynsham Abbey. Therefore, a sequence appears to have been established with these two dated assemblages.

In the Lower Thames valley, the site at Hurst Park, East Molesey (Andrews 1996) may belong to a transitional middle Bronze Age/late Bronze Age phase of activity. Only one vessel from the site has

been attributed to the middle Bronze Age, a finger-impressed cordoned urn. A total of 995 other flint-tempered sherds was assigned to the late Bronze Age. However, one unusual pit deposit, which unfortunately had been disturbed, contained large parts of two vessels. One of these is a round-shouldered jar with a small everted rim and the other is a flaring, flower pot profile vessel with a compact row of numerous fingertip impressions on the upper girth zone and on the top of the flat, slightly flaring rim. The flower pot vessel is 30cm in diameter and has 10mm thick walls, while the shouldered jar is 50cm in diameter and has 12mm thick walls and wiped surfaces on the exterior. The base of the flower pot profile vessel is more similar to an urn-type base than a late Bronze Age expanded or flared base. They are made from slightly different flint-tempered fabrics: one with a common amount of moderately well-sorted flint < 2mm in size and the other with a moderate amount of well-sorted flint < 2mm in size. Both are classified as being late Bronze Age but it is worth considering whether this purposeful deposit represents another example of the transitional ceramic phase during the later Bronze Age. The 'flower pot' clearly belongs to the middle Bronze Age urn tradition in general shape, nature of the base, and style of decoration. The large jar is clearly of the plainware phase of the late Bronze Age in profile, surface finish and absence of decoration. Both belong to the later Bronze Age based on their fabrics. There is some confusion between the specialists and the excavator as to the nature of the deposition of the vessels in this feature, in particular as to which vessel is the larger of the two (despite the illustration) and whether one vessel was covering the other (compare Andrews 1996, 66, fig. 39, pl. 10 to Laidlaw 1996a, 86, fig. 53). The rest of the flint-tempered pottery from Hurst Park is a mixture of upright rim, round-shouldered jars, convex jars, and a thick-walled hemispherical bowl, none of which are decorated. Therefore, it is not inappropriate to suggest that this assemblage could belong to the end of the second millennium cal BC, and this is suggested by Laidlaw (1996a, 86) but with no supporting reasons. There is no information about the contexts of recovery for this material, other than the special deposit, and no radiocarbon determinations were obtained.

The recognition of transitional forms of later Bronze Age pottery in the Lower Thames area should be more straightforward because of the distinctive array of jars and bowls of late Bronze Age character from Runnymede Bridge, Surrey where radiocarbon determinations place this assemblage firmly in the 9th century cal BC (Needham 1991, 345–53; Ambers and Leese 1996). There are many different types of shouldered jars and bowls in the large assemblages from this site (Longley 1980; Needham 1991; Needham and Spence 1996), and most importantly there are no examples of straight-sided vessels or convex-profile jars.

Wessex: the chalkland landscapes of Berkshire, Wiltshire, Hampshire, Dorset and Sussex

Rams Hill, Oxfordshire (formerly Berkshire) is famous for its association with this transitional period of the later Bronze Age, and has been a key site in the definition of post-Deverel-Rimbury developments in southern England. Located on the northern edge of the Wessex chalk landscape, Rams Hill has been reassessed with new radiocarbon measurements for its many phases of enclosure. The dates fall within the 13th to 10th centuries cal BC, which spans the formal middle-late Bronze Age transition, overlapping the use of Penard and Wilburton metalwork (Needham and Ambers 1994, 225). The illustrated pottery from the original publication (Bradley and Ellison 1975, fig. 3.5) includes a number of very small rim fragments which appear to be hooked rim and simple ovoid jars, upright rim necked vessels, one round-shouldered jar and one more sharply shouldered jar, as well as several straight-sided vessels in a collection of later, decorated material. It is difficult at present to know exactly which of these vessels belongs to which phase of occupation and enclosure construction.

In Wiltshire, the first examples of a possible transitional phase of later Bronze Age pottery which was not actually post-Deverel-Rimbury were published by Chris Gingell (1980; 1992). Gingell recognised that not only was it possible for there to be regional variations in assemblages but that this may have chronological implications. Unfortunately, his sites on the Marlborough Downs were not appropriate for radiocarbon dating due to their disturbed nature. The pottery from Burderop Down in particular consists of a very distinctive regional type of Deverel-Rimbury barrel urn with an applied cordon tucked under a flat, horizontally everted or flared rim (Gingell 1992, 72–3). The cordon is finger-impressed or slashed on different vessels and there are examples of an applied cordon on the girth as well. The unstratified assemblage also contained shouldered jars including both biconical and rounded types, a range of other rims with flaring profiles, a hemispherical bowl, other possible bowls and expanded or pinched bases, all of which can be assigned to the plainware phase of the late Bronze Age, especially because none of it is decorated (ibid., 74-75). From Rockley Down there are other examples of shouldered jars. This site also had middle Bronze Age urn sherds (including one which appears to be a barrel urn) and other regionally specific types which could be accepted as possible transitional vessels (ibid., fig. 71.35–8).

What is interesting is that there are no good examples of convex-profile, ovoid vessels or straight-sided vessels which are so common in the Middle Thames Valley area. However, there are straight-sided vessels within the area from the site at Potterne, near Devizes (Lawson 2000). The midden contained lower zones of material, Zones 14–11 (Morris 2000b, figs 61–2), which are very different in character to the more diagnostic types depicted in the main late Bronze Age decorated assemblage typology. This pottery is thick-walled and either straight-sided or barrel-shaped. The assemblage includes incurved or hooked rim jars, simple ovoid jars, shouldered jars, slack-shouldered jars and flat-topped bowls. Only the shouldered jar and flat-topped bowl types were found in the higher zones of the midden. The discussion of the various types focused on the similarities with middle Bronze Age urns, hooked-rim jars from Aldermaston Wharf and the assemblages from Itford Hill, Sussex and South Cadbury, Somerset. Only 1.6% of the 1299 sherds examined from these zones is decorated, and one of these pieces is most likely to be from a middle Bronze Age urn based on wall thickness and decoration (ibid., fig. 62.165).

The earliest midden layers at Potterne also contained single sherds of Peterborough Ware and Beaker, which unfortunately affected the interpretation of one of the two radiocarbon determinations from Zone 11. The dates were 1630–1130 cal BC (95% confidence, HAR-6982, 3130±100 BP) and 2040–1510 cal BC (95% confidence, HAR-6983, 3430±110 BP), both of which have wide errors resulting in spans of 500 years each. Nevertheless, one pit was also dated (3605, which cut into the bedrock) and this produced a date of 1460–990 cal BC (95% confidence, HAR-8938, 3000±90 BP). The rest of the midden is dated broadly from the 10th to 6th centuries cal BC based on four samples, two each from Zones 4 and 7 (Allen 2000, table 1). The dates from these samples were regarded as suspect, and further radiocarbon dating was recommended (Bayliss 2000, 41).

It may be important to mention that there appears to be no evidence for a transitional phase of ceramic material from the middle Bronze Age to late Bronze Age recovered from the Linear Ditches Project (Bradley *et al.* 1994). This is one landscape location where, despite an abundance of evidence for both periods, there appears to be a strong separation in the types of pottery recovered and reported; there is middle Bronze Age pottery and there is plain late Bronze Age pottery. This division is especially well-represented by the clear-cut division between middle Bronze Age fabrics and late Bronze Age fabrics (Raymond 1994, appendix 2, tables 29 and 30), despite the apparent Deverel-Rimbury origins of at least five settlement locations and the equal amounts of middle Bronze Age and late Bronze Age pottery from the LDP 109 settlement outside the linear ditches system in particular (ibid., fig. 51). However, several of the late Bronze Age illustrated sherds are straight-sided or convex-profile vessels with fingertip impressions on the top of the rim and straight body sherds with fingertip impression like bucket urns (ibid., 53, figs 53.12, 53.14–15, 53.23–5) which could be transitional in nature rather than specifically late Bronze Age.

In Hampshire, the evidence is slightly different as it comes from the middle Bronze Age end of the spectrum. Excavation of the rich middle Bronze Age Deverel-Rimbury cemetery at Kimpton, located outside Andover, revealed five phases of pyre burning and deposition of many barrel, bucket and globular urns as well as sherd groups and cremated bones associated with a complex flint platform (Dacre and Ellison 1981). In particular, however, phase E contained three vessels described as post-Deverel-Rimbury in type. Two of these are illustrated, including one plain vessel and one with very slight fingertip impressions on the upper quarter of the vessel (ibid., figs 19.E4, 19.E28). Phase E, however, also has 19 globular urns, ten bucket urns (two described as Lower Thames Valley vessels), and five accessory cups. Phase G contained nine pots described as late Bronze Age, including a slack-profiled jar or bowl, a carinated jar, a wide-mouthed jar, a round-shouldered jar, a high-shouldered jar, a straight-walled vessel, a carinated jar and an unillustrated carinated bowl (ibid., figs 20–2). These are predominantly made from coarse, flint-tempered fabrics containing large inclusions, and it was noted that these fabrics are markedly coarser than the urn fabrics (Davies 1981), although a few of the urns have similar fabric codes. What is so significant is that these post-Deverel-Rimbury and late Bronze Age vessels were all found complete or nearly complete within the funerary complex. The phase G burials were interred in relatively deep holes beneath distinct but badly eroded circular flint mounds around the margins of the flint platform.

This funerary context of recovery appears to be a Hampshire theme. Another special complex of vessels found in two nearby locations, one in a burial complex (this time an early Bronze Age ring ditch) and the other directly into the land nearby, was found at Twyford Down (Walker and Farwell 2000). The ring ditch was interpreted as a favoured location for structured deposition due to the presence of both middle Bronze Age urns and late Bronze Age vessels within the flint and ash deposits and the agricultural soils of this ditch. One of the vessels, a slightly convex but basically straight-walled form with slight finger impressions (ibid., fig. 23.8), is remarkably similar to a phase G vessel from Kimpton (Dacre and Ellison 1981, fig. 20.G3), and was found in the same context as another apparently late Bronze Age plain vessel which is much smaller but equally simple in profile. This continuity of deposition, first an early Bronze Age collared urn rim in the centre of the ring ditch area, followed by middle Bronze Age urns with cremation burials and then non-middle Bronze Age pottery in the ditch itself without burials, is extended to an area about 30m to the south-west of the ditch where six non-middle Bronze Age vessels were deposited (Walker and Farwell 2000, fig. 25.18–23). These represented formerly complete or semi-complete vessels of large size, individually placed in pits without cremated remains. Three are convex-profile jars, one is extremely similar to a

bucket urn with finger-impressed girth cordon while another is a very small shouldered jar, two have bases similar to middle Bronze Age urns and one has a row of pre-firing perforations for attaching a soft lid. These vessels were found as individual items in pits cut into the chalk. Two of the three fabrics are flint-tempered but differ from the middle Bronze Age flint fabrics from this site in that the texture is coarser, with large, poorly-sorted angular inclusions. The other is labelled a flint fabric type, but the description is distinctively sandy (moderate to common amount less than 0.5mm) with only a rare to sparse amount of flint (less than 3mm across). These two sites, Kimpton and Twyford Down, demonstrate the challenge of characterising and classifying later Bronze Age pottery during this transition period.

A third site in Hampshire, Winnall Down (Fasham 1985), had a late Bronze Age phase as well as evidence of middle Bronze Age activity. The middle Bronze Age pottery consists of redeposited, thick-walled, heavily flint-tempered sherds in an early Iron Age enclosure ditch and a possible urned cremation, but the late Bronze Age is represented by an extraordinary assemblage of sherds from at least five vessels found together in a posthole (ibid., fig. 51, 4–9). These include four thin-walled, undecorated convex-profile types and an additional vessel with an expanded base which would not be out of place in a transitional assemblage. The posthole is from either a fenceline or the windbreak for a post-built roundhouse. Other sherds from the site that were thought to be late Bronze Age in character include a hemispherical bowl and an upright but slightly flared rim from a small, necked jar. It is most likely that this assemblage is later in date than the Twyford Down vessels, based on the thinner vessel walls, the lack of any decoration and the presence of the expanded base, but the similarity in simplicity of the vessel profiles is important to note.

One more site from Hampshire needs to be mentioned: Grange Road, Gosport (Hall and Ford 1994). This site, located 1km from the shore on a relatively flat terrace of the River Alver, consists of pits and postholes which have been reconstructed into various possible structures and associated features. The pottery from Area A is flint-tempered and undecorated, with one exception. The vessel forms, once again, consist of flower pot profile, straight-sided, and convex/ovoid jars with two upright rims, slack-shouldered jars, one sharply everted rim vessel, and expanded bases. The only bowl is straight-sided as well, and is decorated with pinching of the rim on the interior and exterior. One of the convex-profile, nearly hooked rims illustrated was perforated at the pre-firing stage 20mm below the rim. The pottery from this site is not typical of the late Bronze Age, as is mentioned in the pottery report, although it is assigned to the post-Deverel-Rimbury repertoire of the late Bronze Age as a plain assemblage and compared to Yapton in West Sussex (Timby 1994).

An assemblage of late Bronze Age-earliest Iron Age pottery from Balksbury, Andover (Wainwright and Davies 1995) provides a useful closure to the discussion of dated deposits of later Bronze Age date in Hampshire. The pottery was recognised as typical of this period both on the basis of stratigraphic relationships and the types present (Rees 1995), and subsequently confirmed by two radiocarbon dates: phase II bank, 1395–410 cal BC (95% confidence; HAR-442, 2740±170 BP) and posthole 3464, 1160–820 cal BC (95% confidence, HAR-5127, 2800±70 BP). The range of vessels illustrated from the posthole (ibid., fig. 63, 7–14) includes two tall shouldered/carinated bowls, a round-shouldered bowl, four necked jars including one with fingertip decoration on the exterior of the rim, and a vessel with a sharply inturned rim profile. This group of pottery in partic-ular and a similar key group from a pit (ibid., fig. 63, 2–6) would not be out of place within a plain assem-blage of late Bronze Age pottery from the Thames Valley. The pottery from this phase is overwhelm-ingly made from coarse or fine flint-tempered non-sandy fabrics (ibid., fig. 62a, fabrics 7 and 9).

East of Hampshire, there are two important assemblages from Sussex which need reviewing. Black Patch is one of the most famous later Bronze Age settlement sites in southern Britain (Drewett 1982), and reinterpretation has demonstrated that it consists of two chronologically distinct occupation phases (Russell 1996). The pottery was originally examined as a single phase assemblage and it was declared that "no late Bronze Age types can be identified within the Black Patch groups" (Ellison 1982, 362) but there is now scope for re-examination of the material in the light of this rephasing. The pottery contains obvious middle Bronze Age types, including several bucket urns and at least five globular urns (ibid., figs 30.6, 30.18–24, 31.25–6, 31.32, 31.34–6). However, there is a common vessel form, Sussex type 2, an ovoid or straight-sided jar, which may represent a non-Deverel-Rimbury component within the Black Patch assemblage (ibid., figs 30.2, 30.7–15). Its similarity to vessels from Green Park does not require further emphasis, but the presence of knobs on some examples demonstrates the transitional nature of these vessels. Radiocarbon dating of six samples of grain from three pits located at Hut Platform 4 (pits 3–5) produced significant results but only ten body sherds (210 g) were associated with the food deposits: 1130–800 cal BC (95% probability, HAR-2939, 2780±80 BP); 1430–1040 cal BC (95% proba-bility, HAR-2940, 3020±70 BP); 1400–990 cal BC (95% probability, HAR-2941, 2970±70 BP); and 1020–820 cal BC (95% probability, BM1643, 2790±40 BP). A similar range of dates was established for three samples of grain from another pit (49) from Hut Platform 1: 1410–970 cal BC (95% probability, HAR-3735, 2970±80 BP); 1520–1120 cal BC (95% probability, HAR-3736, 3080±70 BP); and 1220–830 cal BC (95% probability, HAR-3737, 2850±70 BP). These dates are recognised by Ellison as confirming the general middle Bronze Age dating of the assem-blage, "although they are rather later, on average, than the only other date obtained for such an assem-blage in Sussex (Itford Hill: GrN-6167, 2950±35 BP)" (ibid., 364). The Itford Hill settlement pottery curiously consists predominantly of middle Bronze Age urns (Burstow and Holleyman 1957, 194–200, figs 20–4) but there is a statement that several sherds are late Bronze Age in type (ibid., fig. 24.d-j). This distinction between obvious middle Bronze Age urn assemblages and those which have both elements of middle Bronze Age and non-Deverel-Rimbury types was first recognised in Sussex at Plumpton Plain. The Site A assemblage was typical of the middle Bronze Age but that from Site B belonged to a non-Deverel-Rimbury range of forms but still maintained some elements of middle Bronze Age character (Hawkes 1935; Barrett 1980). Research to determine whether carbonised residues remain on any of this material needs to be conducted in order to provide samples for radio-carbon dating of these vessels.

In addition, what is most unusual is that there are two base sherds illustrated for Black Patch, one made from a fabric consisting of a micaceous clay matrix with sand and flint inclusions in it and the other made from a sandy fabric, which are distinc-tively not middle Bronze Age in character (ibid., fig. 31.37, 31.39), but no mention of their considerable difference from the heavily flint-tempered middle Bronze Age pottery is made. Therefore, there is every possibility that one of the Black Patch phases of occupation could represent a transitional ceramic phase during the later Bronze Age. Plain assem-blages of late Bronze Age type are well-recognised in Sussex, such as those from Yapton (Hamilton 1987) and Selsey (Thomas 2001).

The evidence from Wessex would not be complete without briefly mentioning sites in Dorset. The Eldon's Seat assemblage from the Isle of Purbeck, one of the most famous sites where non-Deverel-Rimbury pottery was recovered along with late Bronze Age pottery (Cunliffe and Phillipson 1968), should be seen as a classic example of the transitional phase in the earliest levels at the site, referred to as Eldon's Seat I. The pottery actually consists of a few middle Bronze Age urns (ibid., fig. 12.31–2, 12.36, 12.39–41) as well as transitional types (ibid., fig. 12.43–5) and regional variants of these (ibid., figs 10.1, 11.10–14, 11.17). There are also shouldered vessels and straight-sided vessels with thin walls, which were recovered from occupation layers and structural features stratified beneath deposits containing more typical decorated late Bronze Age types. There is only one bowl from this phase and it is not closely stratified. More recently, excavations just outside of Dorchester at Coburg Road revealed a later Bronze Age post-built settle-ment beside a line of Bronze Age ring ditches (Smith *et al.* 1992). The pottery has been recognised as similar in many respects to the Eldon's Seat I assem-blage (Cleal 1992).

Back to the Lower Kennet Valley: Green Park 1–3 and Moores Farm

As mentioned above, the primary fill of waterhole 2690 at Green Park 3 was dated to the 15th and 14th centuries cal BC. Five plain body sherds from three different fabrics were recovered from this context (2689), comprising fabrics F5 and F20 (middle and late Bronze Age type) and F6 (late Bronze Age type). A large quantity of middle Bronze Age, transitional and late Bronze Age pottery was found stratified above this fill (Tables 2.8–9; Figs 2.17.6, 2.18.7–12 and 2.19.13–22). Similar situations occur for three of the four other features sampled for radiocarbon dating. Radiocarbon samples from waterhole 3091 produced dates of 1388–1130 cal BC (KIA19180) and 1395–1047 cal BC (KIA19181), and the feature contained sherds from a middle Bronze Age globular urn as well as plain body sherds from various vessels made from either middle Bronze Age, middle/late Bronze Age and late Bronze Age fabrics in other contexts. Waterhole 2373 produced dates of 1501–1307 cal BC (KIA19184) and 1383–1051 cal BC (KIA 19185) from a context with no pottery, but contexts above this produced plain sherds of middle/late Bronze Age and late Bronze Age fabric pottery. Waterhole 3263 produced dates of 1434–1214 cal BC (KIA19186) and 1388–1129 cal BC (KIA19187) and 11 sherds in fabric F22 from a single, probably middle Bronze Age urn (based on fabric alone).

At Green Park 2 large quantities of transitional and late Bronze Age pottery were identified, but were found separate from the middle Bronze Age pottery, which was associated with field boundary ditches and cremation burials. The Moores Farm collection contains an impressive amount of middle Bronze Age pottery from settlement occupation but no evidence of any transitional or late Bronze Age forms or fabrics.

TRANSITIONAL LATER BRONZE AGE (TLBA) POTTERY

This survey has shown that serious consideration must be given to assemblages of later Bronze Age type which appear to be: (1) not typical of the plain assemblage array of shouldered jars and bowls of the late Bronze Age, but (2) do include specific types from the full repertoire, in particular the straight-sided vessels and convex-profile jars, and (3) may be found directly in association with middle Bronze Age urns or (4) without any evidence of associated middle Bronze Age material. It is not best practice to label this material post-Deverel-Rimbury, as the types may be contemporary. This pottery is difficult to recognise or to separate from other later Bronze Age pottery, especially when plain body sherds are the most frequent material. The contexts whence the sherds may derive can be funerary locations, settlement features or special deposits. This material appears to date to the second half of the second millennium cal BC, predating the plainware pottery of the late Bronze Age. This transitional material has been recovered throughout central southern England on all types of landscapes. It is suggested that the terminology 'transitional later Bronze Age' or TLBA may suitably describe this material. It is certainly less common than truly late Bronze Age pottery of 10th to 9th centuries cal BC date, and therefore seems to have a role more similar to that of pottery in the middle Bronze Age.

THE FUTURE

The characterisation of later Bronze Age pottery is very challenging, due to the gradual evolution of forms, the similarities of fabrics and the deposition of different types within the same deposits. The significance of the Green Park 1–3 and Moores Farm discoveries has been placed within a local context by discussing other sites on which TLBA pottery has been identified, such as Pingewood and Brimpton. The subtleties of the pottery from the distinct, transitional period has been emphasised in this project and TLBA pottery has been placed well within the second half of the second millennium cal BC. It is now no longer possible to ignore these special assemblages or hide behind the label 'post-Deverel-Rimbury'. This important pottery is now a well-recognised, wider regional phenomenon which may have local variations. However, we still know very little about the dating of this material, its manufacture and its use. Therefore the following points are suggested to improve this situation.

When middle Bronze Age and late Bronze Age pottery is encountered or expected in a field project, ceramic specialists of this period must be able to advise on the focus of further excavation. At Gosport, Hampshire, features were only half excavated and yet the pottery was reported at the post-excavation stage to be extraordinarily significant and unique for the area. A more flexible approach to fieldwork is important for the future, with features fully excavated in order to provide the best possible pottery assemblage sample available. For example, the careful excavation and recording of the first half of features would be normal practice, but once middle or late Bronze Age pottery is recovered a different strategy of rapid scooping of the contents from the second half should be considered. For ditch sections, a tactic of machining out the contents of ditches in additional 2–5m sections, after detailed hand-excavated sections have been recorded, should be considered. We know so little about later Bronze Age pottery assemblages that every opportunity of recovery within financial limitations must be attempted in order to maximise the size of the assemblage.

Always, wherever suitable samples are encountered, radiocarbon dating must be considered an essential aspect of fieldwork and publication. Financial provision of at least six pairs of samples from every project suspected of having middle

Bronze Age-late Bronze Age pottery should be estimated for at the budgeting stages. In addition, a regional radiocarbon dating assessment should be organised to determine whether any of these assemblages are associated with suitable samples for C14 determinations. Such a re-assessment produced important new dating evidence which contributed to the understanding the sequences and timespan of occupation at Rams Hill (Needham and Ambers 1994).

In order to determine what later Bronze Age pottery was used for, records should be kept of the surface treatments and usewear evidence and middle Bronze Age-late Bronze Age pottery fabrics and forms should be quantified by context. This information should be either published or made available online. Illustrated vessels should always detail this information. This would provide basic data about the pottery recovered and provide the means for assessing the archaeology and past human behaviour without recourse to time-consuming re-examination of the individual sherds or vessels in archive stores. A research project using absorbed lipid residue analysis should also be conducted to find out what middle Bronze Age and TLBA pots were used for.

Chapter 6: Prehistoric settlement at Green Park and Moores Farm – an overview

Introduction

Green Park 3 and Moores Farm cannot be understood in isolation, as they form only part of an intensively investigated archaeological landscape. This chapter discusses the results from the two sites in the context of the other work to date in the Green Park/Moores Farm landscape (Fig. 1.2), including the Green Park 1 and 2 excavations (Moore and Jennings 1992; Brossler *et al.* 2004), the Hartley Court Farm (OA 1991a) and Green Park Substation (OA 2001) evaluations and the Reading Sewage Treatment Works watching brief (OA 2002). The key issue that will be explored is: how did the inhabitation of this landscape develop through prehistory? Particular attention will be paid to the character of middle Bronze Age settlement and land use, as it is here that the evidence from Green Park 3 and Moores Farm makes the greatest contribution.

In order to better understand the development of this landscape, comparative evidence will also be drawn from the wider area of the Lower Kennet Valley, defined here as the stretch of the river downstream from the confluence with the Enborne. Many prehistoric sites have been excavated out in this area (Fig. 6.1), mainly in advance of gravel quarrying, though much of this work was carried out on a rescue basis prior to the 1990s under less than ideal conditions.

Land and water

Green Park and Moores Farm occupy a fairly flat and low-lying gravel terrace landscape to the south of the modern course of the River Kennet. The area is crossed by numerous palaeochannels, which show that shifting or braided river systems existed in the area during the earlier Holocene, though none of the channels can be closely dated. At Moores Farm, two palaeochannels demarcated the northern and southern edges of the main area of prehistoric settlement. It seems likely that the southern channel had largely silted up by the early Iron Age, as pottery of that date was found within a layer overlying the edge of the channel. A palaeochannel 350m to the north-east of Green Park 3 at Area 3000B (Green Park 2) had largely silted up by later Bronze Age (Robinson 2004).

Today, seasonal flooding affects much of the area. However, claims that the area therefore could not have supported permanent settlement or arable farming in later prehistory (Johnston 1985; Lobb and Rose 1996, 82) fail to take into account changes in hydrology over the last two to three thousand years (Moore and Jennings 1992, 120). Current evidence suggests that the onset of frequent overbank flooding in the Lower Kennet Valley did not occur before the late Bronze Age at the earliest (Collins *et al.* 2006); in the Thames Basin as a whole it is commonly a feature of the Iron Age/Roman period onwards (Booth *et al.* 2007, 17-18). This is consistent with the evidence from the Green Park/Moores Farm landscape. At Moores Farm, alluvial layers sealed many of the Bronze Age and early Iron Age features, while at Green Park 1, Area 2000, similar layers sealed Romano-British features (Robinson 1992).

Early prehistoric communities

Mesolithic

Good evidence for Mesolithic activity was found at Moores Farm, where small-scale occupation occurred in an area close to the northern palaeochannel. Two hollows or tree throw holes contained early Mesolithic flint assemblages, and further Mesolithic flintwork was recovered from later features and from the subsoil, suggesting the existence of surface scatters. The flint assemblage includes a range of retouched forms, indicating that a variety of activities were carried out at the site. The features at Moores Farm fit into a wider pattern of Mesolithic use of tree throw holes and natural hollows across southern Britain (Evans *et al.* 1999). Evidence was much sparser at Green Park 3, where the excavations produced only a few pieces of residual flintwork broadly dated to the Mesolithic or early Neolithic. In the wider Green Park landscape, no evidence for a Mesolithic presence was identified in the flint assemblages from Green Park 1 and 2. A Mesolithic blade was recovered from the Substation evaluation, however, and a group of microliths was found in a single evaluation trench at Hartley Court Farm, *c* 200m from a palaeochannel.

The evidence from the Green Park/Moores Farm landscape is suggestive of relatively brief and small-scale episodes of occupation, a pattern that seems to hold for the Lower Kennet Valley as a whole. The best evidence comes from the Kennet floodplain, where Mesolithic flint scatters sealed by peat or alluvium have been found at Haywards Farm, Theale (Lobb and Rose 1996, 75) and Ufton Nervet (Allen and Allen 1997), the latter site possibly representing a specialised, temporary kill and butchery

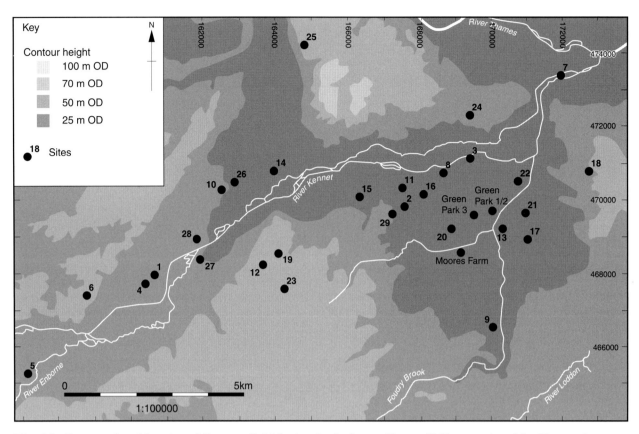

Fig. 6.1 Excavated prehistoric and Romano-British sites in the Lower Kennet Valley mentioned in Chapter 6.
1: Aldermaston Wharf; 2: Amner's Farm, Burghfield; 3: Anslow's Cottages; 4: Beenham; 5: Brimpton; 6: Cod's Hill; 7: Crane Wharf, Reading; 8: Cunning Man, Burghfield; 9: Diddenham Manor Farm, Grazeley; 10: Englefield; 11: Field Farm, Burghfield; 12: Field Farm, Sulhamstead; 13: Hartley Court Farm, Shinfield; 14: Haywards Farm, Theale; 15: Heron's House, Burghfield; 16: Knight's Farm, Burghfield; 17: Little Lea Park; 18: Marshall's Hill, Reading; 19: Meales Farm, Sulhamstead; 20: Pingewood; 21: Reading Football Club; 22: Reading Sewage Treatment Works; 23: Shortheath Lane, Sulhamstead; 24: Southcote; 25: Sulham; 26: Theale Ballast Hole; 27: Ufton Nervet (Allen and Allen 1997); 28: Ufton Nervet (Manning 1974); 29: Wickhams Field, Burghfield. © Crown Copyright 2013, Ordnance Survey 100005569

site (Chisham 2006). On the gravel terraces, a small flint scatter has been found adjacent to a palaeo-channel at Field Farm, Burghfield (Butterworth and Lobb 1992), and individual pieces of Mesolithic flint have been recovered at Pingewood (Care 1985, 33) and Anslow's Cottages (Harding 1992, 106). Further stray finds of Mesolithic flintwork, particularly tranchet axes, have been made at a number of places along the river Kennet corridor, along with a few on the higher plateau gravel around Sulhamstead (Lobb and Rose 1996). The evidence as a whole suggests that the floodplain and lower gravel terraces were the main focus of Mesolithic activity, with locations close to watercourses often favoured. While it is assumed that much of the landscape would have been forested at this time, river margins may have been characterised by a mosaic of woodland, low vegetation and grasses which would probably have made them attractive to Mesolithic hunter-gatherers (Chisham 2006).

The evidence for widespread but small-scale activity in the Lower Kennet Valley can be contrasted with the situation in the Middle Kennet Valley between Woolhampton and Hungerford, an area

famed for its high concentration of large, stratified Mesolithic sites. Sites such as Thatcham Reedbeds, which produced an assemblage of 18,400 flints, are of a quite different order of magnitude from the Lower Kennet sites and may have been repeatedly revisited or perhaps even continually occupied over extended periods of time (Chisham 2006). Chisham (ibid.) suggests that the Middle Kennet Valley was the 'main base area' for Mesolithic groups in the region, from which visits to surrounding areas such as the Lower Kennet Valley were made.

Early Neolithic

No evidence for early Neolithic activity was found at either Green Park 3 or Moores Farm, aside from the few pieces of residual flint from Green Park 3 ascribed a broad Mesolithic/early Neolithic date. Elsewhere in the wider Green Park landscape, the only good evidence for occupation in this period comes from Green Park 1, where a cluster of pits in Area 7000 produced a flint assemblage argued to include elements of both earlier and later Neolithic industries (Bradley and Brown 1992, 89). The interpretation was that the assemblage is transitional in date, although an alternative possibility would be that this location was revisited over an extended period of time through the course of the Neolithic.

The paucity of evidence for early Neolithic activity in the Green Park/Moores Farm landscape is replicated within the Lower Kennet Valley as a whole. The only feature of this period yet identified is a single isolated pit at Field Farm, Burghfield, containing a few flints and a single piece of plain pottery (Butterworth and Lobb 1992, 7). Otherwise, evidence is essentially limited to occasional finds of diagnostic early Neolithic flint, such as a leaf-shaped arrowhead from Wickhams Field, Burghfield (Harding 1996). An alder stake from Kennet palaeochannel deposits at Crane Wharf, Reading, has been radiocarbon dated to 3820–3570 cal BC (Har-7028: 4950±80 BP), but there were no other associated artefacts (Hawkes and Fasham 1997).

From this it might be concluded that the Lower Kennet Valley was not densely inhabited at this time. However, the possibility that early Neolithic activity has simply not been recognised should also be considered. Until recently, it has been common practice in the middle Thames Valley to date plain, flint-tempered pottery to the late Bronze Age. However, recent work at Heathrow led to the reclassification of much of this material as early Neolithic plain ware, substantially increasing the evidence for early Neolithic activity at the site (Framework Archaeology 2006, 32). The late Bronze Age plain ware assemblages of the Lower Kennet Valley sites might thus repay re-evaluation, to investigate whether they too might reveal an early Neolithic element. In particular, the 'intrusive' late Bronze Age pottery recorded in many of the Neolithic pits at Green Park 1 (Moore and Jennings 1992, 6) may be open to reassessment.

Middle Neolithic to early Bronze Age

From the middle Neolithic onwards, a human presence in the landscape becomes more tangible. At Moores Farm, two features – a pit and a posthole – contained middle Neolithic Impressed Ware pottery and worked flint. The two semi-complete pottery vessels from the pit probably represent a deliberate deposit. An unstratified later Neolithic oblique arrowhead was also recovered. Subsequent activity at the site is represented by a few residual sherds of Beaker and early Bronze Age pottery. No features of this period were identified at Green Park 3, although the majority of the flint assemblage was ascribed a broad later Neolithic/early Bronze Age date, and one residual sherd of Beaker pottery was also found. Within the wider Green Park/Moores Farm landscape, a middle/later Neolithic segmented ring ditch was uncovered at Green Park 2 (Area 3017). Two samples of animal bone from the upper ditch fills were radiocarbon dated to the early 3rd millennium cal BC (NZA 9411: 2900–2580 cal BC; NZA 9478: 2920–2620 cal BC), though a third

produced a date of 1740–1440 cal BC (NZA 9508). An unurned cremation burial was found in the same upper ditch fill as the latter sample, and may have been interred long after the monument was first constructed. The ring ditch formed the focus for a dispersed group of pits, postholes and tree throw holes, many of which produced Neolithic flintwork. One pit also contained two sherds of Impressed Ware pottery, and another a single sherd of Grooved Ware. Activity continued 60m to the north in Area 7000 (Green Park 1), where as noted above a group of pits produced a flint assemblage argued to show aspects of both earlier and later Neolithic industries. Three further ring ditches in the Green Park area produced no finds but could date broadly to this period. A tiny ring ditch (3m diameter) was found at Area 3100 (Green Park 1). A C-shaped ditch found to the north of Green Park at Reading Sewage Treatment Works had an internal diameter of 13m and enclosed an irregular hollow or tree throw hole (Fig. 6.2). A more typical ring ditch, 15m in diameter, was uncovered 150m to the south of Green Park 3 in the Pingewood excavations (Lobb and Mills 1993).

Elsewhere in the Lower Kennet Valley, numerous ring ditches—presumed in most cases to represent levelled round barrows—are known from cropmark evidence (Fig. 6.3). Most occur on the river terrace gravels, and in particular in two distinct clusters to the west of Green Park/Moores Farm in the Burghfield and Englefield areas, though there is also a further cluster on the higher ground around Ufton Nervet and Mortimer Common (Gates 1975; Butterworth and Lobb 1992, fig. 58). Where excavated, a number of these ring ditches have produced late Neolithic and/or early Bronze Age pottery and flint, as at Field Farm, Burghfield (Butterworth and Lobb 1992), Amner's Farm, Burghfield (Lobb 1985), Englefield (Healy 1993) and Beenham (Anon. 1964, 99; Holgate 1988, table 29). Some of these ring ditches seem to have been foci for contemporary activity, being associated with pits or flint scatters. At Field Farm, a sequence can be seen in which a hollow containing a Neolithic hearth and an Impressed Ware vessel was later enclosed by a ring ditch that produced a radiocarbon date of 2130–1710 cal BC (HAR-9142: 3560±70 BP) from a lower fill; three cremation burials contained within Collared Urns were found close to the inner edge of the ditch. Away from known burial monuments, traces of occupation are sparse. A middle Neolithic pit containing Impressed Ware pottery has been found at Wickhams Field, Burghfield (Crockett 1996), but otherwise evidence is limited to a few residual or unstratified finds such as a late Neolithic flake and Beaker sherds from Anslow's Cottages (Butterworth and Lobb 1992). A paucity of structural features associated with settlement in the late Neolithic and early Bronze Age is a common pattern in many areas of southern England, and suggests that material was often deposited in surface spreads or middens rather than cut features (Garrow 2006).

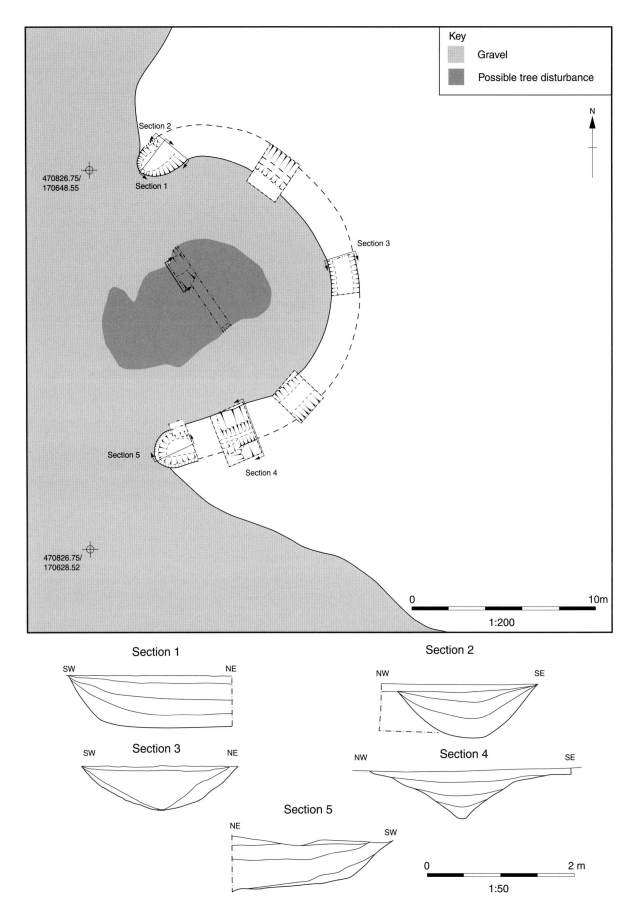

Fig. 6.2   C-shaped ring ditch, Reading Sewage Treatment Works

Little is known of the contemporary environment of the Lower Kennet Valley, although at Anslow's Cottages it has been argued that alder carr on the floodplain had been partly cleared for grazing by the late Neolithic/early Bronze Age, with the higher gravel terrace supporting some arable agriculture (Butterworth and Lobb 1992, 172).

The evidence suggests that the Lower Kennet Valley was similar to much of southern England during this period in that settlement was fairly mobile, with people moving through the landscape on a seasonal basis, coming together and dispersing at different times of year. Burial monuments provided 'fixed points' in the landscape that were foci for repeated visits or seasonal gatherings (Brück 1999a). In this way the monuments may have helped to articulate claims to land and resources, perhaps instituting a system of land tenure that prefigured the field systems of the later Bronze Age (see below).

Later Bronze Age settlement and farming

Middle Bronze Age settlement at Green Park 3 and Moores Farm

At both Green Park 3 and Moores Farm, field boundary ditches were laid out during the middle Bronze Age, and waterholes or pit-wells were constructed to secure the supply of water for people and livestock. Artefacts from the field boundaries and waterholes, as well as scattered pits and other features, provide evidence for episodes of settlement within the field systems.

At Green Park 3, a fairly regular layout of rectangular fields was constructed. Five waterholes were distributed across the field system, all located close to field edges or corners. One of the waterholes produced a piece of 'plashed' roundwood suggesting that the field boundaries were augmented by hedges. The main period of use of both the field system and waterholes appears to have been in the middle Bronze Age. Radiocarbon dates from the lower fills of the waterholes indicate that these were in active use between *c* 1450–1250 cal BC. The ceramics from the waterholes and field boundary ditches consist mostly of middle Bronze Age Deverel-Rimbury wares, but also include some non-Deverel-Rimbury or 'transitional' material. Morris (Chapters 2, 4 and 5) argues that both pottery types were in contemporary use during the later 2nd millennium BC at this site, but the possibility that some of the deposition of non-Deverel-Rimbury pottery relates to continued use of the field system into the late Bronze Age 'proper' cannot be discounted. Other than the material from the field boundary ditches and waterholes, evidence for occupation was limited to two small pits. Overall, finds from the Bronze Age features were generally very sparse, though with a distinct clustering in the north-western part of the excavated area, in and around waterhole 2690 (Fig. 2.3). The sparseness of the features and finds from the site as a whole could

imply that it was peripheral to a settlement core lying outside the excavated area, but this need not necessarily be the case given the slight character of much of the middle Bronze Age settlement evidence from the wider region (see below).

The field system at Moores Farm was laid out across the area between the two palaeochannels. While the full extent of the field system was not uncovered, it seems to have consisted of fields of varying sizes and forms, demarcated by both straight and curving ditches. In some places the field boundaries consisted of a pair of parallel ditches, which may have lain either side of a bank or hedge, as seen in other Bronze Age field systems in the region (Yates 1999, 165–6). Middle Bronze Age occupation within the field system was concentrated in Area 16, where shallow pits, postholes, and two possible ovens were found in a loose swathe 125m across. No buildings could be identified, and the sparse distribution of finds gives little indication of any focus to the activity. A number of contemporary waterholes were also found within the field system, scattered around the periphery of the settlement area. There is little evidence that the field system continued in use beyond the middle Bronze Age. No diagnostic late Bronze Age finds were recovered from the field boundary ditches or waterholes, and it seems likely that the ditches had already largely silted up by the time the site was resettled in the early Iron Age (see below). Fragments of two late Bronze Age-type type ovoid jars were, however, recovered from the site as unstratified material.

It has often been argued that later Bronze Age field systems in southern England were primarily associated with livestock husbandry (Pryor 1996; Yates 2007). The environmental evidence from the waterholes at Green Park 3 and Moores Farm might support this. Pollen analysis, augmented by insect evidence at Green Park 3, suggests an open landscape dominated by grassland; cereals provide no more than 2% of the pollen totals at either site. Given, however, that cereal pollen tends not to travel far from its source, it remains possible that some arable cultivation was occurring in the vicinity. Either way, the sparse charred plant remains provide no evidence for large-scale cereal processing at either site; just a few grains of barley were found, along with a single grain of wheat from Moores Farm. Survival of faunal remains was poor, but cattle, sheep/goat, horse and red deer were present at both sites, with pig also found at Moores Farm.

The repertoire of artefacts recovered from the two sites was fairly limited, including pottery, worked flint and saddle querns. Wooden bowls, a wooden ladle and a shale bracelet fragment were also found within the waterholes at Green Park 3 (see below). Thus while food processing and consumption were certainly taking place, direct evidence for crafts such as textile production or metalworking is lacking. It is notable that there are no examples of the cylindrical fired clay 'loomweights' (or oven bricks: Woodward 2009) found at Green Park 1 and 2 and many other later Bronze Age sites in the Lower Kennet Valley (Bradley *et al.* 1980; Johnston 1985; Lobb 1990; Piggott 1938).

Waterholes: use and decommissioning

Waterholes or pit-wells are a characteristic feature of later Bronze Age field systems and settlements in southern England. Indeed, the later Bronze Age was the period in which such features first appear in the archaeological record in any numbers (Evans 1999; Yates 2007).

At Green Park 3, the waterholes could be divided into two categories. There were three teardrop-shaped waterholes, each with a sloping access ramp leading to a timber-revetted platform, and two steep-sided waterholes that lacked surviving timber structures. Coincidentally or not, each of the steep-sided waterholes appears to have been paired with a ramped waterhole, one pair occurring within the eastern block of the field system and the other in the western block. At Moores Farm, only steep-sided waterholes were present, none of which produced any evidence for timber structures. It is likely that the two categories of waterhole were used and thought of in different ways. It would be tempting to suggest that one type of waterhole provided water for human consumption and the other for livestock, but this is difficult to demonstrate. In fact, it is not obvious that either type of waterhole was particularly well suited for use by livestock. During times when the water level was low, many of the steep-sided waterholes would have required ladders or a suspended bucket to draw water. The ramped waterholes could be directly accessed, but it is questionable whether the wooden revetment/ platform structures would have survived for long under livestock trampling. It is of course possible that livestock were watered from either category of feature through the rather labour intensive method of using buckets to transport water to nearby troughs; alternatively they were simply driven to rivers or other natural water sources.

Another characteristic which distinguishes the two categories of waterhole is the nature of the material deposited within them during and after their period of use. While the steep-sided water-holes generally produced few finds, the ramped, timber-revetted waterholes at Green Park 3 contained some unusual objects (Table 2.2). Material entering the waterholes while they were still in use included wooden vessels, a human tibia fragment and a buzzard bone. After the waterholes had gone out of use, material deposited in their upper fills included a large group of pottery sherds (waterhole 2690) and a shale bracelet fragment from a source *c* 120km away in Dorset (waterhole 3091). Small amounts of cremated human bone were also recovered from the upper fills of two of the waterholes. Any wooden objects within the upper fills would of course not have survived.

Material recovered from later Bronze Age water-holes is often interpreted in terms of 'special', 'structured' or ritual deposition (Yates 2007, 16; Lambrick 2009, 285, 287). This is particularly the case where complete artefacts or other 'odd' finds occur. Examples from the Thames Valley include a complete globular urn placed at the base of middle Bronze Age waterhole at Kingsmead Quarry, Horton, Berkshire (TWA n.d.) and complete pots and a Neolithic stone axe head from waterholes at Perry Oaks, West London (Framework Archaeology 2006). The lower fill of a late Bronze Age waterhole at Green Park 1 (see below) contained a worked human skull fragment, shaped into a disc and perforated, along with a perforated wooden disc of a similar size – perhaps a representation of a second skull. Human remains have also been recovered from later Bronze Age waterholes at sites such as Shorncote Quarry, Gloucestershire (Brossler *et al.* 2002) and Watkins Farm, Northmoor, Oxfordshire (Allen 1990, 8–10). Brück (1999b) has drawn attention to comparable deliberate deposits in a range of feature types within later Bronze Age settlements, arguing that these acts of deposition served to mark significant points in the life cycle of the settlement and its inhabitants, such as the foundation or break up of a household unit. It is possible that the wooden objects and human tibia from the lower fills of the ramped waterholes at Green Park 3 were deliberate deposits of this kind that marked the construction of the waterholes, or served as offerings to maintain a supply of good, fresh water. The significance of the material from the upper fills of the waterholes is more difficult to resolve. Morris (Chapter 2) suggests that pottery from the upper fills of waterhole 2690 was carefully selected to include particular elements of both Deverel-Rimbury and non-Deverel-Rimbury vessels. This is an intriguing possibility, but overall the fragmented and mixed character of the pottery and other material from the upper fills of the waterholes arguably shows little to distinguish it from general 'occupation' or midden material. The presence of small amounts of cremated human bone within two of the waterholes may seem inconsistent with this. However, similar tiny deposits of cremated human bone are commonly found at later Bronze Age settlements in association with otherwise typical occupation material (Brudenell and Cooper 2008). At Green Park 2 (Area 3000B), for example, three pits and postholes within the later Bronze Age settlement area each contained 1–11g of cremated bone (Boyle 2004b). It has generally been assumed that cremated bone deposits of this kind were deliberate and meaningful, often being described as 'token burials' (Brück 2006a, 2006b; Guttmann and Last 2000). This approach has been critiqued by Brudenell and Cooper, who argue for more attention to the complexities of depositional processes at later Bronze Age sites. They argue that cremated human bone may often have been incorporated into middens or the general occupation matrix some time before their ultimate deposition. "It has perhaps too often been assumed that formality was enacted at the moment that human fragments were interred in the ground, rather than much earlier in their pre-depositional histories...By the time that human remains were caught up in cut features of the settlement, their previous identities, and even their presence in the material being deposited, may not have been clear" (2008, 29–30). While the material from the upper fills of the waterholes thus need not have been consciously 'structured', it remains possible that there was some significance behind the incorporation of midden or occupation material into these features at the time of their decommissioning. The fact that it was specifically the ramped, timber-revetted waterholes that were a focus for such acts of deposition could possibly hint that these were particularly important as sources of water for human consumption.

Interpreting the field systems of the Green Park/ Moores Farm landscape

The fields at Moores Farm and Green Park 3 formed only part of a wider pattern of later Bronze Age land division extending across the local landscape (Fig. 6.3). The Green Park 3 fields appear to be a direct continuation of the rectilinear field system uncovered 200m to the north-east in Area 3000B/3100 (Green Park 1 and 2), which followed an identical NNE-SSW axis. This shared axis breaks down further to the north, in Areas 5000, 6000 and 7000 (Green Park 1), where an irregular group of fields or enclosures on varying alignments has been uncovered. A few ditches probably representing further field boundaries were also found to the east in Areas 3, 5 and 6 (Green Park 1). The field boundary ditches investigated during the Green Park 1 excavations were ascribed to the late Bronze Age, though dating evidence was evidently scant; no pottery from the ditches is illustrated in the report, and it appears that the only diagnostic late Bronze Age form recovered was a single coarse jar from Area 7000 (Moore and Jennings 1992, table 15). Those ditches investigated during the Green Park 2 excavations contained both middle and late Bronze Age pottery, though only in the upper fills (Brossler *et al.* 2004, 15). Importantly, however, a clear stratigraphic sequence could be seen in Area 3000B/3100 whereby the field system was replaced by a 'nucleated' late Bronze Age settlement (see below). Elsewhere in the Green Park/Moores Farm landscape, two ditches containing Bronze Age pottery and flint were encountered in the Substation evaluation, and at Hartley Court Farm a number of shallow ditches were uncovered that may belong to this period, although few finds were recovered.

Later Bronze Age fields thus covered much of the Green Park/Moores Farm landscape, extending across a total area of *c* 2 x 2km. However, it should be stressed that the fields did not form a single, coherent system similar to the very large coaxial landscapes seen in some other parts of the Thames Valley, although at locations such as the Heathrow area of west London these coaxial systems (eg Framework Archaeology 2006, fig. 3.1) are only part of the story, as subsequent work has demnstrated the existence of broadly contemporary coaxial and 'aggregate' field landscapes, as well as unenclosed 'common' land (eg Framework Archaeology 2010, fig. 3.1) and increasing diversity of field system arrangements (ibid., 375). At Green Park/Moores Farm, on a similar scale, although less intensively examined, there were small blocks of fields on varying alignments, possibly with unenclosed areas between (such as Area 3017 at Green Park 2). It is should also be noted that the fields show more than one phase of development. At both Moores Farm and Green Park 1 and 2 (Area 3000B/3100), ditches were realigned and fields added and altered over time. Overall, the evidence is suggestive of a landscape that developed fairly organically over an extended period, rather than being created in a single grand act of landscape planning. Compared to the large-scale coaxial landscapes seen elsewhere, the Green Park/Moores Farm field systems may have been created within a very different social context. Tenure may have been articulated on a more local level, with decisions being made by smaller social units (cf. Johnston 2005; Cooper and Edmonds 2007).

It is likely that this process of decision-making referenced pre-existing landscape arrangements or systems of tenure. Elsewhere in southern England, later Bronze Age field systems often respected or were aligned upon earlier monuments such as barrows or ring ditches. It has thus been argued that these monuments were in effect precursors of the field systems, marking claims to land which were subsequently developed or made more explicit by the ditched field boundaries (Evans and Knight 2000; Johnston 2005; Yates 2007, 134; Cooper and Edmonds 2007, 133). In the Green Park landscape, it is notable that the ring ditch in Area 3100 and that found in the Pingewood excavations (see above) together form a NNE-SSW alignment identical to axis followed by the surrounding field system (Fig. 6.3). In fact, a major ditch corner within the field system lay directly adjacent to the ring ditch in Area 3100. While the lack of finds from the ring ditches leaves their chronological relationship to the field system unproven, it can be suggested that the fields were laid out following an existing alignment of monuments.

There is as yet no evidence that the creation of field systems in the Green Park/Moores Farm landscape was replicated elsewhere in the Lower Kennet Valley. It has been claimed that ditches found in an evaluation 2km to the south-west of Moores Farm at Diddenham Manor Farm, Grazeley represent a middle Bronze Age field system (Yates 1999, 158; 2007, 152), but in fact these features produced no dating evidence (Lobb and Rose 1996, 121). There is no sign that field systems continued

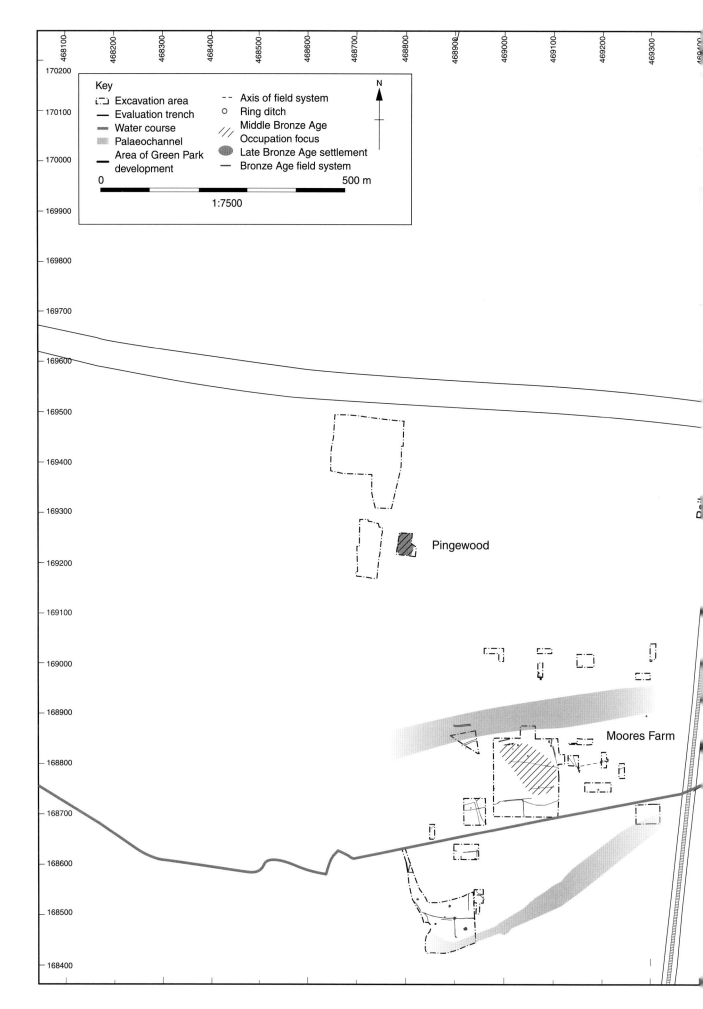

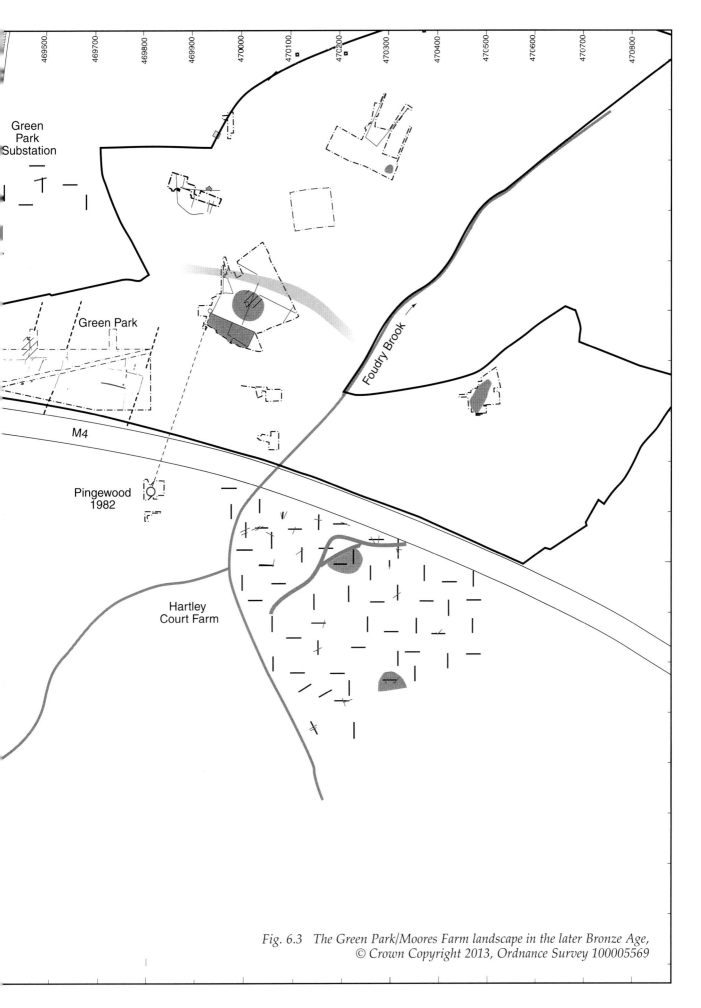

Green
Park
Substation

Green Park

Foudry Brook

M4

Pingewood
1982

Hartley
Court Farm

*Fig. 6.3   The Green Park/Moores Farm landscape in the later Bronze Age,
© Crown Copyright 2013, Ordnance Survey 100005569*

along the gravel terrace to the west of Green Park/Moores Farm at excavated sites such as Pingewood (Johnston 1985), Field Farm (Butterworth and Lobb 1992), Knight's Farm or Aldermaston Wharf (Bradley *et al.* 1980), despite the presence of later Bronze Age occupation in each case. Further excavation could alter the picture, of course, and it should also be acknowledged that shallow field boundary ditches might have been missed in the problematic conditions of some of the earlier rescue excavations in the Kennet Valley. Nonetheless, it does seem that ditched field systems were not an essential element of settlement complexes in this period.

The development of later Bronze Age settlement in the Green Park/Moores Farm landscape and beyond

As we have seen, middle Bronze Age occupation within the field systems at Green Park 3 and Moores Farm left only slight archaeological traces in the form of shallow pits and postholes, and sparse scatters of finds from field boundaries and waterholes. Any buildings must have been constructed in a manner that did not deeply penetrate the ground. Elsewhere in the Green Park/Moores Farm landscape, middle Bronze Age settlement evidence is similarly 'scrappy'. In Area 3000B (Green Park 2), occupation within the field system was attested by a few sherds of pottery recovered from the field boundary ditches and a waterhole, and a single pit containing a semi-complete Deverel-Rimbury vessel. An urned cremation burial radiocarbon dated to 1260–840 cal BC was also found adjacent to a field boundary. In Areas 5 and 7000 (Green Park 1), some late Bronze Age settlement features produced small quantities of middle Bronze Age pottery, but contemporary features were elusive.

The inhabitation of this landscape changed character in the late Bronze Age, with the appearance of well-defined settlements associated with plain ware TLBA pottery (see Morris, Chapter 5) in Areas 5 and 3000B/3100 (Fig. 6.3). In Area 5, two clusters of post-built roundhouses were uncovered, with associated four- and six-post 'granary' structures, fence lines and pits. Twenty roundhouses were present in total, although many of these overlapped, so that the number of buildings standing at any one time must have been much lower. While plain ware pottery predominated, small amounts of decorated pottery were also recovered, indicating that the settlement continued to be occupied into the latter part of the late Bronze Age or the earliest Iron Age. This material was concentrated in the southern cluster of roundhouses, suggesting a southwards shift in the focus of occupation over time. The late Bronze Age settlement in Area 3000B/3100 consisted of two discrete clusters of roundhouses, four- and six-post structures, pits and waterholes. It is clear that the settlement post-dated the field system in this area, demonstrated by the fact that a number of settle-

ment features cut the field boundary ditches. Fifteen roundhouses were identified, though again there were many overlaps. A sharply demarcated 'blank' area between the two settlement clusters could represent a thoroughfare or trackway. Decorated wares were concentrated in the southern cluster, again suggesting a southwards shift in the focus of occupation over time. Probably at around the same time as this southwards settlement shift, a large burnt mound began to accumulate at the northern edge of the site. Pollen analysis of one of the waterholes associated with the settlement in Area 3000B/3100 produced greater evidence for arable cultivation (8% cereal pollen: Scaife 2004) than the middle Bronze Age waterholes at Green Park 3 and Moores Farm, perhaps implying a shift to increased cereal production during the late Bronze Age. Elsewhere in the Green Park/Moores Farm landscape, pit clusters representing smaller-scale foci of late Bronze Age activity were found in Areas 3017 (Green Park 2) and 7000 (Green Park 1), and two concentrations of late Bronze Age features were found in the Hartley Court Farm evaluation.

There is abundant evidence for middle and late Bronze Age settlement elsewhere in the Lower Kennet Valley, forming one of the densest known concentrations of occupation of this period in southern England. During the middle Bronze Age, several sites are known on the gravel terrace to the west of Green Park and Moores Farm. The 1977 excavations at Pingewood uncovered a swathe of pits and postholes in an area 50m across, producing 10kg of Bronze Age pottery. Some of the postholes were interpreted as belonging to fence lines or buildings, though in no case is the plan of these structures clear (Johnston 1985). The pottery included both Deverel-Rimbury and non-Deverel-Rimbury material, and Morris (Chapter 5) argues that this represents a 'transitional' assemblage similar to that from Green Park 3. A subsequent watching brief showed that the excavated features at Pingewood formed part of a much more extensive, dispersed spread of later Bronze Age occupation, though few details are available (Lobb and Mills 1993). To the west of Pingewood, at the adjacent sites of Knight's Farm (Bradley *et al.* 1980) and Field Farm (Butterworth and Lobb 1992), Burghfield, middle Bronze Age pits and postholes were found across an extensive area in and around a major ring ditch cluster. Features dating to the late Bronze Age and earliest Iron Age were also found, and the evidence suggests a polyfocal, shifting settlement pattern. At Field Farm, cremation burials contained within Deverel-Rimbury vessels were interred within or close to a number of ring ditches, one of which had previously been a focus for burial during the early Bronze Age. Fragments of middle Bronze Age pottery not associated with human remains were also found in the fills of several ring ditches at this site. Nearby, ring ditches at Heron's House (Bradley and Richards 1980) and Amner's Farm (Lobb 1985) also produced Deverel-Rimbury pottery, in the latter case inserted into the upper fills of a monument that had previously seen use in the early Bronze Age. Further to the west, at Brimpton, hollows and soil layers overlying a silted palaeo-channel contained finds including pottery, animal bone and a bronze spearhead (Lobb 1990). As at Green Park 3 and Pingewood, the pottery assemblage combines Deverel-Rimbury and 'transitional' elements (Morris, Chapter 5). Little is known of settlement on higher ground surrounding the valley, but a middle Bronze Age cremation burial has been found close to a ring ditch at Field Farm, Sulhamstead (Stoten 2008), and Deverel-Rimbury cremation cemeteries not associated with monuments are known at Sulham (Shrubsole 1907; Barrett 1973) and Shortheath Lane, Sulhamstead (Lobb 1992).

During the late Bronze Age, in addition to the scattered occupation at Knight's Farm and Field Farm, Burghfield, a settlement has been investigated on the gravel terrace at Aldermaston Wharf (Bradley *et al.* 1980). A pair of roundhouses was uncovered, lying within a fairly compact cluster of pits and postholes, associated with plain ware TLBA pottery. Large quantities of pottery and other finds were recovered, comparable in size to the assemblages found at Green Park 1 and 2 (Fig. 6.4). On the Kennet floodplain at Anslow's Cottages, a timber structure found at the edge of a palaeochannel is interpreted as a possible landing stage or revetment. One of the timbers produced a radiocarbon date of 840–510 cal BC (HAR-9186: 2570±70 BP), placing it in the latter stages of the late Bronze Age or in the early Iron Age. Burnt flint concentrations at the edge of the river channel could represent burnt mounds. Late Bronze Age pottery was recovered from pits and palaeochannel fills, though it was argued that there was no permanent settlement on the site during this period (Butterworth and Lobb 1992). Late Bronze Age activity is also attested at Cod's Hill (Lobb and Rose 1996, 81), Reading Football Club, Theale Ballast Hole and Marshall's Hill, though few details are known about these sites. At Reading Football Club, a short distance to the east of Green Park, late Bronze

Age/early Iron Age pottery has been recovered from a palaeochannel and a pond (TWA 1997; 1999). At Theale Ballast Hole, late Bronze Age pottery and cylindrical loomweights were recovered during quarrying in the early 20th century (S Piggott 1935; C M Piggott 1938). At Marshall's Hill, on the high ground overlooking the eastern end of the Kennet Valley, a circular earthwork described as a possible disc barrow was observed in 1907–9 but subsequently destroyed without record. Late Bronze Age/early Iron Age pottery (including haematite-coated wares) was found 'within' the earthwork, and Bronze Age metalwork in its vicinity, but there is no stratigraphic context for these finds (Seaby 1932). Bradley (1986) has suggested that the site could have been a high-status late Bronze Age ringwork similar to examples known elsewhere in the Thames Valley, and Yates (1999; 2007) includes it in his class of late Bronze Age 'aggrandised enclosures'. However, the enclosure appears to have been very small and seems unlikely to have been related to this category of site (Allen *et al.* 2010, 250).

Drawing together the evidence from Green Park/Moores Farm and other local sites, the following observations can be made about the inhabitation of the Lower Kennet Valley between *c* 1500–800 BC. The stereotype of middle Bronze Age settlement in southern Britain is of farmsteads or hamlets consisting of a cluster of roundhouses and other structures, often set within an enclosure – an image derived largely from excavations on the chalk downlands of Wessex and Sussex (Brück 2000, 285; 2007, 25). Although a number of middle and transitional Bronze Age occupation sites have now been found in the Lower Kennet Valley, none correspond to this stereotype. Rather, the signature of settlement consists of loose swathes of pits and postholes, and deposits of pottery and other material within field boundary ditches, waterholes and ring ditches. The postholes indicate that structures of some kind existed, but as no clearly interpretable building plans survive these were probably quite lightly built. Whether these occupation areas represent permanent, long-lasting settlements must

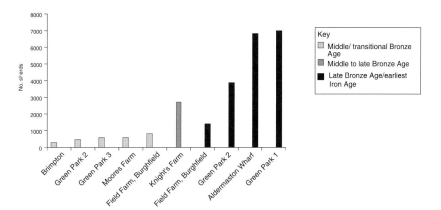

Fig. 6.4   Pottery assemblages from later Bronze Age sites in the Lower Kennet Valley, quantification by numbers of sherds

be open to question. An alternative possibility would be that there was a pattern of shifting settlement within this landscape of fields and burial monuments, with people perhaps moving on a seasonal basis or at intervals of a few years. The situation changed in the late Bronze Age with the appearance of well-defined settlements with more robust post-built roundhouses at Green Park 1–2 and Aldermaston Wharf, similar buildings occurring in alsightly different context at Hartshill Copse (Collard *et al.* 2006). Crucially, it is clear that one of the Green Park settlements post-dated the abandonment of the network of field boundaries at this site. Ring ditches were also no longer maintained during this period, or at least ceased to be a focus for deposition of burials or artefacts. It is notable that many of roundhouses at the Green Park settlements were rebuilt one or more times on the same spot, suggesting a long-term investment in place of residence not seen at the middle Bronze Age sites (cf Brück 1999b; 2007). It is also instructive to compare the quantities of finds recovered from the middle and late Bronze Age sites in the area. Figure 6.4 shows the size of the pottery assemblages from sites for which data is available. This is only a crude measure, which takes no account of variations in the areas or proportions of features excavated, but it does demonstrate that late Bronze Age sites typically produce much greater quantities of material. This may be a reflection of a trend towards longer and more intense occupation in a single location, although changes in depositional practices could also have played a role.

It could be merely fortuitous that well-ordered middle Bronze Age farmsteads and hamlets producing large quantities of finds have not been found in the Lower Kennet Valley, and further excavation may yet change the picture. It is possible, for example, that the main focus of settlement in this period was in a different part of the landscape, away from the fields and monuments on the gravel terraces. However, the possibility that middle and late Bronze Age settlements were genuinely very different in character should be entertained. Looking beyond the Lower Kennet Valley, the stereotypical middle Bronze Age 'farmstead' has been equally elusive in neighbouring parts of the Middle Thames region, despite extensive excavation over the past two decades (Ford 2003, 157; Lambrick 2009). Excavated field systems at sites such as Eton Rowing Lake (T Allen pers. comm.) and Weir Bank Stud Farm, Bray (Barnes and Cleal 1995) have produced scattered traces of middle Bronze Age occupation similar to those seen at Green Park and Moores Farm, with buildings again difficult to identify. A post-built roundhouse was found within the Bray field system, but this produced late Bronze Age pottery as well as Deverel-Rimbury material and probably post-dated the use of the field system (Barnes and Cleal 1995, 48), mirroring the sequence at Green Park 1–2. Many of the field systems in the wider

Middle Thames region respected barrows or ring ditches (eg at Eton Rowing Lake), which often continued to be foci for activity. For example, a ring ditch at Cippenham near Slough contained what is described as a 'midden deposit' in its upper fill, comprising middle Bronze Age pottery, flint, fired clay and charcoal. While this deposit could have resulted from some form of mortuary ritual, the excavator argues that it is more likely to represent the residues of occupation in the vicinity of the monument (Ford 2003).

The middle Bronze Age has often been seen as a turning point in southern British prehistory, marking a decisive shift from the 'ritual landscapes' of the Neolithic and early Bronze Age to the more familiar settled agricultural landscapes that characterise later periods (eg Yates 2007). The appearance of field systems at this time is certainly a significant development, likely to relate to developments in farming practices, even if assumptions of widespread 'intensification' of agriculture at this time can be questioned (Brück 2000). In the Lower Kennet and Middle Thames, however, the evidence suggests that in at least some respects the middle Bronze Age may not have been so very different from the early Bronze Age. The newly laid out field systems often respected existing monuments and hence perhaps existing tenurial arrangements. The traces of middle Bronze Age occupation found within and beyond the field systems are suggestive of a pattern of dispersed, shifting settlement, challenging the assumption that the appearance of fields must have gone hand in hand with the appearance of permanent farmsteads (Lambrick 2009). The continued significance of barrows and ring ditches as foci for burial and other activity also links the middle Bronze Age to the preceding period. Perhaps the construction of field systems, rather than marking an entirely new regime of settled agriculture, aimed to regulate land allotment in the context of an existing system of shifting settlement. Only in the late Bronze Age do we see the appearance of well-defined settlements with recognisable domestic buildings, which could occupy the same location for generations. The maintenance of field boundaries was probably abandoned at this time in many places, as at Green Park and Moores Farm, and across the region ring ditches seem to have lost much of their role as focal points in the landscape, to judge by the paucity of late Bronze Age finds. These developments may mark an important change in the way that the relationship between people and landscape was articulated. Before, family or community ties to land had been physically expressed by burial places and field systems, which contrasted with the ephemeral nature of settlements. Now, there was greater emphasis on the place of residence, expressed by the construction of more robust and permanent timber buildings, and the deposition of greater quantities of material culture in the domestic sphere.

It should be stressed that these arguments are specific to the Lower Kennet Valley and adjacent areas of the Middle Thames. Other regions of southern Britain, such as the chalklands of Wessex and Sussex (see above) clearly show different trajectories. This underscores the importance of acknowledging regional variation during the later Bronze Age.

Early Iron Age settlement shift

As we have seen, decorated late Bronze Age pottery shows that the late Bronze Age settlements at Green Park Areas 5 and 3000B/3100 continued to be occupied into the closing stages of the Bronze Age or the earliest part of the Iron Age, albeit on a reduced scale and with a slight southwards shift in focus in each case (Morris 2004, 78–80). It seems clear, however, that these settlements had been abandoned by the latter stages of the early Iron Age. In contrast, Moores Farm was resettled around this time. A swathe of early Iron Age pits and postholes was found across the area previously occupied by the middle Bronze Age settlement, focused on a discrete cluster of pits set into a shallow hollow (pit group 2042), which produced a large proportion of the finds from the site. Two radiocarbon dates from the pit group calibrate to the late 8th to 4th centuries BC, and the pottery suggests that this can be narrowed down to *c* 700–400 BC (Brown, Chapter 4). The significance of the pit group is unclear, partly as a result of difficulties in disentangling the stratigraphic relationships of the individual pits. The pits are difficult to explain as quarries, but equally they do not closely resemble the cylindrical or bell-shaped storage pits known from other Iron Age sites. One possibility could be that the dense tangle of features relates to a multiple phase building of some kind; certainly, the sub-circular area of *c* 9m across occupied by the pit group falls within the size range of contemporary round-houses. Aside from pottery, finds from the early Iron Age settlement included saddle querns and fired clay loomweights or oven bricks. Environmental and economic evidence was scant, though cattle, horse, pig and red deer bone was recovered, along with a few grains of wheat and barley.

Elsewhere in the Lower Kennet Valley, there are a few other sides belonging to the period following *c* 800 BC. The neighbouring late Bronze Age sites of Knights Farm and Field Farm, Burghfield, seem to show at least some continuity of occupation into the early Iron Age. At Knight's Farm, the latest radiocarbon date of 750 cal BC–50 cal AD (BM-1595: 2240±120 BP) was associated with a fingertip-decorated vessel of late Bronze Age or early Iron Age type (Bradley *et al*. 1980, 274), while at Field Farm a good early Iron Age pottery assemblage was recovered from a single pit (Butterworth and Lobb 1992, 46). At Wickhams Field, an enclosure and trackway were laid out during the early Iron Age (Crockett 1996), and pottery of this period has also been recovered from Theale Ballast Hole (Piggott 1938). The finds from Moores Farm and Wickhams Field dispel earlier arguments that this part of the Kennet Valley 'was clearly abandoned' in the early Iron Age (Lobb and Rose 1996, 84), though interpretation of the character of settlement and land use in this period remains difficult, in part due to the paucity of environmental evidence.

The end of prehistory

Occupation at Moores Farm had ceased by the end of the early Iron Age, and there is no evidence for further significant activity at the site prior to the post-medieval period. Alluvial layers sealed many of the Bronze Age and early Iron Age features, suggesting that increased wetness and seasonal or periodic flooding became an issue at some point from the later prehistoric period onwards. However, as the date of these alluvial deposits is uncertain it is not known whether flooding was a factor in the abandonment of the early Iron Age settlement.

At Green Park 3, a series of ditches demarcating boundaries or enclosures was established in the middle to late Iron Age. Other contemporary features were limited to a few shallow pits and a late Iron Age cremation burial placed within a wheel-thrown vessel. The low density of finds and paucity of charred plant material from the pits and ditches suggest that the main focus of occupation lay outside the excavated area, although no other evidence for later Iron Age activity has yet been found elsewhere at Green Park. The Iron Age boundaries developed into a more regular, rectilinear field system in the 1st to 2nd centuries AD. The sparse finds indicate that these boundaries remained peripheral to contemporary settlement. The Romano-British fields were probably associated with the settlement 250m to the east in Area 2000 (Green Park 1), where enclosures and pits ranging in date from the 1st to 4th centuries AD were uncovered (Moore and Jennings 1992). The fields at Green Park 3 appear to have formed one element of much more widespread land division across the Green Park area during the Roman period. Further Romano-British fields or enclosures have been found in Area 7000 (Green Park 1), 600m to the north-east of Green Park 3 (Moore and Jennings 1992), and at Pingewood, 150m to the south (Lobb and Mills 1993). Further possible Romano-British field boundaries were encountered during the evaluation at Hartley Court Farm, 200m to the south-east of Green Park 3, though these could be associated with the late 3rd to 4th century settlement found at the southern end of the evaluated area (OA 1991a; Keevill 1992). Probable ploughsoils of Roman date found in the vicinity of the settlement in Area 2000 indicate that arable farming was carried out.

A pattern of dense later Iron Age and Roman settlement and enclosure can be seen across the Lower Kennet Valley, an area that lay within the hinterland of the late Iron Age 'oppidum' and Roman town of Silchester, 10km to the south-west of Green Park. At Little Lea Park, 2km south-east of Green Park 3, a small middle Iron Age enclosure developed into a larger ladder-like enclosure system with associated roundhouses during the late Iron Age and Roman period (Lambrick 2009, 117, there labelled 'Lower Lea Farm'). At Pingewood, 1km south-west of Green Park 3, excavations within an extensive cropmark complex identified at least two late Iron Age cremation burials and a settlement of the 1st-2nd centuries AD, comprising a series of enclosures flanking a trackway (Johnston 1985). On the Kennet flood-plain, a late Iron Age cremation burial and Roman occupation levels have been found at the Cunning Man site (Boon and Wymer 1958). Further to the east, excavated sites include a middle Iron Age settlement at Southcote (Piggott and Seaby 1937); middle to late Iron Age activity at Theale Ballast Hole (S Piggott 1935; C M Piggott 1938); successive

middle to late Iron Age and late Roman settlements at Aldermaston Wharf (Cowell *et al.* 1978); Roman settlement enclosures and a trackway at Wickhams Field (Crockett 1996); late Iron Age and Roman enclosures at Ufton Nervet (Manning 1974); and a Roman settlement at Meales Farm, Sulhamstead (Lobb *et al.* 1990). While a number of theses sites show continuity from the later Iron Age into the Roman period, it is notable that continuity from the early to later Iron Age is generally absent. The one possible exception is Theale Ballast Hole, where both early and later Iron Age pottery were recovered, but the absence of stratigraphic information for these finds (made during quarrying in the early 20th century) leaves the relationship between the two phases of occupation unclear. The evidence from the Lower Kennet Valley as a whole thus seems to match that from the Green Park/Moores Farm landscape in suggesting a dislocation in the settlement pattern between the early and later Iron Age.

Bibliography

Allen, J R L and Allen, S, 1997 A stratified prehistoric site from the Kennet floodplain at Ufton Nervet, Berkshire, *Berkshire Archaeol J* **75**, 1–8

Allen, M J, 2000 Taphonomy and species of the samples, in Lawson 2000, 40–1

Allen, T, 1990 *An Iron Age and Romano-British enclosed settlement at Watkins Farm, Northmoor, Oxon*, Thames Valley Landscapes Monograph: the Windrush Valley **1**, Oxford

Allen, T, Cramp, K, Lamdin-Whymark, H and Webley, L, 2010 *Castle Hill and its landscape; Archaeological Investigations at the Wittenhams, Oxfordshire*, Oxford Archaeol Monogr No. **9**, Oxford

Ambers, J and Leese, M, 1996 The radiocarbon results and their interpretation, in Needham and Spence 1996, 78–82

Andersen, S T, 1979 Identification of wild grass and cereal pollen, *Danmarks Geologiske Undersøgelse Årbog* **1978**, 69–92

Andrews, P, 1996 Hurst Park, East Molesey, Surrey: riverside settlement and burial from the Neolithic to the early Saxon periods, in Andrews and Crockett 1996, 51–104

Andrews, P and Crockett, A, 1996 *Three excavations along the Thames and its tributaries, 1994*, Wessex Archaeol Rep **10**, Salisbury

Anon., 1964 Archaeological notes from Reading Museum, *Berkshire Archaeol J* **61**, 96–109

Barclay, A, 2001 Later prehistoric pottery, in Barclay *et al.* 2001, 127–39

Barclay, A, 2002 Ceramic lives, in *Prehistoric Britain: the ceramic basis* (eds A Woodward and J D Hill), 85–95, Oxford

Barclay, A, Bradley, R, Hey, G and Lambrick, G, 1996 The earlier prehistory of the Oxford region in the light of recent research, *Oxoniensia* **61**, 1–20

Barclay, A, Boyle, A and Keevill, G D, 2001 A prehistoric enclosure at Eynsham Abbey, Oxfordshire, *Oxoniensia* **66**, 105–62

Barnes, I and Cleal, R M J, 1995 Neolithic and Bronze Age settlement at Weir Bank Stud Farm, Bray, in Barnes *et al.* 1995, 1–51

Barnes, I, Boismier, W A, Cleal, R M J, Fitzpatrick, A P and Roberts, M R, 1995 *Early settlement in Berkshire*, Wessex Archaeol Rep No **6**, Salisbury

Barrett, J, 1973 Four Bronze Age cremation cemeteries from Middlesex, *Trans London Middlesex Archaeol Soc* **24**, 111–34

Barrett, J, 1980 The pottery of the later Bronze Age in lowland England, *Proc Prehist Soc* **46**, 297–319

Barrett, J and Bradley, R, 1980 The later Bronze Age in the Thames Valley, in *Settlement and society in the British later Bronze Age* (eds J C Barrett and R Bradley), BAR Brit Ser **83**, 247–69, Oxford

Bayliss, A, 2000 Results, in Lawson 2000, 41–2

Bennett, K D, Whittington, G and Edwards, K J, 1994 Recent plant nomenclatural changes and pollen morphology in the British Isles, *Quaternary Newsletter* **73**, 1–6

Birks, H J B, 1973 *Past and present vegetation of the Isle of Skye: a palaeoecological study*, Cambridge

Blake, J H, 1903 *The geology of the country around Reading*, London

Boast, R, 1995 Fine pots, pure pots, Beaker pots, in Kinnes and Varndell 1995, 69–80

Boon, G C and Wymer, J J, 1958 A Belgic cremation burial from Burghfield (Cunning Man site), 1956, *Berkshire Archaeol J* **56**, 46–53

Booth, P, Dodd, A, Robinson, M, and Smith, A, 2007 *The Thames through time; the archaeology of the gravel terraces of the Upper and Middle Thames. The early historical period: AD 1-1000*, Oxford Archaeology Thames Valley Landscapes Mono **27**, Oxford

Boyle, A, 1992 Human remains, in Moore and Jennings 1992, 98

Boyle, A, 2001 Shale, in Barclay *et al.* 2001, 144

Boyle, A, 2004a Shale bracelet, in Brossler *et al.* 2004, 98–9

Boyle, A, 2004b Human skeletal assemblage, in Brossler *et al.* 2004, 106–10

Bradley, P, 2004 Worked flint, in Brossler *et al.* 2004, 45–57

Bradley, R, 1980 Pottery, in Bradley *et al.* 1980, 232–42

Bradley, R, 1985 Prehistoric pottery, in Johnston 1985, 26–8

Bradley, R, 1986 The Bronze Age in the Oxford area: its local and regional significance, in *The archaeology of the Oxford region* (eds G Briggs, J Cook and T Rowley), 38–48, Oxford

Bradley, R and Brown, A, 1992 Flint artefacts, in Moore and Jennings 1992, 89–93

Bradley, R and Ellison, A, 1975 *Rams Hill: a Bronze Age defended enclosure and its landscape*, BAR Brit Ser **19**, Oxford

Bradley, R and Hall, M, 1992 Contexts, chronology and wider associations, in Moore and Jennings 1992, 71–82

Bradley, R and Richards, J, 1980 The excavation of two ring ditches at Heron's House, Burghfield, *Berkshire Archaeol J* **70**, 1–7

Bradley, R, Lobb, S, Richards, J and Robinson, M, 1980 Two late Bronze Age settlements on the Kennet gravels: excavations at Aldermaston

Wharf and Knight's Farm, Burghfield, Berkshire, *Proc Prehist Soc* **46**, 217–95

Bradley, R, Entwistle, R and Raymond, F, 1994 *Prehistoric land divisions on Salisbury Plain: the work of the Wessex Linear Ditches Project*, English Heritage Archaeol Rep **2**, London

Bronk Ramsey, C, 1995 Radiocarbon calibration and analysis of stratigraphy: the OxCal program, *Radiocarbon* **37**, 425–30

Bronk Ramsey, C, 2001 Development of the radio-carbon program OxCal, *Radiocarbon* **43**, 355–63

Brooks, D and Thomas, K W, 1967 The distribution of pollen grains on microscope slides, 1: The non randomness of the distribution, *Pollen and Spores* **9**, 621–9

Brossler, A, Gocher, M, Laws, G and Roberts, M, 2002 Shorncote Quarry: excavations of a late prehistoric landscape in the Upper Thames Valley, 1997 and 1998, *Trans Bristol Gloucestershire Archaeol Soc* **120**, 37–87

Brossler, A, Early, R and Allen, C, 2004 *Green Park (Reading Business Park). Phase 2 excavations 1995: Neolithic and Bronze Age sites*, Thames Valley Landscapes Monogr **19**, Oxford

Brown, N, 1995 Ardleigh reconsidered: Deverel-Rimbury pottery in Essex, in *Unbaked urns of rudely shape: essays on British and Irish pottery for Ian Longworth* (eds I A Kinnes and G Varndell), Oxbow Monogr **55**, 123–44, Oxford

Brück, J, l999a What's in a settlement? Domestic practice and residential mobility in early Bronze Age southern England, in *Making places in the prehistoric world* (eds J Brück and M Goodman), 52–75, London

Brück, J, 1999b Houses, lifecycles and deposition on middle Bronze Age settlements in southern England, *Proc Prehist Soc* **65**, 145–66

Brück, J, 2000 Settlement, landscape and social identity: the early-middle Bronze Age transition in Wessex, Sussex and the Thames Valley, *Oxford J Archaeol* **19**, 273–300

Brück, J, 2006a Fragmentation, personhood and the social construction of technology in middle and late Bronze Age Britain, *Cambridge Archaeol J* **16**, 297–315

Brück, J, 2006b Death, exchange and reproduction in the British Bronze Age, *European J Archaeol* **9**, 73–101

Brück, J, 2007 The character of late Bronze Age settlement in southern Britain, in *The earlier Iron Age in Britain and the near continent* (eds C Haselgrove and R Pope), 24–38, Oxford

Brudenell, M and Cooper, A, 2008 Post-middenism: depositional histories on later Bronze Age settlements at Broom, Bedfordshire, *Oxford J Archaeol* **27**, 15–36

Burleigh, R, Clutton-Brock, J and Gowlett, J, 1991 Early domestic equids in Egypt and western Asia, in *Equids in the ancient world, vol II* (R H Meadow and H-P Uepermann (eds), 9–11, Wiesbaden

Burstow, G P and Holleyman, G A, 1957 Late Bronze Age settlement on Itford Hill, Sussex, *Proc Prehist Soc* **8**, 167–212

Butterworth, C A and Lobb, S J, 1992 *Excavations in the Burghfield Area, Berkshire*, Wessex Archaeol Rep **1**, Salisbury

Care, V, 1985 The flint assemblage, in Johnston 1985, 33–5

Chisham, C, 2006 The upper Palaeolithic and Mesolithic of Berkshire, unpublished draft resource assessment for the *Solent-Thames Archaeological Research Framework*

Cleal, R M J, 1984 The later Neolithic in eastern England, in *Neolithic studies: a review of some current research* (eds R Bradley and J Gardiner), BAR Brit Ser **133**, 135–58, Oxford

Cleal, R M J, 1992 Pottery, in Smith *et al.* 1992, 36–9

Cleal, R M J, 1995 Pottery fabrics in Wessex in the fourth to second millennia BC, in Kinnes and Varndell 1995, 185–94

Cleal, R M J and Raymond, F, 1990 The prehistoric pottery, in *The Stonehenge Environs Project* (ed. J Richards), English Heritage Archaeol Rep **16**, 233–46, London

Collard, M, Darvill, T and Watts, M, 2006 Ironworking in the Bronze Age? Evidence from a 10th century BC settlement at Hartshill Copse, Upper Bucklebury, West Berkshire, *Proc Prehist Soc* **72**, 367-421

Collins, P E F, Worsley, P, Keith-Lucas, D M and Fenwick, I M, 2006 Floodplain environmental change during the Younger Dryas and Holocene in northwest Europe: insights from the lower Kennet Valley, south central England, *Palaeogeography, Palaeoclimatology, Palaeoecology* **233**, 113–33

Cooper, A and Edmonds, M, 2007 *Past and Present. Excavations at Broom, Bedfordshire 1996–2005*, Cambridge

Copley, M, Berstan, R and Evershed, R, 2002 *Was dairying an important element of animal husbandry in prehistoric Britain? Organic residue analysis of Bronze Age pottery vessels from Potterne*, unpubl. archive report, School of Chemistry, Univ. Bristol

Cowell, R W, Fulford, M G and Lobb, S, 1978 Excavations of prehistoric and Roman settlement at Aldermaston Wharf 1976–77, *Berkshire Archaeol J* **69**, 1–35

Crockett, A, 1996 Iron Age to Saxon settlement at Wickhams Field, near Reading, Berkshire: excavations on the site of the M4 Granada Reading Motorway Service Area, in Andrews and Crockett 1996, 113–70

Cunliffe, B, 2005 *Iron Age communities in Britain*, 4th edn, London

Cunliffe, B and Phillipson, D W, 1968 Excavation at Eldon's Seat, Encombe, Dorset, England, *Proc Prehist Soc* **34**, 191–237

Dacre, M and Ellison, A, 1981 A Bronze Age urn cemetery at Kimpton, Hampshire, *Proc Prehist Soc* **47**, 147–203

Daniel, P, 2009 *Archaeological excavations at Pode Hole Quarry – Bronze Age occupation on the Cambridgeshire fen edge*, BAR Brit Ser **484**, Oxford

Darvill, T, 1987 *Prehistoric Britain*, London

Davies, S M, 1981 The late Bronze Age Pottery, in A Bronze Age urn cemetery at Kimpton, Hampshire (M Dacre and A Ellison), *Proc Prehist Soc* **47**, 185

Dewey, H and Bromehead, C E N, 1915 *The Geology of the Country around Windsor and Chertsey*, London

Drewett, P, 1979 New evidence for the structure and function of middle Bronze Age round-houses in Sussex, *Archaeol J* **136**, 3–11

Drewett, P, 1982 Later Bronze Age downland economy and excavations at Black Patch, East Sussex, *Proc Prehist Soc* **48**, 321–400

Earwood, C, 1993 *Domestic wooden artifacts*, Exeter

Ellison, A B, 1975 *Pottery and settlements of the later Bronze Age in southern England*, unpubl. PhD thesis, Univ. Cambridge

Ellison, A, 1978 The Bronze Age, in *Archaeology in Sussex to 1500 A.D.* (ed. P L Drewett), CBA Res Rep **29**, 30–7, London

Ellison, A, 1980 Deverel-Rimbury urn cemeteries: the evidence for social organisation, in *Settlement and society in the British later Bronze Age* (eds J C Barrett and R Bradley), BAR Brit Ser **83**, 115–26, Oxford

Ellison, A, 1982 Middle Bronze Age pottery, in *Archaeology in Sussex to 1500 A.D.* (ed. P L Drewett), CBA Res Rep **29**, 361–8, London

Evans, C, 1999 The Lingwood wells: waterlogged remains from a first millennium BC settlement at Cottenham, Cambridgeshire, *Proc Cambridge Antiq Soc* **87**, 11–30

Evans, C and Knight, M, 2000 A fenland delta: later prehistoric land-use in the lower Ouse reaches, in *Prehistoric, Roman and post-Roman landscapes of the Great Ouse valley* (ed. M Dawson), CBA Res Rep **119**, 89–106

Evans, C, Pollard, J and Knight, M, 1999 Life in woods: tree-throws, 'settlement' and forest cognition, *Oxford J Archaeol* **18**, 241–54

Faegri, K and Iversen, J, 1989 *Textbook of modern pollen analysis*, 4 edn (eds K Faegri, P E Kaaland and K Krzywinski), Chichester

Fasham, P J, 1985 *The prehistoric settlement at Winnall Down, Winchester*, Hampshire Fld Club Archaeol Soc Monogr **2**, Gloucester

Ford, S, 1987 Chronological and functional aspects of flint assemblages, in *Lithic analysis and later British prehistory* (eds A G Brown and M Edmonds), BAR Brit Ser **162**, 67–85, Oxford

Ford, S, 2003 *Excavations at Cippenham, Slough, Berkshire, 1995–7*, TVAS Monogr **3**, Reading

Ford, S, and Roberts, M R, 1995 Discussion, in Excavations at Park Farm, Binfield, Berkshire, 1990: An Iron Age and Romano-British settlement and two Mesolithic flint scatters (M R Roberts), in Barnes *et al.* 1995, 130–2

Framework Archaeology 2006 *Landscape evolution in the Middle Thames Valley. Heathrow Terminal 5 excavations volume 2*, Oxford and Salisbury

Framework Archaeology 2010 *Landscape evolution in the Middle Thames Valley. Heathrow Terminal 5 excavations volume 1, Perry Oaks*, Oxford and Salisbury

Froom, F R, 1972 A Mesolithic site at Wawcott, Kintbury, Berkshire, *Berkshire Archaeol J* **66**, 23–44

Froom, F R, 1976 *Wawcott III: A stratified Mesolithic succession*, BAR Brit Ser **27**, Oxford

Garrow, D, 2006 *Pits, settlement and deposition during the Neolithic and early Bronze Age in East Anglia*, BAR Brit Ser **414**, Oxford

Gates, T, 1975 *The Middle Thames Valley: an archaeological survey of the river gravels*, Reading

Gent, H, 1983 Centralized storage in later prehistoric Britain, *Proc Prehist Soc* **49**, 243–67

Gibson, A, 1995 First impressions: a review of Peterborough Ware in Wales, in Kinnes and Varndell 1995, 23–39

Gibson, A, 2002 *Prehistoric pottery in Britain and Ireland*, Stroud

Gingell, C, 1980 The Marlborough Downs in the Bronze Age: the first results of current research, in *Settlement and society in the British later Bronze Age* (eds J C Barrett and R Bradley), BAR Brit Ser **83**, 209–22, Oxford

Gingell, C, 1992 *The Marlborough Downs: a later Bronze Age landscape and its origins*, Wiltshire Archaeol Soc Monogr **1**, Stroud

Gingell, C J and Lawson, A J, 1984 The Potterne Project: excavation and research at a major settlement of the late Bronze Age, *Wiltshire Archaeol Mag* **78**, 31–4

Gingell, C J and Lawson, A J, 1985 Excavations at Potterne, 1984, *Wiltshire Archaeol Mag* **79**, 101–8

Gingell, C J and Morris, E, 2000 Pottery, Lawson 2000, 136–77

Grant, A, 1982 The use of tooth wear as a guide to the age of domestic ungulates, in *Ageing and sexing animal bones from archaeological sites* (eds R Wilson, C Grigson and S Payne), BAR Brit Ser **109**, 91–108, Oxford

Guttmann, E B A and Last, J, 2000 A Late Bronze Age landscape at South Hornchurch, Greater London, *Proc Prehist So* **66**, 319-359

Hall, M, 1992 The prehistoric pottery, in Moore and Jennings 1992, 63–71

Hall, M and Ford, S, 1994 Archaeological excavations at Grange Road, Gosport, 1992, *Proc Hampshire Fld Club Archaeol Soc* **50**, 5–34

Halstead, P, 1985 A study of mandibular teeth from Romano-British contexts at Maxey, in *Archaeology and environment in the lower Welland Valley* (F M M Pryor and C A I French), East Anglian Archaeol **27**, 219–24

Hamilton, S, 1987 Late Bronze Age pottery, in The excavation of a late Bronze Age site at Yapton,

West Sussex, 1984 (D Rudling), *Sussex Archaeol Collect* **125**, 51–67

Harding, P A, 1992 The flint, in Butterworth and Lobb 1992, 73–8

Harding, P A, 1996 Worked flint, in Crockett 1996, 141–2

Hawkes, C C F, 1935 The pottery from the sites on Plumpton Plain, *Proc Prehist Soc* **3**, 39–59

Hawkes, J W and Fasham, P J, 1997 *Excavations on Reading waterfront sites, 1979–88*, Wessex Archaeol Rep **5**, Salisbury

Heal, V, 1991 The technology of the worked wood and bark, in Needham 1991, 140–1

Healy, F, 1993 The excavation of a ring ditch at Englefield by J Wymer and P Ashbee, 1963, *Berkshire Archaeol J* **74**, 9–25

Healy, F, Heaton, M and Lobb, S J, 1992 Excavations of a Mesolithic site at Thatcham, Berkshire, *Proc Prehist Soc* **58**, 41–76

Hey, G, forthcoming *Yarnton: Neolithic and Bronze Age*, Oxford

Holgate, R, 1988 *Neolithic settlement in the Thames Basin*, BAR Brit Ser **194**, Oxford

IFA, 1999 *Institute of Field Archaeologists standards and guidance for excavation*, London

Inizan, M-L, Roche, H and Tixier, J, 1992 *The technology of knapped stone*, Meudon

Jacobi, R, 1978 The Mesolithic of Sussex, in *Archaeology in Sussex to AD 1500* (ed. P L Drewett), CBA Res Rep **29**, 15–22, London

Jacobson, G L and Bradshaw, R H W, 1981 The selection of sites for palaeovegetational studies, *Quaternary Research* **16**, 80–96

Jarvis, R, 1968 *The soils of the Reading district*, Harpenden

Jennings, D, 1992 Small Finds, in Moore and Jennings 1992, 93–7

Johnson, B, 1975 *Archaeology and the M25, 1971–1975*, Aldershot

Johnston, J, 1985 Excavations at Pingewood, *Berkshire Archaeol J* **72**, 17–52

Johnston, R, 2005 Pattern without a plan: rethinking the Bronze Age coaxial field systems on Dartmoor, south-west England, *Oxford J Archaeol* **24**, 1–21

Keevill, G D, 1992 A frying pan from Great Lea, Binfield [sic], Berkshire, *Britannia* **23**, 231–3

Kinnes, I and Varndell, G, 1995 *Unbaked urns of rudely shape: essays on British and Irish pottery for Ian Longworth*, Oxbow Monogr **55**, Oxford

Kloet, G S and Hincks, W D, 1977 *A check list of British insects, 2 edn (revised): Coleoptera and Strepsiptera*, Royal Entomological Society of London, Handbook for the Identification of British Insects **11**, pt 3, London

Laidlaw, M, 1996a Pottery, in Andrews and Crockett 1996, 81–91

Laidlaw, M, 1996b Pottery, in Andrews and Crockett 1996, 142–50

Lambrick, G, (with Robinson, M and contributions by Allen, T), 2009 *The Thames through time; the archaeology of the gravel terraces of the Upper and Middle Thames. Volume 2: The Thames Valley in late prehistory: 1500 BC–AD 50*, Oxford Archaeol Thames Valley Landscapes Monogr No. **29**, Oxford

Langmaid, N G, 1978 *Prehistoric pottery*, Aylesbury

Lawson, A J, 1976 Shale and jet objects from Silchester, *Antiq J* **105**, 241–76

Lawson, A J, 2000 *Potterne 1982–5: Animal husbandry in later prehistoric Wiltshire*, Wessex Archaeology Rep **17**, Salisbury

Lobb, S J, 1985 Excavation of two ring ditches at Burghfield by R A Rutland, 1969, *Berkshire Archaeol J* **72**, 9–16

Lobb, S J, 1990 Excavations and observations of Bronze Age and Saxon deposits at Brimpton, 1978–9, *Berkshire Archaeol J* **73**, 43–54

Lobb, S J, 1992 Excavation at Shortheath Lane, Abbotts Farm, Sulhamstead, in Butterworth and Lobb 1992, 73–8

Lobb, S J and Mills, J M, 1993 Observations and excavations in the Pingewood area: Bronze Age, Romano-British and medieval features, *Berkshire Archaeol J* **74**, 85–93

Lobb, S J and Morris, E L, 1993 Investigation of Bronze Age and Iron Age features at Riseley Farm, Swallowfield, *Berkshire Archaeol J* **74**, 37–68

Lobb, S J and Rose, P G, 1996 *Archaeological survey of the Lower Kennet Valley, Berkshire*, Wessex Archaeology Rep **9**, Salisbury

Lobb, S J, Richards, J and Bradley, R, 1980 Pottery, in Bradley *et al.* 1980, 265–74

Lobb, S J, Mees, G and Mepham, L, 1990 Meales Farm, Sulhamstead. Archaeological investigation of Romano-British and medieval features, 1985–87, *Berkshire Archaeol J* **73**, 55–65

Longley, D, 1980 *Runnymede Bridge 1976: Excavations on the site of a late Bronze Age settlement*, Surrey Archaeol Soc Res Vol **6**, Guildford

Manning, W H, 1974 Excavations on late Iron Age, Roman and Saxon sites at Ufton Nervet, Berkshire, in 1961–1963, *Berkshire Archaeol J* **67**, 1–61

Masefield, R, 2003 A later Bronze Age well complex at Swalecliffe, Kent, *Antiq J* **83**, 47–121

McKinley, J, 1997 The cremated human bone from burial and cremation related contexts, in *Archaeological excavations on the route of the A27 Westhampnett Bypass, West Sussex, 1992. Volume 2: the cemeteries* (A P Fitzpatrick), Wessex Archaeol Rep **12**, 55–73, Salisbury

McNee, B, 2000 *A study of the use of middle Bronze Age urns in southern England*, unpubl. undergraduate dissertation, Univ. Southampton

McOmish, D, 1996 East Chisenbury: ritual and rubbish at the British Bronze Age-Iron Age transition, *Antiquity* **70**, 68–76

Mepham, L N, 1992a Pottery, in Butterworth and Lobb 1992, 40–8

Mepham, L N, 1992b Pottery, in Butterworth and Lobb 1992, 108–14

Mepham, L N, 1992c Other vessels, in Butterworth and Lobb 1992, 77–8

Montague, R, 1995 Stone, in Barnes and Cleal 1995, 24–5

Moore, J and Jennings, D, 1992 *Reading Business Park: A Bronze Age landscape,* Thames Valley Landscapes: The Kennet Valley **1**, Oxford

Moore, P D and Webb, J A, 1978 *An illustrated guide to pollen analysis*, London

Moore, P D, Webb, J A and Collinson, M E, 1991 *Pollen analysis*, 2 edn, Oxford

Morris, E L, 1994 Production and distribution of pottery and salt in Iron Age Britain: a review, *Proc Prehist Soc* **60**, 371–93

Morris, E L, 2000a Residues and vessel use, in Lawson 2000, 157

Morris, E L, 2000b Dating, in Lawson 2000, 157–66

Morris, E L, 2002 Staying alive: the function and use of prehistoric ceramics, in *Prehistoric Britain: the ceramic basis* (eds A Woodward and J D Hill), 54–61, Oxford

Morris, E L, 2004 Later prehistoric pottery, in Brossler *et al.* 2004, 58–91

Morris, E L, 2006 The prehistoric pottery, in Ironworking in the Bronze Age? Evidence from a 10th century BC settlement at Hartshill Copse, Upper Bucklebury, West Berkshire (M Collard, T Darvill, and M Watts), *Proc Prehist Soc* **72**, 367–421

Morris, E L and Mepham, L, 1995 Pottery, in An early Iron Age settlement at Dunston Park, Thatcham (A P Fitzpatrick, I Barnes and R M J Cleal), in Barnes *et al.* 1995, 77–84

Needham, S, 1991 *Excavation and salvage at Runnymede Bridge 1978: the late Bronze Age water-front site*, London

Needham, S, 1996 Chronology and periodisation in the British Bronze Age, *Acta Archaeologica* **67**, 121–40

Needham, S and Ambers, J, 1994 Redating Rams Hill and reconsidering Bronze Age enclosure, *Proc Prehist Soc* **60**, 225–43

Needham, S and Spence, T, 1996 *Refuse and disposal at Area 16 East Runnymede*, London

OA, 1989 Burghfield: Moores Farm, Pingewood: archaeological assessment report, unpubl.

OA, 1991a Hartley Court Farm, Shinfield, Reading, Berkshire: archaeological assessment report, unpubl.

OA, 1991b Hopkiln Farm, Shinfield, Reading, Berkshire: archaeological surface collection survey report, unpubl.

OA, 2000 Green Park Areas 9 and 10, Reading, Berkshire: archaeological evaluation report, unpubl.

OA, 2001 Proposed site for Option 2 Substation and H V Electricity Reinforcement Works, Green Park, Reading, Berkshire: archaeological evaluation report, unpubl.

OA, 2002 Sewage Treatment Works, Reading, Berkshire: watching brief report, unpubl.

O'Connell, M, 1990 Excavations during 1979–1985 of a multi-period site at Stanwell, *Surrey Archaeol Collect* **80**, 1–62

PCRG, 1997 *The study of later prehistoric pottery: general policies and guidelines for analysis and publication*, Prehistoric Ceramics Research Group Occ Pap **1** and **2**

Piggott, C M, 1938 The Iron Age pottery from Theale, *Trans Newbury Dist Fld Club* **8**, 52–60

Piggot, C M and Seaby, W A, 1937 Early Iron Age site at Southcote, Reading, *Proc Prehist Soc* **3**, 43–57

Piggott, S, 1935 An early settlement at Theale, near Reading, Berks, *Trans Newbury Dist Fld Club* **7**, 146–9

Pitts, M W and Jacobi, R M, 1979 Some aspects of change in flaked stone industries of the Mesolithic and Neolithic in southern Britain, *J Archaeol Sci* **6**, 163–77

Poole, C, 1991 Objects of baked clay, in *Danebury: an Iron Age hillfort in Hampshire. Vol. 5. The excavations, 1979–1988: the finds* (B Cunliffe), 382–404, London

Poole, C, 1995 Study 14: Loomweights versus oven bricks, in *Danebury: an Iron Age hillfort in Hampshire. Volume 6: a hillfort community in perspective* (B Cunliffe), CBA Res Rep **102**, York, 285-6

Pryor, F, 1996 Sheep, stockyards and field systems: Bronze Age livestock populations in the Fenlands of eastern England, *Antiquity* **70**, 313–24

Raymond, F, 1994 The pottery, in Bradley *et al.* 1994, 69–90

Rees, H, 1995 Later prehistoric and Romano-British pottery and briquetage, in Wainwright and Davies 1995, 57–82

Reimer, P J, *et al.*, 2004 *Radiocarbon* **46**, 1029–58

Robinson, M, 1992 Soils, sediments and hydrology, in Moore and Jennings 1992, 5

Robinson, M, 2004 Palaeochannel: soils, sediments and hydrology, in Brossler *et al.* 2004, 116

Robinson, M and Hubbard, R N L B, 1977 The transport of pollen in bracts of hulled cereals, *J Archaeol Sci* **4**, 197–9

Rocque, J, 1761 *A topographical survey of the county of Berkshire in 18 sheets*

Roe, F, 2004 Worked stone, in Brossler *et al.* 2004, 94–8

Rowlands, M J, 1976 *The production and distribution of metalwork in the middle Bronze Age in southern Britain*, BAR Brit Ser **31**, Oxford

Russell, M, 1996 Problems of phasing: a reconsideration of the Black Patch middle Bronze Age 'nucleated village', *Oxford J Archaeol* **15**, 33–8

Scaife, R G, 2004 Pollen analysis of a Bronze Age waterhole, in Brossler *et al.* 2004, 111–13

Seaby, W A, 1932 Some pre-Roman remains from south Reading, *Berkshire Archaeol J* **36**, 121–5

Shaffrey, R, 2003 The rotary querns from the Society of Antiquaries' excavations at Silchester, 1890–1909, *Britannia* **34**, 143–74

Shaffrey, R, 2006 *Grinding and milling. Romano-British rotary querns made from Old Red Sandstone*, BAR Brit Ser **409**, Oxford

Shepherd, W, 1972 *Flint. Its origin, properties and uses*, London

Shrubsole, O A, 1907 A burial place of the Bronze Age at Sulham, Berks, *Proc Soc Antiq* **21**, 308–14

Silver, I A, 1969 The ageing of domestic animals, in *Science in archaeology* (eds D Brothwell and E Higgs), 283–302, London

Smith, R J C, Rawlings, M and Barnes, I, 1992 Excavations at Coburg Road and Weymouth Road, Fordington, Dorchester, 1988 and 1989, *Proc Dorset Nat Hist Archaeol Soc* **114**, 19–45

Stace, C, 1991 *New flora of the British Isles*, Cambridge

Sterner, J, 1989 Who is signalling whom? Ceramic style, ethnicity and taphonomy among the Sirak Bulahey, *Antiquity* **63**, 451–60

Stoten, G, 2008 Prehistoric features at Field Farm, Sulhamstead: excavations in 2000, *Berkshire Archaeol J* **77**, 11–15

Stuiver, M, Reimer, P J, Bard, E, Beck, J W, Burr, G S, Hughen, K A, Kromer, B, McCormac, G, van der Plicht, J and Spurk, M, 1998 INTCAL98 radio-carbon age calibration, 24,000–0 cal BC, *Radiocarbon* **40**, 1041–83

Taylor, M, 1998 Wood and bark from the enclosure ditch, in *Etton: excavations at a Neolithic cause-wayed enclosure near Maxey, Cambridgeshire, 1982–7* (F Pryor), English Heritage Archaeol Rep **18**, 115–60, London

Taylor, M, 2001 The wood, in *The Flag Fen Basin* (F Pryor), 167–228, London

Taylor, M, 2004 Worked wood, in Brossler *et al.* 2004, 100–3

Thomas, J, 1991 *Understanding the Neolithic*, London

Thomas, M S, 2001 Two early first millennium BC wells at Selsey, West Sussex and their wider significance, *Antiq J* **81**, 15–50

Timby, J R, 1989 The pottery, in *The Silchester Amphitheatre: excavations of 1979–85* (M G Fulford), Britannia Monogr **10**, 80–110, London

Timby, J, 1994 The Pottery, in Hall and Ford 1994, 19–25

Timby, J, 2000 The pottery, in *Late Iron Age and Roman Silchester. Excavations on the site of the Forum-Basilica 1977, 1980–86* (M Fulford and J Timby), Britannia Monogr **15**, 180–312

Tomalin, D, 1992 The Deverel-Rimbury and late Biconical Urn domestic ceramic assemblage from Bishops Cannings Down, in Gingell 1992, 71–86

Tomalin, D, 1995 Cognition, ethnicity and some implications for linguistics in the perception and perpetration of 'Collared Urn art', in Kinnes and Varndell 1995, 101–12

TWA (Trust for Wessex Archaeology), 1986 Reading Business Park: Axiom 4, archaeological evaluation 1986, unpubl.

TWA (Trust for Wessex Archaeology), 1997 Reading Football Club, Smallmead Tip Site, Reading, *CBA Wessex Newsletter* **April 1997**, 10

TWA (Trust for Wessex Archaeology), 1999 Reading Gate Retail Park, Berkshire, *CBA Wessex Newsletter* **April 1999**, 16

TWA (Trust for Wessex Archaeology), n.d. Kings-mead Quarry, Horton (www.wessexarch.co.uk/projects/berkshire/Horton). Accessed August 2008.

Van de Noort, R, Ellis, S, Taylor, M and Weir, D, 1995 Preservation of archaeological sites, in *Wetland Heritage of Holderness – an archaeological survey* (R Van de Noort and S Ellis), 341–56

Wainwright, G J and Davies, S M, 1995 *Balksbury Camp, Hampshire: excavations 1973 and 1981*, English Heritage Archaeol Rep **4**, London

Walker, K and Farwell, D, 2000 *Twyford Down, Hampshire: archaeological investigations on the M3 motorway from Bar End to Compton, 1990–93*, Hampshire Fld Club Monogr **9**, Salisbury

Ward, G K and Wilson, S R, 1978 Procedures for comparing and combining radiocarbon age determinations: a critique, *Archaeometry* **20**, 19–31

Wilkinson, D, 1992 *Oxford Archaeological Unit field manual*, unpubl.

Woodward, A, 1992 Discussion, in Butterworth and Lobb 1992, 75–7

Woodward, A, 2009 Fired clay, in *Excavations at Bestwall Quarry, Wareham 1992–2005, Volume 1: the prehistoric landscape* (L Ladle and A Woodward), Dorset Nat Hist and Archaeol Soc Monograph **19**

Yates, D T, 1999 Bronze Age field systems in the Thames Valley, *Oxford J Archaeol* **18**, 157–70

Yates, D T, 2007 *Land, power and prestige. Bronze Age field systems in southern England*, Oxford

Young, C J, 1977 *The Roman pottery industry of the Oxford region*, BAR Brit Ser **43**, Oxford

Index

Aldermaston Wharf, Berks 27-8, 108, 110-11, 126-8, 130

alluviation 129

Amner's Farm, Burghfield, Berks 119, 126

animal bone
  butchery 98
  buzzard 17, 39, 122
  cremated 47
  horse 39, 53, 60-1, 65, 98, 121
    skeleton 65, 98
  red deer 39, 59, 61, 98-9, 109, 121, 129
  special deposit 99
  in waterhole 61, 65, 98-9

Anslow's Cottages, Berks 109, 118-19, 121, 127

antler, red deer 59, 99

arable agriculture 41-2, 102, 121, 126, 129

Ashford Common, Sunbury, Middlesex 86

Balksbury Camp, Hants 107, 113

Beenham, Berks 119

Binfield, Berks 75

Black Patch, Sussex 107, 113

bowl, wooden 2, 17, 121

box, wooden 38

bracelet
  copper alloy 50
  shale 13, 17, 35, 121-2

Bray, Berks 34

Brimpton, Berks 108, 114, 127

bronze working, crucible 109

Burderop Down 111

burial
  cattle 3
  cremation 3, 119
    early Bronze Age 119
    late Bronze Age 3, 126
    late Iron Age 6, 45, 129-30
    middle Bronze Age 3, 38-9, 109, 112, 126-7
    middle to late Bronze Age 27
    in waterhole 13, 17, 122
  grave goods 45
  in waterhole 13-14, 38
  inhumation
    crouched 2
    middle to late Bronze Age 21
    late Bronze Age   3
  burnt mound 3, 126-7

Cippenham, Berks 128

clay pipe 47, 50

Coburg Road, Dorchester, Dorset 113

Cod's Hill, Beenham, Berks 127

coin, Roman 2

copper alloy
  bracelet 47, 50
  earring 47, 50

Crane Wharf, Reading, Berks 119

cropmarks 2, 6

crucible, bronze-working 109

Cunning Man, Burghfield, Berks 130

Diddenham Manor Farm, Grazeley, Berks 123

dowel, wooden 38

dung beetle 43

Dunston Park, Thatcham, Berks 96-7

earring, copper alloy 47, 50

Eldon's Seat, Dorset 113

Englefield, Berks 119

Eton Rowing Lake, Dorney, Bucks 128

Eynsham Abbey, Oxon 27-8, 30, 35, 107, 109

Field Farm, Burghfield, Berks 26-7, 30, 81, 85, 96-7, 109, 118-19, 126, 129

Field Farm, Sulhamstead, Berks 127

field system 3
  abandonment of 128
  medieval 3
  middle Bronze Age 53, 55, 57, 121, 123, 126, 128
  middle to late Bronze Age 9
  recutting of 47
  Roman 45, 129

fired clay
  loomweight 65, 69, 97, 121, 129
  oven brick 60, 65, 69, 97, 122, 129

flax retting 3

flintwork
  arrowhead 76
    oblique 76 119
    leaf-shaped 119
  Bronze Age 70, 75
  bullhead flint 22, 70-1
  later Bronze Age 23
  Mesolithic 9, 21-2, 53, 70, 71-3, 75-6, 117
  microburin 72 3, 75
  microlith 72, 75, 117
    manufacture of 72-3, 75
  middle Neolithic 119
  Neolithic 3, 21-2, 70, 73, 75, 118-19
  scraper 72, 75-6
  tranchet axe 118

flooding 117, 129

Forest of Dean, Glos 50

granary (four- and six-post structure) 3, 70, 126
  early Iron Age 70

middle Bronze Age 60
Grange Road, Gosport, Hants 112, 114
grassland 41-2, 100, 121
Green Park Substation, Berks 6, 117, 123

Hartley Court Farm, Berks 6, 117, 123, 126, 129
Hartshill Copse, Upper Bucklebury, Berks 96, 128
Haywards Farm, Theale, Berks 117
hearth, early Iron Age 69
Heathrow Airport, London 119, 123
hedge 35, 121
Heron's House, Burghfield, Berks 108, 126
Hopkiln Farm, Berks 6
horseshoe 47
Hurst Park, East Molesey, Surrey 110

Isle of Purbeck, Dorset 113
Itford Hill, Sussex 111, 113

Kimpton, Hants 112
Kingsmead Quarry, Horton, Berks 122
Knight's Farm, Burghfield, Berks 27, 30, 86, 96,
    108, 126, 129

ladle, wooden 14, 35, 38, 121
land tenure 121, 123, 128
landing stage 127
Little Lea Park, Berks 130
livestock husbandry 121
Lower Kennet Valley, archaeology of 2

Marlborough Downs, Wilts 111
Marshall's Hill, Berks 127
Meales Farm, Sulhamstead, Berks 130
Mesolithic
    flintwork 53, 71-3, 70, 75-6, 117-18
    settlement 75, 117-18
    tree-throw hole 117
metalwork
    Penard phase 109, 111
    Taunton phase 109
    Wilburton phase 109, 111
midden 106, 111, 119, 128
Mortimer Common, Berks 119

Neolithic
    flintwork 9, 70, 73, 75, 118
    pit 3, 53, 118-19
    posthole 53, 119
    settlement 118-19
    tree-throw hole 119

oven, middle Bronze Age 60

palaeochannel 3, 53, 109, 117, 121, 127
Park Farm, Binfield, Berks 75
Perry Oaks, London 122
Petters Sports Field, Egham, Surrey 35
Pingewood, Berks 6, 26-8, 34, 75, 108, 114, 118-19,
    123, 126, 129-30
pit
    alignment 3

flax retting 3
    Neolithic 3, 53, 118-19
Plumpton Plain, Sussex 113
Pode Hole, Cambs 38
posthole, Neolithic 53, 119
Potterne, Wilts 93, 96, 107, 111
pottery
    accessory cup 112
    Alice Holt industry 49
    All Cannings Cross 96
    All Cannings Cross-Meon Hill 96
    Ardleigh 81
    Beaker 9, 24, 53, 78, 81, 83-4, 111, 119
    charred residue 81, 87, 93, 106
    deliberate deposit 13, 21, 47
    Deverel-Rimbury 108-9, 111, 121, 126-7
        barrel urn 25-6, 30, 34, 84, 86, 88, 103-4,
            111-12
        bucket urn 26, 30, 59, 84, 86, 88, 91-2, 103-4,
            108-9, 112-13
        globular urn 25-6, 30, 34, 84, 86-8, 92, 103-4,
            109, 112-14, 122
        use of 105
    Dorset black burnished ware 49
    early Bronze Age 53, 81, 84, 119
        biconical urn 53, 81, 84
        collared urn 112, 119
    early Neolithic 119
    flint temper 106
    Grooved Ware 119
    knobbed vessel 86, 110
    miniature vessel 110
    Neolithic Impressed Ware 53, 78, 80, 83, 111, 119
        Fengate style 53, 78, 80-1, 84
        Mortlake style 53, 78, 80, 84
    Oxfordshire colour-coated ware 50
    Oxfordshire white ware 50
    perforated 13, 27-8, 86, 112
    post-Deverel-Rimbury 26, 30, 86, 96, 105-6, 109,
        111-12, 114
        bowl 105-6
        cup 106
        decorated ware 108-9, 126
        miniature vessel 106
        plain ware 108-9, 111-14, 126
        use in feasting 106
    samian ware 50
    Silchester ware 49
    Surrey-Hampshire white ware 50
    transitional later Bronze Age 9, 24, 26-8, 30, 86,
        103, 106-11, 113-14, 121, 126-7

quern
    rotary 47, 50
    rubber 97-8
    saddle 13, 34, 97-8, 121, 129

Rams Hill, Berks 111, 115
Reading Football Club, Berks 127
Reading Sewage Treatment Works, Berks 6, 117,
    119
residency pattern 87

ring ditch 119, 128
  C-shaped 6, 119
  early Bronze Age 112, 123, 126
  middle Bronze Age 126-7
  Neolithic, segmented 3, 119
ringwork, late Bronze Age 127
Riseley Farm, Swallowfield, Berks 49
Rockley Down, Wilts 111
roundhouse
  late Bronze Age 3, 126-8
  late Iron Age-Roman 130
  middle Bronze Age 128
Runnymede Bridge, Surrey 35, 110

Sarsen stone 34, 97
Selsey, Sussex 113
settlement
  early Bronze Age 119
  late Bronze Age 123, 126, 128
  Mesolithic 75, 117-18
  middle Bronze Age 121, 126-7
  Neolithic 118-19
  Roman 129-30
settlement mobility
  middle Bronze Age 128
  Neolithic and early Bronze Age 121
shale
  bracelet 13, 17, 35, 121-2
  Kimmeridge 35
  vessel 6
Shorncote Quarry, Glos 122
Shortheath Lane, Sulhamstead, Berks 26, 85-7, 127
Silchester, Hants 49-50, 130
South Cadbury, Somerset 111
Southcote, Berks 130
spearhead
  bronze 127
  side-looped socketed 109
Stanwell, Middlesex 13
Sulham, Berks 127
Sulhamstead, Berks 118
Swalecliffe, Kent 13

Thatcham, Berks 75, 118
Theale Ballast Hole, Berks 96, 127, 129-30

trackway
  late medieval/post-medieval 47
  middle Bronze Age 55
tree-throw hole
  Mesolithic 117
  Neolithic 119
Twyford Down, Hants 112

Ufton Nervet, Berks 49, 117, 119, 130

vessel, wooden 13-14, 17, 38, 106, 122

waterhole 3, 9, 57, 60-1, 121-2
  animal bone in 39, 61, 65, 98-9, 122
  cess-like deposit in 19
  cremated human bone in 13, 17, 38-9, 122
  deposition in 13, 122
  deposition of wood in 38
  human bone in 13-14, 38, 122
  pottery in 30, 114
  radiocarbon dating 9, 20
  ramped 13, 122
  steep-sided 13, 17, 122
  types of 13, 122
  wooden structure in 13, 17, 35, 122
Watkins Farm, Northmoor, Oxon 122
Wawcott, Berks 75
weight, clay 109
Weir Bank Stud Farm, Bray, Berks 87, 128
Wickhams Field, Burghfield, Berks 96-7, 119, 129-30
Wilsford Shaft, Wilts 38
Winnall Down, Hants 112
wood
  bowl 121
  box 38
  dowel 38
  ladle 35, 38, 121
  plank 35
  vessel 13-14, 17, 38, 106, 122
woodland clearance 41-2
woodworking 35

Yapton, Sussex 112-13
Yarnton, Oxon 38